FIRE IN

ON BEING A MAN

THE BELLY

FIRE IN

ON BEING A MAN

THE BELLY

SAM KEEN

BANTAM BOOKS
NEW YORK • TORONTO • LONDON • SYDNEY • AUCKLAND

FIRE IN THE BELLY

A Bantam Book / April 1991

Bantam New Age and the accompanying figure design as well as "the search for meaning, growth and change" are trademarks of Bantam Books, a division of Bantam Doubleday Dell Publishing Group, Inc.

Grateful acknowledgment is made for permission to reprint the following:
   Excerpts from quatraines 558 and 1794 from Open Secret: Versions of Rumi, *Threshold Books, 139 Main St., Room 403, Brattleboro, VT 05301. Excerpts from "No Worst, There Is None . . ." by Gerard Manley Hopkins taken from* Poems of Gerard Manley Hopkins, *Oxford University Press. Quoted material from "Living In the Office" by Timothy Haight appeared in* The Whole Earth Review, *27 Gate Five Road, Sausalito, CA 94965, subscription price $20.*
   Excerpts from Scenes from the Corporate Life *by Earl Shorris.*

Library of Congress Cataloging-in-Publication Data

Keen, Sam.
   Fire in the belly : on being a man / Sam Keen.
      p.   cm.
   ISBN 0-553-07188-2
   1. Men—Psychology.   2. Men—United States—Psychology.
   3. Masculinity (Psychology)   I. Title.
   HQ1090.K44   1991
   305.32—dc20   90-19474
                                                       CIP

Published simultaneously in the United States and Canada

Bantam Books are published by Bantam Books, a division of Bantam Doubleday Dell Publishing Group, Inc. Its trademark, consisting of the words "Bantam Books" and the portrayal of a rooster, is Registered in U.S. Patent and Trademark Office and in other countries. Marca Registrada. Bantam Books, 666 Fifth Avenue, New York, New York 10103.

PRINTED IN THE UNITED STATES OF AMERICA

0   9   8   7   6   5

Especially for:

James Donaldson
Bill Jersey
Richard Ruopp
Earl Scott
Heartful men.
Friends for three decades.

Jananne Lovett-Keen
With whom
irreconcilable differences
have stimulated the growth of love.

ACKNOWLEDGMENTS:

Dr. Ofer Zur and I have shared ideas for three years about war, gender and the changing ideals of manhood.

Leslie Meredith, an editor with a wide-ranging mind, a gentle spirit and a sharp red pencil has criticized, suggested, cut, tightened and helped beyond the call of duty.

A man must go on a quest
to discover the sacred fire
in the sanctuary of his own belly
to ignite the flame in his heart
to fuel the blaze in the hearth
to rekindle his ardor for the earth.

CONTENTS

I

INTRODUCTION
The Making of a Man

II

THE RITES OF MANHOOD

III

TAKING THE MEASURE OF A MAN

IV
A PRIMER FOR NOW AND FUTURE HEROES

V
MEN AND WOMEN: COMING TOGETHER

INTRODUCTION:

THE MAKING
OF A MAN

INVITATION
TO A JOURNEY

The year I was seventeen I received many messages from my classmates, my family, and my culture about what was required to be a *real man:*

Join the fraternity.
Get a letter in football, baseball, or basketball.
Screw a lot of girls.
Be tough; fight if anybody insults you or your girl.
Don't show your feelings.
Drink lots of beer (predrug era).
Be nice—don't fight or drink.
Dress right—like everybody else: penny loafers, etc.
Get a good job, work hard and make a lot of money.
Get your own car.
Be well liked, popular.

My grandmother gave me a Bible with a note that said: "Read this every day, Big Boy—it will make you a *real man.*"

I felt I was probably destined to fail at being a man. I didn't drink, smoke, or swear. I was the only one in P. S. duPont High School in Wilmington, Delaware, who wore cowboy boots. I did not shave, had only a sparse crop of pubic hair, and was embarrassed in the locker room. I never got a letter in a major sport. To this day I avoid anyone who was in my high school class, especially old football heroes. I hated fraternities. The only thing that saved me from being a complete geek was that I had a car and a girlfriend, although the car was only a Model A Ford and the girlfriend was not a cheerleader.

Today I look at an old picture of that seventeen-year-old boy. He is dressed for the senior prom in a rented white dinner jacket—lanky, loose-jointed, too-large hands on hips, the pose clearly adopted from Gary Cooper. Next to him stands his girlfriend, Janet, already looking mature, dressed in the traditional white gown with the traditional purple orchid, filled with the traditional dreams of settling down. They are both virgins. I see hints in his ungainly adolescent body of the man he will become. In the forward-leaning head, slightly sunken chest, and forward-curved shoulders is the form of a question mark. In the awkwardness of his pose I see him trying to be suave for the occasion and play the man while he still feels himself to be a boy. I know he will feel boyish, not a man among men, well into his mature years.

But it is his face that moves me most. Open. Shining. Filled with a strange power of innocence and strong dreams. His mask of sophistication hides the painful sensitivity he fears is a mark of his inadequacy as a man. I do not see, but remember well, the loneliness, the uncertainty, the feeling of being both proud and embarrassed by the secret life the boy was living.

His clandestine life included many activities not on any list of requirements for being a *real man:* keeping a diary; exploring nearby woods and longing for the wilderness; sleeping under the stars; taking long walks alone; waiting and watching to see what would happen when a cowbird laid its eggs in a vireo's nest; masturbating and imagining the woman of his dreams; wondering about the limits of his mind; exploring his dark moods; writing poetry; reading books and playing with ideas; loving his parents; agonizing about war, poverty, injustice, torture; wanting to do something to make the world better.

Today I honor the boy, knowing that he knew far more about manhood than he thought he knew. For instance, the week after the prom, he set out on his walkabout, a trip across the U.S., working on a wheat harvest, ranches, carnivals, etc. Hidden in his young heart was a craving to discover his own definition of manhood. Father to the man who is writing this book, he did not know it but he had already set out on a pilgrimage, a quest to find the Grail.

Deep down, the tectonic plates that have supported the modern world are shifting. Revolutions are daily occurrences; the centers of power are moving. Ancient enemies are making common cause. Paradigms and worldviews are changing overnight. Yesterday's certainties are today's superstitions. Today is all chaos and creativity. As the sign down at the local Chevron station says: "If you aren't harried, worried, and a little bit nuts you don't understand what's going on around here." Nobody can predict the shape of tomorrow's world.

The earthquake that is shaking men and women, their roles and interrelationships, is part and parcel of this shifting of the world culture's tectonic plates. The changes in our gender roles are only one aspect of the upheaval that accompanies the death of one epoch and the birth of another. And we will be in the birth process for several generations.

For most of what feminists rightly call Western his-story men were considered the norm for humanity, the standard by which sanity and virtue were judged, and women were considered mysterious, suspect, and slightly deviant. Freud articulated the standard opinion when he asked with supposed seriousness, "What does a woman want?" Until recently, women were characterized as the gender with the problem. But nearly a generation ago, women began to lead the revolution in gender. Feminist philosophers, theologians, poets, and social activists have gone a long way toward articulating a systematic critique of modern society, redefining female identity, and securing equal rights. They have made it abundantly clear that the answer to Freud's question is, and has always been, obvious to men of goodwill. First and foremost, women want what they have been denied—justice, equality, respect, and power.

Today the question that is the yeast in the social dough is: What do men want? The traditional notions of manhood are under attack and men are being called upon to defend themselves, to change, to become something other than what they have been. The matter was summarized in a recent *Newsweek* article on "Guns and Dolls"[1]:

"Perhaps the time has come for a new agenda. Women, after all, are not a big problem. Our society does not suffer from burdensome amounts of empathy and altruism, or a plague of nurtur-

ance. The problem is men—or more accurately, maleness. . . .
Men are killing themselves doing all the things that our society
wants them to do. At every age they're dying in accidents, they're
being shot, they drive cars badly, they ride the tops of elevators,
they're two-fisted drinkers. And violence against women is in-
credibly pervasive. Maybe it's men's raging hormones, [or] . . .
because they're trying to be a *man*."

Ask most any man, "How does it feel to be a man these
days? Do you feel manhood is honored, respected, celebrated?"
Those who pause long enough to consider their gut feelings will
likely tell you they feel blamed, demeaned, and attacked. But
their reactions may be pretty vague. Many men feel as if they are
involved in a night battle in a jungle against an unseen foe. Voices
from the surrounding darkness shout hostile challenges: "Men
are too aggressive. Too soft. Too insensitive. Too macho. Too
power-mad. Too much like little boys. Too wimpy. Too violent.
Too obsessed with sex. Too detached to care. Too busy. Too
rational. Too lost to lead. Too dead to feel." Exactly what we are
supposed to become is not clear.

Men have only recently begun to explore new visions and
definitions of manhood. At no time in recent history have there
been so many restless, questioning men. Granted, this yeasty
brotherhood is still a minority, but it is a powerful ferment. As
yet, there is little literature that speaks to these questing men.
The most spiritually adventurous men of our time have moved
out on the frontier beyond the reporters, the popularizers, the
psychologists, the so-called "experts" about men. Go into a good
bookstore and ask if they have a section on women's studies and
you will be shown a rich variety of books on social theory,
linguistics, biographies of forgotten heroines, women's poetry,
studies of the goddess, histories of feminism, etc. Ask if they
have a men's studies section and you will be shown a small one
with titles relating to (1) gay experience; (2) diatribes about men's
inadequacies and failures (*Men Who Hate Women and the
Women Who Love Them, What to Do When He Won't Change,
The Peter Pan Syndrome,*[2] etc., ad nauseam); or (3) something
called "men's liberation," which sounds suspiciously like
warmed-over feminism with a reverse twist. Not much here to
stir the head, the heart, or the gonads.

This book is an attempt to fill this lack. It is not *One-
Minute Masculinity* or simple answers for simple men. It is for a
new kind of man who is being forged in the crucible of the chaos
of our time. It is for men who are willing to undertake a spiritual

journey beginning with the disillusioning awareness that what we have agreed to call "normal" is a facade covering a great deal of alienation. But it goes beyond the valley of the shadow to celebrate a new vision of manhood—a vision of man with fire in his belly and passion in his heart. The path it follows is the ancient way of the hero's journey that involves departure from everyday normality; descent into the strange land of dis-ease, demons, dreadful powers, treasures, and maidens guarded by dragons; and, finally, a return home to the heart of the ordinary.

I structured the book along the lines of something Paul Tillich, perhaps the greatest philosopher-theologian of our time, was fond of saying. "Every serious thinker," he said, "must ask and answer three fundamental questions: (1) What is wrong with us? With men? Women? Society? What is the nature of our alienation? Our dis-ease? (2) What would we be like if we were whole? Healed? Actualized? If our potentiality was fulfilled? (3) How do we move from our condition of brokenness to wholeness? What are the means of healing?"

An overview of the book:

In the *Introduction* I argue that men cannot find themselves without first separating from the world of WOMAN.

In *The Rites of Manhood* I argue that our modern rites of passage—war, work, and sex—impoverish and alienate men.

In *Taking the Measure of a Man* I argue that authentic manhood has always been defined by a vision of how we fit into the universe and by the willingness to undertake an appropriate task or vocation—which have changed at various times in history.

In *A Primer for Now and Future Heroes* I trace the spiritual journey into the self men must undertake in our time and sketch a portrait of the resulting heroic virtues.

In *Men and Women Coming Together* I explore the reconciliation and common vocation of men and women.

I did not include an entire chapter on men and their fathers, although this relationship is addressed throughout the book. Recently, many men have become aware of the wound they suffer from the absence of their fathers and the vacuum they feel in not having been initiated into manhood. How often I have heard the lament, "Dad, where were you? I never knew you." A generation ago, under the influence of pop psychology, we began to blame men's problems on Mom and momism. The charge was that, with father away, she ruled the roost and sissified her sons. Now the tide has changed and father is becoming the new target of blame. In this book, I try to go beyond the psychological wound created by the missing father and concentrate on the political, economic, and mythic sources of men's dis-ease. I have chosen to homogenize the father-son theme with other themes in order to emphasize what I believe to be the most central source of men's alienation—the absence of a sense of abiding meaning, or as I prefer to say "vocation," in our lives.

A word about the sources on which this book depends.

Discerning the signs of the times is risky business. We all know at a gut level that major changes are occurring. As women enter more equally into the economic order and increasingly define themselves in terms of money, position, and power there is some shifting deep in the male and female psyche. Nobody yet fully understands the implications of this change. Once upon a time we depended on omens, oracles, and divination to determine the secret meaning of events. Nowadays, sociologists and psychologists design polls and controlled studies that give us reams of statistical information about surface events but little wisdom and even less vision of what we may become. This book does draw on a statistical analysis of a research poll on "ideal men" that Dr. Ofer Zur and I conducted and published in *Psychology Today* in March and November 1989 (see Appendix). But keep in mind that our best market research predicted the success of the Edsel and "information specialists" in the CIA failed to predict the religious uprising in Iran or the collapse of governments in Eastern Europe. In any of the human sciences a "scientific" study is only as good as the intuition of those conducting it.

Most of the views, judgments, and insights of this look at contemporary men and their issues come from two quite unscientific sources.

The first source is my half-century-long study of the life of one man—myself. Instead of hiding behind an objective, "scientific" analysis, my only privileged access to the meaning and the spirit of my age, to the difficulty and splendor of being a man, is the data of my own experience. The journey described in this book is the one I am taking. Its questions are my questions. As Henry David Thoreau wrote in *Walden:* "I should not talk so much about myself if there were anybody else whom I knew as well." What I have to offer a reader is not the truth about men, for even when I borrow other eyes, minds, and hearts to help me explore the complex reality of manhood, I remain a WASP, a Westerner, a heterosexual, a husband (twice), a father, and a philosopher (a "meaning junkie"). This book is not an encyclopedia of male experience, for a gay man, an Asian, an American Indian, indeed, any other man would tell a different story. But I am convinced we are most likely to touch something universal when each of us speaks personally and witnesses to the sliver of truth we have refined from our individual experience.

The second source of my knowledge is from longtime friendships with a few men and participation in a group of a dozen or so men that have been meeting every Wednesday since 1978. Over the years this group, which called itself simply The Men, or sometimes SPERM (Society for the Protection and Encouragement of Righteous Manhood), has challenged, loved, appreciated, changed, and taught me more about the common agonies and aspirations of men than any book or "scientific" study. The voices you hear in this book will frequently be those of this circle of friends, who remain anonymous to protect the innocent, the guilty, and the privacy of the group.

And finally, some words to women.

This book is primarily an effort to get inside the dilemmas and delights, confusions and cares of modern men, but its audience is both sexes. When I first started giving seminars on "Understanding Men" I was surprised to find that half the participants were women, mostly weary veterans of many engagements in the battle between the sexes. They had been disappointed and hurt by fathers, brothers, husbands, lovers, sons, bosses, and male friends, but were not vindictive. All had been strengthened and nurtured by feminism. None had come to the seminars to find a platform to vent old anger. Almost without exception the women came because they realized that after a lifetime of trying to relate to men they still didn't understand them. Many women said, "What I want from this seminar is to be a fly on the wall and listen to what men have to say." After a particularly affecting weekend in which men had talked to each other about the longing they felt for the fathers they never knew, and about the horror, guilt, and psychic wounds of warfare, a woman who had been silent rose and said, "I have been married twice, and had several other relationships that ended badly. Like most women I have always 'listened' to men, but until today I never heard them. I have never heard men talk to other men with such depth and love. And I never imagined what it was like for men to live with the knowledge that they must be prepared to kill, or with the actual horror of battle. This weekend I feel like I have been in a room with giants. I thank you for letting me listen."

Much of the following exploration of men's journeys will

resonate with women. While it explores the meaning of being a person from within the horizons of male experience, the story of injury and promise it tells will be equally relevant to both sexes. Women may often find themselves saying, "That is the way it is for me, too." We are more profoundly united by our common humanity than separated by gender. Nevertheless, I try to avoid comparisons and stick to the exposition of men's experience, because at the moment men need to concentrate on recollecting and savoring their uniqueness. The most hopeful thing we can do to end the war between the sexes is merely to witness to each other, tell our stories, and listen quietly.

I suggest that you read this book with two different colored markers in hand and underline those passages that fit and those that do not fit your experience. More than most books, this is an invitation to a conversation. I hope it will start men talking among themselves and men and women talking to each other. Creating new visions of manhood and womanhood is a venture that will involve us for years to come.

IT'S A WOMAN'S WORLD

I had recently been divorced after a seventeen-year marriage. My children were living a thousand miles away. I was madly in love with a beautiful young woman. She was rapidly slipping away from me and I could already feel the other man, a dark moody poet, lurking in the shadows. No hour passed when I did not plot ways of luring her back to me, making her love me. In my daydreams I became irresistible, lighthearted, a powerful lover. I held her lightly, encouraged her, took pleasure in her growth, selflessly gave myself to fulfill her needs and desires. In real life, she didn't return my phone calls and our nights together were becoming rare and terrible. To protect myself against the coming loss, I had already provided myself with another lover to fill my empty hours and lonely nights. Sweet lust to heal the wound of a failed romance.

My life was coming apart at the seams.

One day I went to talk with Howard Thurman, a friend for twenty-five years, true witness, grandson of a slave, mystic, philosopher, a man acquainted with darkness and the journey of the spirit. Through a long afternoon we talked and sipped bourbon. I told him about the pain of the divorce and my disintegrating romance. He asked about my children.

And then he told me two stories:

"When I was a boy in Florida I used to go fishing. The best fish were to be caught just at the point where the bay met the ocean, but there was only a short time between the tides when you could stay in the calm water. When the tide began to change you couldn't row against it. You had to go in the direction it was sweeping you."

"Once there was a man who loved a woman beyond all measure. He sailed away with her and one day came to an uninhabited island. Leaving her on the boat, he explored the interior, and deep in the forest he came upon a stone image of an unknown god. It radiated such a sense of power that he fell on his knees and prayed for his beloved: 'May her life be full and happy. May our love develop in a way that will be fulfilling for her.' As he headed back he came to a hilltop, and as he looked out across the water he saw his boat and his lover sailing away. His prayer had been answered."

The last thing he said before I left was probably the single most important bit of advice I ever got about being a man. "Sam," he said, "there are two questions a man must ask himself: The first is 'Where am I going?' and the second is 'Who will go with me?' *If you ever get these questions in the wrong order you are in trouble.*"

When I left Howard's book-lined study, I knew the tide had changed. I stopped at every bar along my way and had a shot of bourbon to feed my pain, until my being turned liquid. The rivulets of grief for a lost marriage, for absent children, for the ending of an impossible romance all flowed together and I found myself walking and weeping, but knowing the time had finally come to sever the umbilical cord that attached me to the goddess who was to have been my salvation. I found a phone booth and called her. For the first time in weeks she answered. "I know it is time for you to go," I said. "As much as I want to be with you, I know there is no way for us to remain lovers. I am too old and too raw to be casual about love and you are too young to be faithful and make graceful commitments. Go, without deception or guilt. I love you. Good-bye."

I didn't change into Superman when I stepped out of the phone booth. I was still weeping. But as I trudged up the steep San Francisco hills I could feel an electric, erotic power surge up through my legs, boil into my belly, and rise into my chest. I walked for hours, awash in the turmoil of clashing emotions, grieving and coming alive. Finally the clashing waves of bay and ocean quieted, the waters grew still, and I went home to rest and begin a new life.

It was slow in dawning on me that WOMAN had an overwhelming influence on my life and on the lives of all the men I knew.

I am not talking about women, the actual flesh-and-blood creatures, but about WOMEN, those larger-than-life shadowy female figures who inhabit our imaginations, inform our emotions, and indirectly give shape to many of our actions.

As befits divinities, demons, and archetypes, these phantasms of our imagination will appear in uppercase letters while flesh-and-blood women will appear in lowercase letters as befits mortals.

From all outward appearances, I was a successfully individuated man. I had set my career course early, doggedly stuck to the discipline of graduate school through many years and degrees, and by my midthirties was vigorously pursuing the life of a professor and writer. Like most men, I was devoting most of my energy and attention to work and profession.

But if the text of my life was "successful independent man," the subtext was "engulfed by WOMAN." All the while I was advancing in my profession, I was engaged in an endless, anxious struggle to find the "right" woman, to make my relationship "work," to create a good marriage. I agonized over sex—Was I good enough? Did she "come"? Why wasn't I always potent? What should I do about my desires for other women? The more troubled my marriage became, the harder I tried to get it right. I worked at communication, sex, and everything else until I became self-obsessed.

Divorce finally broke the symbiotic mother-son, father-daughter pattern of my first marriage. With high hopes for freedom and ecstasy I began "exploring my sexuality," as was required of all "real" men in California during the sexual revolution of the late sixties, and looking once again for Ms. Right. As my obsession with WOMAN grew it finally occurred to me that maybe I should undertake psychotherapy à la Jung. Perhaps if I got to know my feminine side I would not be so dependent upon women for my pleasure and succor. But therapy seemed only to push me deeper into the arms of WOMAN. For several introspective years I juggled the predicates of gender and wondered constantly: Am I receptive, nurturing, intuitive, sensuous, yielding—"feminine"—enough? Am I initiatory, decisive, rational, aggressive—"masculine"—enough? Between dealing with the images of WOMAN in my head, the women in my life, and the "feminine" aspects of my psyche, I was drowning in the dark waters of WOMAN'S world.

Man's Unconscious Bondage to WOMAN

Cliché and common wisdom tell us that "it's a man's world." In the accepted mythology of our time, men are independent and women dependent; men dominate and women yield; men make history and women provide emotional support. Folklore, lately expanded into a cottage industry of books about the uncommitted male, has it that men are phobic about intimacy, are tongue-tied about emotions, and generally keep an antiseptic distance between themselves and females of their species. At best, or so the complaint goes, we end up committing ourselves because we want a secure sexual connection. Otherwise we follow George Washington's advice and avoid entangling alliances. Real men don't depend on women. We stand tall and alone. In locker rooms all across America, boys who are just beginning to sprout pubic hair learn the ancient adolescent litany of the five F's that prescribes the proper relationship with women: Find 'em, fool 'em, feel 'em, fuck 'em and forget 'em.

Over the last century, the one solid truth established by psychologists is that the human psyche is constructed out of opposition, contradiction, and paradox. In problems of logic, contradictory statements cannot be true; in the psyche, *only* contradictions are true. Self-image and shadow are Siamese twins, and the psyche is equally formed by the conscious and unconscious. Whatever appears to be true on the surface is linked to an opposite truth beneath the surface. What you see is *not* what you get. We are who we appear to be *and* our opposite or mirror image. One of Freud's best rules of thumb for determining what a person was unconsciously feeling was: "A negation is as good as an affirmation." Listen with the third ear and you will hear the echo.

"It's not the money, it's the principle." (It's the money.)
"I'm not mad, but . . ." (I'm mad.)
"I don't depend on women." (I depend on women.)

I would guess that a majority of men never break free, never define manhood by weighing and testing their own experience. And the single largest reason is that we never acknowledge the primal power WOMAN wields over us. The average man spends a lifetime denying, defending against, trying to control, and reacting to the power of WOMAN. He is committed to remaining unconscious and out of touch with his own deepest feelings and experience.

The chains that bind us most tightly are those we refuse to acknowledge.

We begin to learn the mysteries unique to maleness only when we separate from WOMAN'S world. But before we can take our leave we must first become conscious of the ways in which we are enmeshed, incorporated, inwombed, and defined by WOMAN. Otherwise we will be controlled by what we haven't remembered.

The secret men seldom tell, and often do not know (consciously) is the extent to which our lives circle around our relationships to WOMAN. It takes half a lifetime of struggle for us to win a separate identity. We are haunted by WOMAN in her many manifestations. She is the center around which our lives circle. WOMAN is the mysterious ground of our being that we cannot penetrate. She is the audience before whom the dramas of our lives are played out. She is the judge who pronounces us guilty or innocent. She is the Garden of Eden from which we are exiled and the paradise for which our bodies long. She is the goddess who can grant us salvation and the frigid mother who denies us. She has a mythic power over us. She is at once terrifying and fascinating.

We have invested so much of our identity, committed so much of our energy, and squandered so much of our power in trying to control, avoid, conquer, or demean women because we are so vulnerable to their mysterious power over us. Like sandy atolls in a monsoon-swept ocean, the male psyche is in continual danger of being inundated by the feminine sea. And this fragility is not psychological, not neurotic, not a symptom of abnormality, but is an ontological fact rooted in our being. Those men who allow themselves to feel it are stronger, not weaker, than those who pretend they are self-sufficient and autonomous. We emerged from WOMAN and we naturally fear that the individual self we have managed to erect, like a makeshift seawall, may be lost.

At this point the voice of common sense is likely to intrude and object. "Who is this female monster you portray as a black hole into which the male psyche disappears? WOMAN a threat? How? Be clear!" But herein lies the problem. Clarity about WOMAN and women is a hard-won prize that comes near the end, not at the beginning, of a man's journey. Before a man struggles to become conscious of the nature and limits of his virility, *the essence of the threat he feels from WOMAN lies in its vagueness.* She is the soft darkness at the core of his psyche, part of him, not a stranger. We are linked to her in our deepest being, but she remains hidden in a haze just beyond the horizon of our reason and never comes out of the shadows to meet us face to face.

One of the major tasks of manhood is to explore the unconscious feelings that surround our various images of WOMAN, to dispel false mystification, to dissolve the vague sense of threat and fear, and finally to learn to respect and love the strangeness of womankind. It may be useful to think about sexual-spiritual maturation—the journey of manhood—as a process of changing WOMAN into women into Jane (or one certain woman), of learning to see members of the opposite sex not as archetypes or members of a class but as individuals. It is the WOMAN in our heads, more than the women in our beds or boardrooms, who causes most of our problems. And these archetypical creatures—goddesses, bitches, angels, Madonnas, castrators, witches, Gypsy maidens, earth mothers—must be exorcised from our minds and hearts before we can learn to love women. So long as our house is haunted by the ghost of WOMAN we can never live gracefully with any woman. If we continue to deny that she lives in the shadows she will continue to have power over us.

A man's journey in relationship to WOMAN involves three stages. In the beginning he is sunk deep in an unconscious relationship with a falsely mystified figure who is composed of unreal opposites: virgin-whore, nurturer-devouring mother, goddess-demon. To grow from man-child into man, in the second stage, he must take leave of WOMAN and wander for a long time in the wild and sweet world of men. Finally, when he has learned to love his own manhood, he may return to the everyday world to love an ordinary woman.

In the first stage of his journey, or so long as he remains unconscious, the trinity that secretly controls man is: WOMAN as goddess and creatrix, WOMAN as mother and matrix, and WOMAN as erotic-spiritual power.

WOMAN as Goddess and Creatrix

WOMAN was, is, and always will be goddess and creatrix. She is the womb from which we sprang, the ground of our being. Feminists who argue that goddess-worship historically preceded the notion of God as father are certainly correct. What they fail to see is that the goddess, since her historical dethronement, has remained alive and well, and continues to exert power from deep in the hidden recesses of the male psyche. Granted, she has been sentenced to remain in a kind of internal exile, under house arrest, but her power is obvious from the efforts spent to keep her imprisoned.

As our source, the goddess is both historically and psychologically primary. She has been an inevitable symbol of divinity since the beginning of time and remains a sacred presence in the timeless dimension of every psyche. The earliest images we have of WOMAN and divinity are one and the same, stone figurines such as the so-called Venus of Willendorph—women without faces or feet, with ponderous breasts and prominent vulvas. When we look at these early icons of mother-goddesses it doesn't require much empathy to imagine the overwhelming sense of awe men experienced at woman's capacity to give birth. She was at once the revelation and the incarnation of creativity. Her womb was of the same substance as the fruitful earth. She was Mother Nature.

In explaining the continuing power of WOMAN as creatrix over men, psychologists have often reduced the mystery of gender to a matter of "penis envy" or "womb envy." But to name the awe we feel in the presence of the opposite sex "envy" is mean and mistaken. Call it "womb awe" or even "womb worship," but it is not simple envy.

I don't remember ever wanting to be a woman. But each of the three times I have been present at the birth of one of my children I have been overwhelmed by a sense of reverence. As the event of birth approached, the delivery room was bathed in a transcendent light and transformed into a stage for a cosmic drama. It was, quite suddenly, the first day of creation; the Goddess was giving birth to a world. When Jessamyn, my last child, was born, the doctors had to attend to Jananne, my wife. I took off my shirt, put the baby next to my body, and walked and sang her welcome into the world. In that hour all my accomplishments—books I had written, works of will and imagination, small monuments to my immortality—shrank into insignificance. Like men since the beginning of time I wondered: What can I ever create that will equal the magnificence of this new life?

As creatrix, WOMAN addresses an inescapable challenge to a man to justify his existence. She gives birth to meaning out of her body. Biology alone assures her of a destiny, of making a significant contribution to the ongoing drama of life. A man responds to her challenge by simulating creation, by making, fabricating, and inventing artifacts. But while she creates naturally and literally, he creates only artificially and metaphorically. She creates from her corpus; he invents a "corporation," a fictitious legal body with endowed rights of a natural person. Her creation sustains the eternal cycle of nature. Each of his artifacts contributes to making history a series of unrepeatable events. (Sometimes I imagine that the hidden intent of technology is to create a perfect mechanical baby—an automobile, a machine that moves by itself, is capable of perpetual motion, is fed its daily bottle of petroleum, and has its pollution diapered.) In response to the power of the goddess, man creates himself in the image of a god he imagines has fabricated the world like a craftsman working with a blueprint to shape matter into meaningful objects. Much of the meaning men attribute to their work is a response to the question posed to us by WOMAN'S capacity to give life.

WOMAN as Mother and Matrix

WOMAN in her second aspect as mother and matrix, is food, everlasting arms, teacher of language and philosophy, the horizon within which we live and move and have our being. To paraphrase an old hymn, She is "so high you can't get over her, so low you can't get under her, so wide you can't get around her." She exists; therefore I am. Within the warp of her womb our bodies are woven—flesh of her flesh. Within the woof of her arms our minds, spirits, and visions of the world are braided together. She is teacher of the categories by which we will understand ourselves. Her face was our first mirror. A newborn is programmed for immediate face recognition and will spend ninety percent of its waking time focused on the mother. The changing pattern of her face—her smile, her frown, the joy or sadness in her eyes—is the infant's barometer of reality. If she smiles I am good. If she is angry I am bad. There was terror in her disapproving glance, and bliss when her face shone upon us.

Consider the fundamental categories of our emotional and intellectual life that we learn before we are weaned. At the breast we learn: desire, satisfaction, disappointment, anger, fear, authority, expectation, judgment. Little wonder that Hindu philosophers identify WOMAN with Maya—illusion—as well as nurturance. Her body is our first information system. If she is warm and sensuous and loves to hold us, we learn that the world is supported by trustworthy and everlasting arms. If she is tense and unhappy we learn the world is fearful and filled with nameless dangers.

WOMAN, as the mother, continues to have enormous power over our adult lives because her most important lessons are taught wordlessly. She shapes us before we understand language, and therefore her influence is hidden from our adult consciousness. Her instructions remain within us like posthypnotic suggestion. Imagine that long ago your mother wrote and inserted the software disk that preprogrammed your life. She etched the script for your life, inserted a philosophy-of-life program, on the blank pages of your mind. This set of instructions remains in the archaic layers of your psyche and continues to shape your perceptions and feelings well into adulthood. The language in which she wrote is as cryptic and difficult to decipher as ancient hieroglyphics, and yet to break the spell she has woven you must learn to decipher these early messages and bring the wordless information and misinformation into the light of consciousness.

In the degree that Mother remains a shadow presence in the life of a man, he will see himself and all women as if reflected in Mother's eyes. He will perform for them as he performed for her, fearing displeasure, courting approval. The size of his ego and the size of his cock will be determined by what he sees in the mirror she holds. And all the while he will imagine that her judgments are those of the flesh-and-blood women in his life. Just like the song says, he will "marry a girl just like the girl that married dear old Dad," and will love and hate her accordingly. Almost inevitably, men marry Mother unless they have undertaken the long struggle to recognize and exorcise WOMAN from their psyches.

Modern men bear a special burden in relationship to Mother; our task of separation is more difficult than that of traditional men. For most modern sons, Mother is a problem that needs to be solved and we find it difficult to break the symbiotic bond.

Freud said that the first major crisis in a boy's life was severing his attachment to his mother and identifying with his father. In the gospel according to Freud, every boy wants to possess and sleep with his mother and displace his powerful father. But he fears being castrated or killed by the father (a fear substantiated by his observation that women and little girls lack, and therefore must have lost, the penis). About the age of six the son learns to live by the ancient adage, "If you can't beat them, join them." He renounces his desire to be his mother's lover and makes common cause with his enemy—the father. This successful resolution of the Oedipus complex, like ancient initiation rites, involves identification with power, authority, and the values of the father and the male establishment.

If this classical drama of separation from Mother and the initiation of the son by the father sounds strange to our ears it is because the world has changed. Since the industrial revolution, the son is more likely to have remained mama's boy than to have identified with any powerful male authority. The powerful father has been all but replaced by the powerful mother.

Dad is no longer present to teach his sons how to be men. More than any other single factor, this absence of the father from the modern family is what presently disturbs the relationship between mothers and their sons and therefore between men and women, husbands and wives. Where once there was a father, there is now a vacuum. Dad belongs more to the world of work than to the family. He is, or was until recently, the provider, but he is gone from the home most of the time. Someone, using what I call SWAG statistics (Scientific Wild-Ass Guess) has estimated that prior to World War I men spent four hours a day with their children, between World War I and World War II two hours, and since World War II twenty minutes.

There are many variations on the modern mother-son theme, but in some degree most sons were forced to step into the role of husband and lover to their mother. As a friend told me: "Mother made me into the husband my father never was. I was the listener, the helper, the ally in hard times. In a sense I became the man of the house. I was superresponsible, so I never really got a chance to be a kid." While the love between mother and son seldom becomes literally incestuous, it becomes too close for comfort. Rollo May, in a conversation with me, characterized the problem of the son who is too close to his mother as the opposite of that which Freud presented. "The dilemma of the modern son is that he *wins* the Oedipal battle against the father and gets Mother. And then he doesn't know what to do with her because she overwhelms him."

Ambivalence is the consequence of the modern mother-son relationship. The son experiences the mother as nearly omnipotent. She works outside the home, manages the household, and provides for his daily needs. But he learns from the rhetoric and values of the surrounding society that women are less important than men, that child-rearing is an inferior task, that men have real power and authority, and that what counts is success in the public arena of business and politics. So the son is faced with a tragic, schizophrenic choice. If he is to become a man and play a role in the "real" world, he must deny his visceral knowledge of the goodness of Mother's caring power and join the male conspiracy to "keep women in their place," in the missionary position, beneath men.

Meanwhile the son must develop various strategies to deal with the power of Mother. He may surrender, becoming mama's boy, and devote his life to pleasing her, and later his wife or lover. If he takes this tack his relationships with women will be dominated by the desire to perform well, to gain approval, and to avoid female anger or rejection. Or he may take an opposite course and reduce females to either servants or sex objects. The Don Juan male constantly tries to prove his potency by seduction and conquest. The more violent man who is obsessed with pornography or rape is compelled to demean and take revenge of woman in order to deny her power over him.

To be free from and for women, to discover the unique ground of manhood, a man must take leave of Motherland.

WOMAN as Erotic-Spiritual Power

The third aspect of WOMAN is as an irresistible erotic-spiritual force. She is the magnet, and men the iron filings that lie within her field.

It is difficult to give this aspect of WOMAN a familiar name because Western mythology, philosophy, and psychology have never acknowledged its reality. Once, men and women assumed that the goddess controlled all things that flow and ebb—the waxing and waning moon, the rise and fall of tide and phallus. But ever since God became Father, and men have considered themselves the lords over nature (and women), we have defined man as active and WOMAN as reactive. Consequently, we have never developed a language that does justice to WOMAN'S erotic-spiritual power.

In Eastern mythology, notions of gender are reversed. The female principle is seen as active and the male as responsive. Among human beings, lions, and other members of the animal kingdom, the female of the species sends out her invitations on the wind and commands the male's response. He may think he initiates, but her sexual perfumes (pheromones) and inspiring image influence him to action. She is the prime mover, the divine eros, whose power draws him to her. As Joseph Campbell points out,[3] the term Shakti in Hindu mythology names the energy or active power of a male divinity that is embodied in his spouse. "Every wife is her husband's Shakti and every beloved woman her lover's. Beatrice was Dante's. Carried further still: The word connotes female spiritual power in general, as manifest, for instance, in the radiance of beauty, or on the elemental level in the sheer power of the female sex to work effects on the male."

To detect this important aspect of men's experience of WOMAN that our language or philosophy of gender does not name or honor, we have to look at the angelic and demonic extremes of men's sexuality—the ways in which WOMAN figures in the imaginations of artists and rapists.

For many creative men WOMAN is the muse and inspiration for their work. She possesses a semidivine power to call forth their creativity. Without her inspiration they cannot paint, write, or manage. She is the anima, the spirit and soul of a man. Without her a man is only will and intellect and blind force.

At the opposite end of the spectrum the rapist confesses the same experience of the irresistible erotic power of WOMAN. His defense is inevitably: "She tempted me. She wanted it. She seduced me." For a moment, put aside the correct response to such deluded excuses, which is that it is *not* the victim's fault, and consider the raw unconscious experience of WOMAN that underlies rape no less than the inspiration of the artist. In both cases, she is experienced as the active, initiatory power.

When we consider how most "civilized" men have repressed their experience of the power of WOMAN as goddess, mother, and erotic-spiritual motivator, it is easy to understand the reasons that lie in back of the history of men's cruelty to women. We fear, therefore deny, therefore demean, therefore (try to) control the power of WOMAN. There is no need here to rehearse the routine insults and gynocidal hatreds of men toward women. Mary Daly, Susan Griffin, and other feminist thinkers have traced this painful history in brilliant and convincing fashion.

As men we need to recollect our experience, reown our repressed knowledge of the power of WOMAN, and cease establishing our manhood in reactionary ways. If we do not, we will continue to be workers desperately trying to produce trinkets that will equal WOMAN'S creativity, macho men who confuse swagger with independence, studs who anxiously perform for Mother's eyes hoping to win enough applause to satisfy a fragile ego, warriors and rapists who do violence to a feminine power they cannot control and therefore fear.

So long as we define ourselves by our reactions to unconscious images of WOMAN we remain in exile from the true mystery and power of manhood.

Saying Good-bye to WOMAN

The early books about men's liberation, after reacting to the threat or promise of woman's liberation and expressing "the hazards of being male," settled down quickly to solve the problem of how to have good relationships with women. Chapter headings of Herb Goldberg's *The New Male* tell the story: "He. He and She. He and Her Changes. He and His Changes." Or the chapter headings of the same author's *The Inner Male: Overcoming Roadblocks to Intimacy:* "With Women. With Sexuality. With Liberation. With Himself." *Why Men Are the Way They Are* by Warren Farrell bears the subtitle *The Male-Female Dynamic.* Even when men try to liberate themselves, they remain hypnotized by WOMAN.[4]

We can't be comfortable in intimacy with women because we have never been comfortable in being distant from them. Most modern men have never learned the joy of solitude. We have failed to define our identity, our purpose, our raison d'être apart from our relationship with WOMAN. We have, as Howard Thurman said to me, gotten the questions we ask ourselves in the wrong order. Before asking what our journey should be, we ask if she will go with us, or where she wants to go. And having sold our souls for her approval, we are ill at ease.

To become a man, a son must first become a prodigal, leave home, and travel solo into a far country. Alien nation before reconciliation. There can be no homecoming without leave-taking. To love a woman we must first leave WOMAN behind.

Until now, this book has been a prelude. Finally, we are at the fork in the road that separates those who choose to remain unconscious of the sources of their identity as men and those who choose to make the journey into lucid manhood. For those who choose the way of the pilgrim, the first step will be to leave behind questions about women, and relationships to women. Only after we have explored the question of first importance— What is our journey?—can we safely return to the question of second importance—Who will go with us?

I urge you not to cheat. No matter how troubled your

relationships with women, do not skip to the final chapters of this book. The urgency men feel about sex, intimacy, marriage, and getting things right with women is precisely what creates the anxiety that forces us into relationships in which we betray our manhood and do violence to women. Like a good mystery story, the journey toward full manhood is filled with many surprises that make no sense to those who try to learn the conclusion without taking one step at a time.

I invite you to join me on the journey.

THE RITES OF MANHOOD

3

THE INITIATION AND MUTILATION OF MEN

"The information necessary to create a
male is encoded in our DNA, but it takes
all the institutions of a culture to
produce a man. The male body is the
biologically given 'hardware,' the myth of
manhood is the 'software' inserted by
society through a series of formal and
informal rites of passage."
—Sandor McNab.

Traditional Rites of Passage

If an anthropologist from Mars were to study Earth cultures he would notice something very strange. Everywhere he would find a social obsession with manliness. He would find that manhood is considered a chancy thing, a prize, a puzzle difficult to solve, a test to be passed, "the Big Impossible." Men and women alike constantly exhort little boys to "act like a man," be *muy macho*, a big man, a real man, an alpha male. Men live under constant dread of being labeled a sissy, a weakling, a wimp, a queer. Most everywhere they live under pressure, stress, and the constant need to prove themselves by establishing mastery in the arenas of war, work, and women, a near universal creed linking manhood with the socially necessary activities of protecting, providing, and procreating. A people

like the Tahitians who encourage men to be gentle, easy, graceful, generous to strangers, slow to take offense, and unconcerned
with defending masculine "honor" are rare.

Further, in nearly every tribe and nation, ancient as well
as modern, our Martian anthropologist would find seemingly
irrational formal rites and informal customs that are designed to
turn males into men. He would find men encouraged to fight,
drink, brawl, defend their honor, strive without ceasing, and risk
life and limb in order to prove their manliness. He would find
men from the island of Truk undertaking foolhardy expeditions
in tiny dugouts in shark-infested waters to prove their valor;
sponge divers in the Greek Aegean islands scorning the use of
safe diving equipment, risking the crippling effects of bends to
show their manly contempt for death; American miners working
in conditions certain to produce black lung disease; "scrubbers"
in nuclear plants scoffing at the hazards of radiation. Everywhere
the path of manhood involves artificial ordeals and rites of
passage that turn a boy's passage into social maturity into a
second birth trauma.[1]

The cycle of human life naturally suggests that there be
at least four major rites of passage for every person: birth, coming
of age, marriage, and death. The rites celebrating our beginning
and end are necessarily conducted without our consent by those
who are on the stage before and after our time. But between the
parentheses of birth and death, the most important rites are
those when we separate from the opposite sex to learn the
mysteries of our own gender and when we return to join in
marriage and create new life.

Premodern societies knew the overwhelming power of
WOMAN and that boys could only emerge into manhood if they
separated from her and entered for a time into an all-male world.
Male rites of passage were designed to allow boys to escape from
WOMAN'S world long enough to discover the shape of man's
world. They knew that men must resist the danger of being
defined by WOMAN (and vice versa). The sexes were pried apart
and isolated to explore their separate truths before they could
come together.

The rites, rituals, and ceremonies that marked the transition from boyhood to manhood differed from tribe to tribe and
culture to culture. But amid all the variations, from the bar
mitzvah of the Jews to the subincision of the penis among the
Australian aboriginals, we can isolate three phases that were
common. The passage to manhood was a drama with three acts:
separation, initiation, and reincorporation. Joseph Campbell puts
it this way: "The so-called rites of passage which occupy such a

prominent place in the life of a primitive society (ceremonials of birth, naming, puberty, marriage, burial, etc.), are distinguished by formal, and usually very severe, exercises of severance, whereby the mind is radically cut away from the attitudes, attachments, and life patterns of the stage left behind. Then follows an interval of more or less extended retirement, during which are enacted rituals designed to introduce the life adventurer to the forms and proper feelings of his new estate, so that when, at last, the time has ripened for the return to the normal world, the initiate will be as good as reborn."[2]

Act I: Separation. The cultural task of turning a boy into a man begins by the disruption of the primal bond between mother and son. In infancy he and she have been one flesh. But at some point, usually near the onset of puberty, the boy child will be rudely stolen from the encompassing maternal arms, ready or not, and thrust into the virile society of men. In many tribes, the men kidnap the boys and take them to live in the men's clubhouse where they are subject to hazing, discipline, and teachings of the elders.

Some form of painful ordeal inevitably accompanies and dramatizes the separation from the world of WOMAN. The list of minor and major tortures imposed upon initiates reads like a page from the fantasy life of de Sade and includes: lip piercing, scarification, filing or knocking out of teeth, scourgings, finger sacrifices, removal of a testicle, bitings, burnings, eating of disgusting foods, being tied on an ant hill, subincision of the penis, solitary confinement, exile in the wilderness for long periods, sleeping naked on winter nights, etc. Often a boy was sent out into the forest to kill a dangerous animal or an enemy to prove his courage. Among the Plains Indians, fasting, vigils, and sometimes psychedelic drugs were used to induce an altered state of consciousness and a personal vision.

As a general rule, the more a tribe or nation practices warfare the harsher its rites of initiation for boys. In such cultures, the main purpose of the initiation rites for males is to turn civilian boys into military men. The life of a man is the life of a warrior. To be a man one must be able to bear suffering without complaint, to kill, to die. Some tribes, in their effort to create manly virtues, amputate the nipples, since only women should have breasts. The neophyte warrior learns to disdain woman's ways, to reject the sensuous knowledge of the body he learned kinesthetically from his mother, and to deny all that is "feminine" and soft in himself.

Why this connection between masculinity and pain? We can see the logic that underlies such ordeals if we look closely at the typical "primitive" ritual of circumcision. For reasons that are deeply unconscious—or mythic—the male elders of the tribe ordain that boys must bear a scar throughout life to remind them that they are required to sacrifice their bodies to the will of the tribe. To be a man is to leave behind the world of women-nature-flesh-sensuality-pleasure and submit one's will and body to the world of men-culture-power-duty. The implicit message given to a boy when he is circumcised, whether the ritual is performed when he is seven days old or at puberty, is that your body henceforth belongs to the tribe and not merely to yourself.

If we are to understand the male psyche, decipher the baffling male obsession with violence, break the unconscious sadomasochistic game that binds men and women together in erotic combat, and end the habit of war, we must understand the original wound, the scar, around which masculine character has traditionally been constructed.

The rite of circumcision is widely though not universally practiced, but it is the best symbol of the process by which boys are turned into men. That so primitive and brutal a rite continues to be practiced nearly automatically in modern times when most medical evidence indicates that it is unnecessary, painful, and dangerous suggests that circumcision remains a mythic act whose real significance is stubbornly buried in the unconscious. That men and women who supposedly love their sons refuse to examine and stop this barbaric practice strongly suggests that something powerfully strange is going on here that is obscured by a conspiracy of silence. We do not want to look at the cruelty that is systematically inflicted on men or the wound that is deemed a necessary price of manhood.

Imagine, if you dare, that you are small enough to rest complete within your mother's arms, so sensitive that every nerve ending of your flesh reaches out to the unknown world, eager as lips to receive the bounties of the breast. Then, suddenly, you are seized by male giants, taken from your mother's arms (but with her consent), and held down by force. The tender skin covering your penis is cut off (whether by a stone knife or surgical blade is a matter of small difference). Feel the violation of your flesh, your being. (Do not allow yourself the comforting lie that circumcision isn't that painful, the wound heals quickly, and the pain is soon forgotten.) What indelible message about the meaning of manhood would be carved on your body, encoded within the scar tissue of your symbolic wound?

It is possible to interpret the cruelty involved in rites of passage as expressing the unconscious resentment of the fathers against the sons. But more likely the pain inflicted served as a sacrament—an outward and visible sign of an inward change that transforms boys into men. To create a social body requires a sacrifice of our individual desires. The pain of the ordeal, the hazings, and the insults were designed to break down individuality and replace personal identity with the imprint of the tribe.

From the beginnings of recorded human history to the present day the most important tacit instruction boys receive about manhood is: Masculinity requires a wounding of the body, a sacrifice of the natural endowment of sensuality and sexuality. A man is fashioned by a process of subtraction, decision, abstraction, being severed from the "natural" world of WOMAN. We gain manhood by the willingness to bear the mutilation imposed on us by the ruling elders.

Act II: Initiation. The purpose of the torturous rites involved in severing the boy from WOMAN and nature was to deprogram, brainwash, break down the childish identity so that he could be given a new self-understanding. The second act of male initiation took place within the new male womb where the boy was formed into a man. In the men's community a boy learned the encyclopedia of the culture. For months or years he would listen to the stories, the myths, the tales of heros and villains, that gave answers to the perennial questions: Where do we come from? What is our destiny? How should we act? What are the different roles of men and women? He would be apprenticed to men who would teach him the spiritual technology (ritual, chants, dances, ceremonies, healing practices), the practical technology (use of tools, methods of hunting, gathering, growing), and the social skills (the art of husbanding, fathering, and fighting), required to fulfill the obligations of manhood.

Act III: Reincorporation. At the end of the educational phase of initiation a boy was invested with some insignia of manhood—a sword, shield, feather cape, or penis sheath—and given the right to marry and assume adult responsibilities and privileges. Often he would be given a new name that signified his graduation into the status of full manhood. He could then look forward to a future in which he would pass through recognized and honored stages of the male journey until, old and full of days, he would become one of the elders, the repositories of the wisdom of the tribe and the initiators of the young. Full circle.

In many ways rites of passage, cruel as they were, were socially and psychologically economical. They gave both men and women secure identities and a comfortable knowledge of the roles they were to play. Men didn't have to wonder: Am I a man? How do I achieve manhood? The male rite of initiation had the virtue of being a social event. At a specific time a boy underwent a series of ceremonies after which he was pronounced a man. Overnight his identification and social status changed. Things were a bit different for a woman. Although women's rites also frequently involved ordeals and specific ceremonies, typically a girl became a woman at first menstruation. A boy became a man in *chronos*, social time; a girl became a woman in *kairos*, body time, natural time, moon time. This crucial difference became the basis of men's and women's different sense of time, their views of death, their experience of their bodies, and their personality structure.

In summary, we might say that there was good news and bad news in the traditional rites of passage.

The good news was that traditional peoples knew who they were. They had a blueprint of the world and a guidebook for their passage through time. They didn't have the kind of self-doubts we suffer. They didn't have gender confusion. Men and women were able to cooperate because they maintained firm boundaries (and therefore manners) between the sexes. A community with a common story creates a comfortable sense of belonging that is largely absent from modern cities.

The bad news is that traditional rites prevented the development of individuality. Tribal societies ensured conformity by eliminating any time in the life cycle during which freedom could develop. When a boy child or girl child was initiated, childhood ended and maturity began, with no carefree years of adolescence. Adolescence is a modern invention, a time before the onset of responsibility. During this moratorium the not-yet-adult is allowed to rebel, to play, and to experiment. In primitive cultures the son was cast in the same mold as the father. The sacred ways of the ancestors were repeated without alteration. Tribal peoples kept their eyes focused on the past, determined that they should keep the faith of their fathers, repeat their virtues, and remain loyal to their visions of the world. Many tribal societies remained virtually unchanged over hundreds of years, but when change was forced on them they died because they believed a man remained a man only so long as he retained the old, sacred ways.

But history is change. Modern men, anxious as we are, uncertain of ourselves, lost without a map, may be better equipped to survive than our more solid and unquestioning forebears. Paradoxically, our instability may be the key to our strength.

Modern Myths and Modern Men

IBM executives and NFL quarterbacks are as molded by myths and shaped by rites of passage as any Trobriand islander or Apache.

Most accounts of modern life are filled with lamentations about the loss of community, the loss of a uniform myth, the loss of rites of passage. The story we usually hear goes something like this: With the growth of cities, technology, and secularism we lost the cosmic horizon, the religious connection, the ceremonies and celebrations that marked the stages on life's way and the continuity between the generations. There are no longer rites of passage in the modern city because there are no self-conscious communities to administer them. Men's primary loyalty has shifted from clan and family to corporation and state. The fathers have been separated from their sons by the job, and the grandfathers have been exiled to Sun City where they are learning to square dance while their grandsons are being initiated into the virtues of competition at Little League.

A backward glance should serve to make us suspicious of such interpretations. Nearly every generation since the Renaissance has touted itself as "modern," as "the new age," as having arrived at the moment of enlightenment when the quaint superstitions and myths of the past are finally being swept into the dustbin of history. As is the case in every society, the myths and rites that form our minds, emotions, and actions remain largely invisible and unconscious. One of the best ways to discover the living myth of any society is to examine what everyone accepts uncritically as the way things really are. We, for instance, assume that progress, urbanization, and technological innovation are inevitable, and that it is the destiny of the underdeveloped nations to evolve into developed nations. The consensus reality is the myth, but it remains as invisible to the majority as water is to a fish.

The task of any individual who wants to be free is to demythologize and demystify the authority or myth that has unconsciously informed his or her life. We gain personal authority and find our unique sense of self only when we learn to distinguish between our own story—our autobiographical truths—and the official myths that have previously governed our minds, feelings, and actions. This begins when we ask: "What story have I been living? What myth has captivated me?" It ends only when we tell our own story, and authorize our own life rather than accept the official view of things.[3]

If we want to be liberated, we must examine the myriad informal ways our society tells men what is expected of them, and examine the rites that mark the accumulation of the tokens of manhood. As psychologist Bill Layman said to me in conversation, "We live in an age of uninitiated men and we have been bequeathed a sense of loss. We are shaped by what did not pass between the synapses of the generations." But if our fathers and grandfathers failed to initiate us into manhood, we have nevertheless been initiated by substitute fathers, mentors, and authorities. The men's clubhouse and the fraternal circle of elders and heroes may have vanished, but other institutions have arisen to take their place. Without our conscious knowledge or consent we have all been molded by the modern myths of war, work, and sex, which I discuss next.

THE RITE OF WAR AND
THE WARRIOR PSYCHE

If men were Homo sapiens there would
be no war.

I was fourteen when I had my last real fight, with fists and feet and anything handy. I don't remember anymore what it was about, maybe a girl, or a casual insult on the school bus, or maybe it was just because "the enemy" lived across the imaginary line on Bellefonte Street and went to another school. By my reckoning, Charley was a bit of a sissy. Chest caved in, shoulders slumping, he walked with a monkey lope. At any rate, war was declared and we agreed to meet in the vacant lot next to Nancy Ritter's house. At the appointed time, we appeared on the battleground, each accompanied by selected members of our respective tribes. For a while we circled round each other, each waiting for the other to throw the first punch. "You want to start something, you chicken-shit bastard?" "You touch me and I'll bust your ass." We moved closer. Push came to shove, fists flew, and the first one hit me in the nose. "Hell with this," I said. I was better at wrestling than boxing, I strategized. So I ducked, grabbed his legs, and took him to the ground. After much rolling, arm bending, and cursing I ended up on the bottom, unable to move. "Give up," he said. "Or I'll break your arm." He ratcheted my arm up a notch or two and pushed my face into the gravel. "Do you surrender?" "Fuck off." My face hurt, but not as much as my pride. We both knew I was defeated even though I wouldn't surrender, so he released my arm and after a few rounds of mandatory cursing and name-calling we went home.

That night, true to the scenario in the comic books, I vowed I would never again be beaten up by some goddamn sissy. For $3.95 I sent away for a Charles Atlas course and began to transform a ninety-eight-pound weakling into a lean and mean fighting machine. In the secrecy of my room I practiced "dynamic tension," lifted weights, did push-ups and leg lifts. Later I graduated to wrestling. For years, well into my midthirties, I worked out at the YMCA. I perfected my take-downs and pinning combinations and occasionally entered competitions as a light-heavyweight. I was never a champion but I learned to love fighting. And no one rubbed my face in the dirt.

Meanwhile I was studying philosophy and honing the weapons of dialectic, debate, and argumentation. By the time I was a practicing Ph.D. my mind was even more skilled than my body in the art of self-defense. As a professor I engaged in daily combat with colleagues and students. I was good at the academic game, enjoyed it, and played to win. I hardly noticed that, over the years, I had gradually adopted a combative stance toward others—the mind and posture of a warrior. I was much better at fighting than at wondering or loving.

Agents of Violence

Why has the gender that gave us the Sistine Chapel brought us to the edge of cosmocide? Why have the best and brightest exercised their intelligence, imagination, and energy and managed only to create a world where starvation and warfare are more common than they were in neolithic times? Why has the history of what we dare to call "progress" been marked by an increase in the quantity of human suffering?

Could it be that men are determined to be greedy, aggressive, and brutish? Does some selfish gene, some territorial imperative, drive us blindly into hostile action? Is the story of Cain and Abel etched on our DNA? Does excess testosterone condemn us to violence and early heart attacks?

Because men have historically been the major agents of violence, it is tempting to place the blame on our biology and to conclude that the problem lies in nature's faulty design rather than in our willfulness. But all deterministic explanations ignore the obvious: men are systematically conditioned to endure pain, to kill, and to die in the service of the tribe, nation, or state. The male psyche is, first and foremost, the warrior psyche. Nothing shapes, informs, and molds us so much as society's demand that we become specialists in the use of power and violence, or as we euphemistically say, "defense." Historically, the major difference between men and women is that men have always been expected to be able to resort to violence when necessary. The capacity and willingness for violence has been central to our self-definition. The male psyche has not been built upon the rational "I think; therefore I am" but upon the irrational "I conquer; therefore I am."

In what has come to be the normal state of emergency of modern life, we grant the state the power to interrupt the lives of young men, to draft them into the army, and to initiate them into the ritual of violence. Clichés that pass for wisdom tell us: "The army will make a man out of you," and "Every man must have his war."

Induction into the army or, if you are one of the lucky "few" into the marines, involves the same process of systematic destruction of individuality that accompanied initiation in primitive tribes. The shaved head, the uniform, the abusive drill instructors, the physical and emotional ordeal of boot camp, are meant to destroy the individual's will and teach the dogface that the primary virtue of a man is not to think for himself but to obey his superiors, not to listen to his conscience but to follow orders. Like the rites of all warrior societies it teaches men to value what is tough and to despise what is "feminine" and tenderhearted. Nowhere so clearly as in the military do we learn the primitive maxim that the individual must sacrifice himself to the will of the group as it is represented by the authorities.

In the mythic initiation, the neophyte identifies with the tribal heroes. Their story provides the pattern that will be superimposed on his autobiography. That this mythical-mystical mode of initiation is still in force in our so-called modern mind can be seen in the continual references to the great American hero, John Wayne, in the literature that is now coming out of the Vietnam experience. "The war was billed on the marquee as a John Wayne shoot-'em-up test of manhood . . . I had flashes of images of John Wayne films with me as the hero . . . You see the baddies and the goodies on television and at the movies . . . I wanted to kill the bad guy."[4] Early Christians learned that the authentic life was an "imitation of Christ"; initiates in the mystery cults became the god Dionysius; nice American boys going into battle became John Wayne, the mythic man who had been divinized and made immortal by the media.

For the last four thousand years the baptism by fire has been a great male initiation rite. To win the red badge of courage was the mark of a man. Phillip Caputo reporting on Vietnam states the tradition in classical form: "Before the firefight, those Marines fit both definitions of the word *infantry*, which means either 'a body of soldiers equipped for service on foot,' or 'infants, boys, youths collectively.' The difference was that the second definition could no longer be applied to them. Having received that primary sacrament of war, baptism of fire, their boyhoods were behind them. Neither they nor I thought of it in those terms at the time. We didn't say to ourselves, We've been under fire, we've shed blood, now we're men. We were simply aware, in a way we could not express, that something significant had happened to us."[5]

Although only a minority of men actually serve in the military and fewer still are initiated into the brotherhood of those who have killed, all men are marked by the warfare system and the military virtues. We all wonder: Am I a man? Could I kill? If tested would I prove myself brave? Does it matter whether I have actually killed or risked being killed? Would you think more or less of me if I had undergone the baptism of fire? Would I think more or less of myself? What special mystery surrounds the initiated, the veteran? What certification of manhood matches the Purple Heart or the Congressional Medal of Honor?

Men have all been culturally designed with conquest, killing, or dying in mind. Even sissies. Early in life a boy learns that he must be prepared to fight or be called a sissy, a girl. Many of the creative men I know were sissies. They were too sensitive, perhaps too compassionate to fight. And most of them grew up feeling they were somehow inferior and had flunked the manhood test. I suspect that many writers are still showing the bullies on the block that the pen is mightier than the sword. The test shaped us, whether we passed or flunked.

We are all war-wounded.

The Warrior Psyche

To understand men and the twisted relations that exist between men and women, we need to look at what happens to a man when his mind, body, and soul are socially informed by the expectation that he must be prepared to suffer, die, and kill to protect those he loves.

These are not the kinds of topics we usually consider when we think about men. Why not? Why do we so seldom wonder if the habit of war has made men what they are rather than vice versa? The warfare system has become such an accepted part of the social and psychological horizon within which we live, that its formative influence on everything we are and do has become largely invisible. Or to put the matter another way, the warfare system has formed the eyes through which we see war, which means we are encompassed within the myth of war. We assume war is "just the way things are." It is an inevitable outcome of the power dynamics that exist among tribes, groups, nations. And because we rarely examine our basic assumptions about war, generation after generation, we continue to beg the crucial question about the relationship between the warfare system and the male and female psyche.

Lately we have generated a new, and I believe, false hope that women can gain enough power to solve the problems men create. The recent feminist slogan "Peace is Matriotic" reveals in a single phrase the degree to which the warfare system has bewitched us all. It assumes the opposite, that "War is Patriotic," a problem caused by men. But as we will see, the warfare system unfortunately shapes both the male and female psyche equally (although in opposite ways). History offers us the chance to take responsibility and change what we previously considered our fate. What it does not offer is virgin births, pure heroes, guiltless saviors, or morally immaculate groups (the faithful, the bourgeoisie, the moral majority, the sons of God or the daughters of the goddess) whose innocence gives them the leverage to change the course of things in the twinkling of an eye or the length of a sermon.

Our best hope is to see how the war system has been constructed, and then to undertake the hundred-year task of taking it apart piece by piece.

Modern psychology has given us two great intellectual tools that can help us understand the warrior psyche: Freud's idea of "defense mechanisms" and Wilhelm Reich's notion of "character armor."

Freud assumed he was offering an objective, empirical, scientific, and universally valid account of the essential nature of the human psyche. But nowhere was he so much a product of his time as in his assumptions that his own theories were not conditioned by his time and social milieu. Like most nineteenth-century scientists, he assumed he could see reality as if from a god's-eye perspective—the way it really was. But Freud is interesting and useful to us precisely when we see his psychology not as a description of the inevitable structure of the human psyche, but as a psychogram of the way the minds and emotions of men and women have been shaped by the warfare system. His account of the self inadvertently lays bare the logic of the warrior psyche. The psychological landscape he describes, no less than the political landscape Matthew Arnold described in *Dover Beach*, is that of a battlefield where "ignorant armies clash by night."

The psyche, according to Freud, is like a miniaturized nation that is organized to guard against threats real or imagined, from internal or external sources. It is the scene of a perpetual conflict in which the embattled ego is constantly fending off angelic legions and moralistic forces of the superego and the dark powers of the libidinal underworld. Even in the healthy individual there is a continual conflict between the instinctual drives that propel the organism toward gratification and the defenses and counterforces that oppose the expression and gratification.

The weapons used in this struggle, the defense mechanisms, are well honed but for the most part are used automatically, with little awareness. In fact, defense mechanisms, like the propaganda apparatus of a modern state, function best when they censor awareness of the actual (ambiguous) situation of the self. They foster comforting illusions and keep unpleasant realities out of consciousness.

Consider the obvious parallels between the modus operandi of the warfare state and some of the defense mechanisms Freud considered the armamentum of the ego:[6]

Repression, "the exclusion of a painful idea and its associated feeling from consciousness," is like the repression of our genocide against native Americans and the consequent sense of appropriate guilt.

Isolation, the splitting off of appropriate feelings from ideas, is obvious in our habit of thinking calmly about nuclear destruction.

Reaction formation, "replacing an unacceptable drive with its opposite," is at work in naming the MX missile "the peacekeeper."

Displacement, directing an unacceptable wish away from its original to a less threatening object, e.g., occurs when a man rapes a woman to give vent to the anger he feels toward his mother or toward the authorities who brutalized the "feminine" aspects of himself.

Projection, attributing an unacceptable impulse to somebody else, allows us to claim that the enemy is planning to destroy us.

Denial, remaining unaware of the painful reality, is evident in the pretense that we can use nuclear weapons against an enemy without destroying ourselves.

Rationalization, using reasons to disguise one's unconscious motives, is used when we announce to the world that "We sent arms to the Contras only because we wanted to help them remain free, not because we want to dominate Central America."

Wilhelm Reich added a crucial twist to the notion of defense mechanisms. Not only the mind, but the body is formed by living in the ambiance of threat and violence. When we perceive danger, the body immediately prepares itself for fight or flight, glands and muscles switch to emergency status. Adrenaline courses through our system, the heart rate increases, and we assume a "red alert" stance. In the natural course of things, a threat arises and recedes, the lion approaches and retreats or is killed. But a culture that is at war or constantly preparing for a possible war conspires to create the perception, especially among its male citizens, that the threat from the enemy is always present, and therefore we can never let down our guard. "Eternal vigilance is the price of liberty." So men, the designated warriors, gradually form "character armor," a pattern of muscular tension and rigidity that freezes them into the posture that is appropriate only for fighting—shoulders back, chest out, stomach pulled in, anal sphincter tight, balls drawn up into the body as far as possible, eyes narrowed, breathing foreshortened and anxious, heart rate accelerated, testosterone in full flow. The warrior's body is perpetually uptight and ready to fight.

Recently, on an ordinary afternoon, I watched an early stage of the education of a warrior in my side yard. Two boys, four and six years old, were swinging on a rope that hung from a tall limb of an old cottonwood tree. For a while they took turns in an orderly way, but then the bigger boy seized power and began to hog the swing. The little boy protested, "It's my turn," and went over and tried to take the rope. "Bug off!" shouted the big boy, and pushed the little boy roughly to the ground. The man-child struggled to his feet, jaw quivering, fighting to hold back his tears, and said defiantly, "That didn't hurt."

Condition a man (or a woman) to value aggression above

all other virtues, and you will produce a character type whose most readily expressed emotion will be anger.

Condition a woman (or a man) to value submission above all other attitudes and you will produce a character type whose most readily expressed emotion will be sadness.

Depending on how you look at it, aggression may be man's greatest virtue or his greatest vice. If our destiny is to conquer and control, it is the prime mover. If our destiny is to live in harmony, it is the legacy of an animal past. Or maybe it is only focused energy that may be as easily directed toward making a hospital as making war.

Research has shown it is not simple aggression but aggression mixed with hostility that predisposes Type A personalities to heart attacks. Unfortunately, the majority of men, being novices at introspection, have a hard time separating aggression and anger. Thus, the social forces that encourage a man to be an extrovert, hard-driving and iron-willed, prepare him equally for success and a heart attack. (And why does the heart "attack" a man if not because he has become an enemy to his own heart? And why does it most frequently attack a man at 9 A.M. on Mondays?)[7] Arguably, the fact that men die seven to nine years before women on an average is due to the emotions, behavior, and character-armor that make up the warrior psyche. Statistically, in modern times the traditional female stance of submission has proven to have greater survival value than the traditional male stance of aggression. The meek do inherit the earth for nearly a decade longer than the conquistadors. Men pay dearly for the privilege of dominating. As women enter the arenas where competition and conquest are honored above all other virtues, both their character armor and their disease profiles are likely to begin to resemble men's.

In the psyche no less than in a machine, "form follows function." Thus a man's mind-body-spirit that has been informed by the warfare system will necessarily be shaped by the actuality or anticipation of conflict, competition, and combat. The following are some of the characteristics of the warrior psyche:

• A dramatic, heroic stance. The warrior's world is structured on one of the oldest dramatic principles—the conflict between an antagonist and protagonist, a hero and a villain. It is filled with the stuff of which good stories are made: crucial battles, brave deeds, winning and losing. And violent emotions: hate and love, loyalty and betrayal, courage and cowardice. It is not accidental that we speak of the "theater" of war. The warrior finds the meaning of his life in playing a part in an overarching story of the cosmic struggle between good and evil.

- Willpower, decision, and action. The warrior psyche has little time for contemplation, appreciation, and simple enjoyment. It is a mind disciplined to strategic thinking, to the setting of goals and the elaboration of means. It asks "how" rather than "why."
- A sense of the adventure, danger, excitement, and heightened awareness that comes from living in the presence of death. Many men who have been to war confess that for all its horror it was the one time in their lives when they felt most alive. The warrior denies death, lives with the illusion of his own invulnerability and his immortality in being a part of the corps, the brotherhood of Valhalla. By remaining in the excitement of the ambiance of violent death he escapes the anxiety (and courage) of having to live creatively with the prospect of normal death.
- The identification of action with force. When politics reaches a point of impotence the warrior's imagination turns immediately to the use of force. Thus the specter of impotence always shadows the warrior. He must constantly prove he is powerful by his willingness to do and endure violence.
- A paranoid worldview. The warrior is marked by a negative identity; his life is oriented against the enemy, the rival, the competition. He moves with others only when he conspires to make them allies in his struggle against a common enemy.
- Black-and-white thinking. The more intense a conflict becomes, the more we oversimplify issues, and screen information to exclude anything that is not relevant to winning the struggle. The warrior's eye and mind narrow to stereotypes that reduce the enemy to an entity that can be defeated or killed without remorse. In the heat of battle life it is: Kill or be killed; You are either for or against us.
- The repression of fear, compassion, and guilt. The warrior psyche automatically manufactures propaganda that allows it to feel morally self-righteous by transferring blame to the enemy.
- Obsession with rank and hierarchy. The military world is organized on the basis of a hierarchy of command and submission, a pecking order in which the private obeys the corporal, the corporal the sergeant, etc. In such a world rank limits responsibility. Because obedience is required there is always a

THE WARRIOR

Ego ideal Consciously:	*Shadow* Unconsciously:
He is expected to protect, to suffer, to kill, and to die. His body and character are hardened to allow him to fight.	He is fragile and terrified of his tenderness and mortality.
His psyche centers in reason, will. He is spirit, mind.	Moody, lacking skill in dealing with emotion.
He is dominant, cruel, sadistic.	Covertly submissive and passive.
His defining virtue is power.	His controlling fear is impotence.
He strives for independence, self-definition.	He is unconsciously controlled by dependency needs, surrenders to and obeys authority.
He is allowed anger but no tears.	Grief and melancholy cause his depression.
He is supposed to be brave, bold, aggressive.	He represses his fear and shyness.
His sphere of action is public, political.	He has abandoned the familiar and domestic.
He is extroverted, practical, focused, linear, goal oriented; at worst, obsessive and rigid.	He fears feeling, nature, woman, death, all that evades his efforts to control.
As actor he assumes super re-sponsibility and Promethean guilt.	Arrogance and pride shadow his life.

The warfare system inevitably shapes the dance between the genders. Once the actuality or possibility of war becomes the context within which we live, men and women are forced into set roles. This is the choreography of the relationship between the sexes that has dominated the last era of human history.[8]

THE WOMAN

Ego idea Consciously:	*Shadow* Unconsciously:
She is expected to inspire, to nurture, to heal. Her body and character are softened to allow her to care.	She is tough and terrified of her power.
Her psyche centers in emotion and sensation. She is nature, body.	Opinionated, lacking skill in disciplined thinking.
She is submissive, obedient, masochistic.	Covertly manipulative and cruel.
Her defining virtue is warmth.	Her controlling fear is frigidity.
She strives for relationship, belonging.	She is unconsciously controlled by rebellious emotions and fears of self-definition and freedom.
She is allowed tears but no anger.	Resentment and rage cause her depression.
She is supposed to be fearful, shy, passive.	She represses her boldness and aggression.
Her sphere of action is private, domestic.	She has abandoned the worldly and political.
She is introverted, intuitive, unfocused, cyclical, process oriented; at worst, hysterical and atonic.	She fears abstraction, history, man, power politics, all that evades the logic of her heart.
As reactor she becomes victim, blamer, martyr.	Timidity and low self-esteem shadow her life.

rationale denying one's radical freedom—"I was only following orders, doing my duty."
• The degrading of the feminine. To the degree that a culture is governed by a warfare system, it will reduce women to second-class citizens whose function is essentially to service warriors.

Cannon Fodder, Gang Rape, and the War System

In the last generation, the women's movement has made us aware of the ways women have been victims of men's violence. Recent estimates[9] are that, in the U.S., three out of four women will be victims of at least one violent crime in their lifetime. Every eighteen seconds a woman is beaten, and the rate of rape is thirteen times higher than in Britain. Short of some theory that attributes violence to the innate sinfulness of men, the only way we can make sense of this propensity to brutalize women is by looking for the factors that cause men to be violent. We must assume, as they say about computers, "Garbage in, garbage out." Violence in, violence out. Men are violent because of the systematic violence done to their bodies and spirits. Being hurt they become hurters. In the overall picture male violence toward women is far less than male violence against other males. For instance, the F.B.I. reports that of the estimated 21,500 murders in the United States in 1989 two-thirds of the victims were males. What we have refused to acknowledge is that these outrages are a structural part of a warfare system that victimizes both men and women.

The advent of total war and nuclear weapons has recently forced women and children to live with the deadweight of the threat of annihilation that men have always felt in times of war or peace. In the old war code, warriors were expendable but women and children were to be protected behind the shield. Granted, the sanctity of innocence was violated as often as it was respected in warfare. The point is: no one even suggested that men's lives have a claim to the sanctity and protection afforded, in theory, to women and children. It is wrong to kill women and children but men are legitimate candidates for systematic slaughter—cannon fodder.

Every man is "the Manchurian candidate," a hypnotized agent of the state waiting to be called into active service by the bugle call of "Duty," "Honor," "Patriotism." While the official stories all rehearse the glory of the crusade, men harbor the secret knowledge from the time we are young that war is more gory than glory. As a boy, I read the names on the Rolls of Honor on the bronze plaques in churches and memorial auditoriums and imagined what it was like for Harvey Jackson 1927–1945, still a boy at eighteen, to die in the mud on a remote island in the Pacific. And we all saw the crippled veterans who had nothing between their bitterness and despair except war stories and wondered if we would still want to live with such perpetual wounds.

The wounds that men endure, and the psychic scar tissue that results from living with the expectation of being a battle-field sacrifice, is every bit as horrible as the suffering women bear from the fear and the reality of rape. Rise a hundred miles above this planet and look at history from an Olympian perspec-tive and you must conclude that when human beings organize their political lives around a war system, men bear as much pain as women. Our bodies are violated, we are regularly slaughtered and mutilated, and if we survive battle we bear the burden of blood-guilt. When we accept the war system, men and women alike tacitly agree to sanction the violation of the flesh—the rape of women by men who have been conditioned to be "warriors," and the gang rape of men by the brutality of war. Until women are willing to weep for and accept equal responsibility for the systematic violence done to the male body and spirit by the war system, it is not likely that men will lose enough of their guilt and regain enough of their sensitivity to weep and accept respon-sibility for women who are raped and made to suffer the indignity of economic inequality.

If we are to honor as well as be critical of manhood we need to remember that most men went to war, shed blood, and sacrificed their lives with the conviction that it was the only way to defend those whom they loved. For millennia men have been assigned the dirty work of killing and have therefore had their bodies and spirits forged into the shape of a weapon. It is all well and good to point out the folly of war and to lament the use of violence. But short of a utopian world from which greed, scarcity, madness, and ill will have vanished, someone must be prepared to take up arms and do battle with evil. We miss the mark if we do not see that manhood has traditionally required selfless gen-erosity even to the point of sacrifice. "To support his family, the man has to be distant, away hunting or fighting wars; to be tender, he must be tough enough to fend off enemies. To be generous, he must be selfish enough to amass goods, often by defeating other men; to be gentle, he must first be strong, even ruthless in confronting enemies; to love he must be aggressive enough to court, seduce, and 'win' a wife."[10] It was historical necessity and not innate hardness of hearts or taste for cruelty that caused masculinity to evolve into a shell of muscle and will wrapped around a vacuum.

I think what I have said about the warfare system and the warrior psyche is mostly true. But another voice rises up from some primitive depth within myself, the voice of a proud warrior, that I found first in a dream:

I go down into a dark, smoky basement where I am to be initiated into one of the mysteries of manhood. As I enter the room I see that men are sitting around a ring in which two men are fighting. I watch as the fighters batter each other with their fists, but my fascination turns to horror when they pull knives and start slashing at each other. Blood flows. Then one of the fighters stabs and kills the other. I rush from the room in revulsion and moral indignation and report the incident to the police.

I woke from the dream in a sweat, filled with anxiety, unable to go back to sleep. As I began to probe I realized that in the dream I was the "good," moral judgmental observer of the violence and that the fighters were "bad" men. As I lay tossing and turning, it occurred to me to experiment by changing roles in the dream and becoming one of the fighters. After all, it was my dream and all the characters in it were parts of myself. No sooner did I project myself inside the bodies of the fighters than my anxiety vanished and was replaced by a feeling of power and the elation. I was inside the ecstasy of hitting and being hit, lost in the excitement of the battle. I was no longer the moral observer but the warrior lost in the primal battle to survive. And it was not pain I felt but a fierce animal power, raw courage, and the strong knowledge that, if my life was threatened, I would fight with everything in me.

It has been twenty years since my blood-dream, but I remember it vividly because it signaled some kind of change in the depth of my being. It put me in touch with the animal that, if threatened, would defend its life. It told me that although I was moral I was also capable of the primitive amoral violence necessary for survival. After the dream I lost a measure of my fear, paranoia, and feeling of vulnerability, because I knew I would instinctively defend myself if attacked.

This is the dilemma a sensitive man must face: So long as the world is less than perfect the warrior can never wholly retire. It still takes gentleness and fierceness to make a whole man.

THE RITE OF WORK:
THE ECONOMIC MAN

"One does not work to live; one lives to
work." —Max Weber,
Capitalism and the Protestant Ethic

"Have leisure and know that I am God."
—Psalm 65

The summer of 1950 I was eighteen, my brother was
twenty, and we were fancy-free and broke. The only job we
could get was as gandy dancers or trackmen on the Pennsylvania Railroad line between Wilmington and Marcus
Hook. In those days the job of leveling the track had not yet been
automated and was done by a large crew that used jackhammers
to push gravel from the roadbed under the ties.

Monday morning we got up at five and dressed in the old
Levi's and faded shirts we had carefully calculated would not
betray to the other men that we were college boys just on for the
summer. Still sleepy, we ate all the breakfast we could manage,
packed our lunch—four sandwiches apiece, carrots, fruit, cook-
ies, and frozen V-8 juice—and drove off to work on my brother's
motorcycle.

At the work depot the hiring agent took us over and
introduced us to the foreman, Dan Pantelone. Our first surprise
was that, with the exception of Dan and one other man, we were
the only white guys on the gang. We tried to look casual but we

stuck out like virgins in a harem. For one thing, the fact that we didn't have hats or gloves told everyone that we were not used to hard labor under the hot sun.

Once out on the track my anxiety began to rise. Confronted with picks, shovels, sledgehammers, bars, and jackhammers, I suddenly wondered if I would be able to work a full day. I felt sick to my stomach and wanted to go home. But before I could invent a face-saving excuse the foreman came over and told me to help the men who were replacing the steel plates that held the rail to the track. I was handed a sledgehammer and told to help Angel drive the spikes into the tie. It was supposed to go like clockwork—bam, bam, bam, bam, each of us hitting the spike alternately in a regular rhythm. The only problem was that I missed the damn thing more often than I hit it, and hit it with the handle of the hammer more often than the head. Angel, who was twenty-one, black, married with one child, and a four-year veteran of the railroad, looked at me with more tolerance than I expected and said, "Don't worry, boy, you'll get the hang of it." After half an hour blisters were beginning to form on my hands but I was hitting the spike two out of three times. "There, you're getting it, man," Angel said. I felt better, blisters and all.

Time flowed slow and sticky as the tar on the cross ties. Quitting time was only a mirage that vanished as we moved into the heat of the day. Grace notes punctuated the day in the form of occasional breezes that swept off the Delaware River and the shrill whistle of the watchman that signaled us to get off the track and sit for 5 minutes to let a train go by. Finally noon arrived. My brother and I sank down on the bank together and ate, without talking much. "How you doing?" "OK. How about you?" "OK." I fell asleep and dreamt about walking on the beach and diving into the green waves in the cooling dusk. At 12:30 on the minute the whistle blew.

In the afternoon we were introduced to the joys of jackhammering—without gloves. The notion was to use the fifty-pound hammer to force stone under the ties to keep the rails level. Since there were ten hammers connected to a single compressor, the gang had to move at a single pace. One slow man would hold up the whole crew, and I was determined not to be the drag. Revived by lunch I grabbed the hammer hard and started to work. Before the hour was out my hands were battered and I could hardly lift the hammer. Thank God, a long freight forced us off the track. Lampkin, a large, slow-talking man, nearly sixty, came over and sat beside me. "Let me tell you something, boy. Don't grab that hammer so hard. Let it sit gentle in your hands.

And don't lift it when you don't have to. Let it rest on the under lip of the tie and do the work for you. And I'm going to tell you something else. Don't ever start the day any faster than you intend on ending it. You take it easy. This railroad is going to be here when you are dead and gone."

Eons later, when quitting time arrived, we got on the motorcycle and blessed the delicious cool wind in our hair! At home we soaked in tubs of hot and cold water. Our hands, too sore to touch, floated by our sides like bloated bodies of dead soldiers. Immediately after supper, we fell asleep in the living room.

Somehow we got through the week. We learned to wear gloves, hold the hammer easy, walk slowly, and pace ourselves. Friday noon we put the hammers away, got the long bars from the tool box, and went along the stretch of track we had leveled during the week to line it. Sixteen men put bars under the track to lever it one way or the other until it was straight. Someone would begin a work chant, and we would all tap our bars in time and pull together on the beat. "I don't know (Pull)/Believe I will (Pull)/Make my home (Pull)/In Jacksonville (Pull)." The last half hour, we sat around waiting for quitting time, everybody in a good mood. "Now don't you boys spend all your money this weekend on pussy and wine," Lampkin told us. "What do you mean, Lampkin?" Angel said. "Them boys is pretty, not like you. They don't have to pay for pussy." "Shit, man," Lampkin shot back. "Just you ask your wife about me." And everybody laughed.

Quitting time. We raced home, bathed, and took off for the beach for the weekend. Every muscle was sore. The tattoo of the jackhammer still rang in our ears. The stigmata of broken blisters and new calluses marked our hands. But, oh, we did wear our wounds proudly, and cherished every ache like old soldiers fingering campaign ribbons. We had worked with the men, had money in our pockets, and were on our way to see the ladies.

The Bottom Line—Work and Worth

Preparations for the male ritual of work begin even before the age of schooling. Long before a boy child has a concept of the day after tomorrow, he will be asked by well-meaning but unconscious adults, "What do you want to be when you grow up?" It will not take him long to discover that "I want to be a horse" is not an answer that satisfies adults. They want to know what men plan to do, what job, profession, occupation we have decided to follow at five years of age! Boys are taught early that they are what they do. Later, as men, when we meet as strangers on the plane or at a cocktail party we break the ice by asking, "What do you do?"

Formal preparation for the rites of manhood in a secular society takes place first through the institution of schooling. Our indoctrination into the dominant myths, value system, and repertoire of heroic stories is homogenized into the educational process. My fifteen-year-old nephew put the matter more accurately than any social scientist. "Schools" he said, "are designed to teach you to take life sitting down. They prepare you to work in office buildings, to sit in rows or cubicles, to be on time, not to talk back, and to let somebody else grade you." From the first grade onward schools teach us to define and measure ourselves against others. We learn that the world is composed of winners and losers, pass or fail.

The games that make up what we call physical education—football, basketball, and baseball—are minibattles that teach boys to compete in the game of life. Pregame pep talks, like salesmen's meetings, begin with the Vince Lombardi prayer: "Winning isn't the most important thing. It's the only thing." For many boys making the team, from Little League to college, provides the ritual form of combat that is central to male identity.

The first full-time job, like the first fight or first sex, is a rite of passage for men in our time. Boys have paper routes, but men have regular paychecks. Like primitive rites, work requires certain sacrifices and offers certain insignia of manhood. In return for agreeing to put aside childish dalliance and assume the responsibility for showing up from nine to five at some place of work, the initiate receives the power object—money—that allows him to participate in the adult life of the community.

Getting a credit card is a more advanced rite of passage. The credit card is for the modern male what killing prey was to a hunter. To earn a credit rating a man must certify that he has voluntarily cut himself off from childhood, that he has foregone the pleasure of languid mornings at the swimming hole, and has assumed the discipline of a regular job, a fixed address, and a predictable character. The Visa card (passport to the good life) is an insignia of membership, a sign that the system trusts you to spend what you have not yet earned because you have shown good faith by being regularly employed. In modern America going into debt is an important part of assuming the responsibilities of manhood. Debt, the willingness to live beyond our means, binds us to the economic system that requires both surplus work and surplus consumption. The popular bumper sticker "I owe, I owe, so off to work I go" might well be the litany to express the commitment of the working man.

After accepting the disciplines of work and credit, a whole hierarchy of graduated symbolic initiations follows, from first to thirty-second degree. Mere employment entitles one to display the insignia of the Chevette. Acquiring the executive washroom key qualifies one for a Buick or Cadillac. Only those initiated into the inner sanctum of the boardroom may be borne in the regal Rolls-Royce. To the victors belong the marks of status and the repair bills. The right to wear eagle feathers or to sing certain sacred songs was recognized in American Indian tribes to signify the possession of a high degree of power and status, just as in contemporary society certain brand names and logos are tokens of class and rank. A man wears a Rolex not because it tells time more accurately than a $14.95 Timex but because, like a penis shield, it signifies an advanced degree of manhood. In a society where the marks of virtue are created by advertising, possession of stylish objects signifies power. For economic man a Ralph Lauren polo shirt says something very different than its Fruit of the Loom equivalent. The implicit message is that manhood can be purchased. And the expense of the luxury items we own marks our progress along the path of the good life as it is defined by a consumer society.

Within the last decade someone upped the ante on the tokens required for manhood. A generation ago providing for one's family was the only economic requirement. Nowadays, supplying the necessities entitles a man only to marginal respect. If your work allows you only to survive you are judged to be not much of a man. To be poor in a consumer society is to have failed the manhood test, or at least to have gotten a D−. The advertising industry reminds us at every turn that real men, successful men, powerful men, are big spenders. They have enough cash or credit to consume the best. Buying is status. "It's the cost of the toys that separates the men from the boys." The sort of man who reads *Playboy* or *The New Yorker* is dedicated to a life of voluntary complexity, conspicuous consumption, and adherence to the demanding discipline of style.

The rites of manhood in any society are those that are appropriate and congruent with the dominant myth. The horizon within which we live, the source of our value system, and the way we define "reality" are economic. The bottom line is the almighty dollar. Time is money, money is power, and power makes the world go round. In the same sense that the cathedral was the sacred center of the medieval city, the bank and other commercial buildings are the centers of the modern city.

Once upon a time work was considered a curse. As the result of Adam and Eve's sin we were driven from the Garden of Eden and forced to earn our bread by the sweat of our brows. Men labored because of necessity, but found the meaning and sweetness of life in free time. According to the Greeks, only slaves and women were bound to the life of work. Free men discovered the joys and dignity of manhood in contemplation and in the cultivation of leisure. Until the time of the Protestant Reformation the world was divided between the realm of the secular, to which work and the common life belonged, and the realm of the sacred, which was the monopoly of the Church. Martin Luther changed all of this by declaring that every man and woman had a sacred vocation. The plowman and the housewife no less than the priest were called by God to express their piety in the common life of the community. Gradually the notion of the priesthood of all believers came to mean that every man and woman had a calling to meaningful secular work.

In the feudal era manhood involved being the lord of a manor, the head of a household, or at least a husbandman of the land. As the industrial revolution progressed men were increasingly pulled out of the context of nature, family, church, and community to find the meaning of their lives in trading, industry, the arts, and the professions, while women practiced their vocations by ministering to the needs of the home and practicing charity within the community. Gradually, getting and spending assumed the place of greatest importance, virtually replacing all of the old activities that previously defined manhood—hunting, growing, tending, celebrating, protesting, investigating. As "the bottom line" became our ultimate concern, and the Dow Jones the index of reality, man's world shrank. Men no longer found their place beneath the dome of stars, within the brotherhood of animals, by the fire of the hearth, or in the company of citizens. Economic man spends his days with colleagues, fellow workers, bosses, employees, suppliers, lawyers, customers, and other strangers. At night he returns to an apartment or house that has been empty throughout the day. More likely than not, if he is married with children, his wife has also been away at work throughout the day and his children have been tended and educated by another cadre of professionals. If he is successful his security (securus—"free from care") rests in his investments (from "vestment"—a religious garment) in stocks, bonds, and other commodities whose future value depends upon the whims of the market.

Nowadays only a fortunate minority are able to find harmony between vocation and occupation. Some artists, professionals, businessmen, and tradesmen find in their work a calling, a lifework, an arena within which they may express their creativity and care. But most men are shackled to the mercantile society in much the same way medieval serfs were imprisoned in the feudal system. All too often we work because we must, and we make the best of a bad job.

In the secular theology of economic man Work has replaced God as the source from whom all blessings flow. The escalating gross national product, or at least the rising Dow Jones index, is the outward and visible sign that we are progressing toward the kingdom of God; full employment is grace; unemployment is sin. The industrious, especially entrepreneurs with capital, are God's chosen people, but even laborers are sanctified because they participate in the productive economy.

As a form of secular piety Work now satisfies many of the functions once served by religion. In the words of Ayn Rand, whose popular philosophy romanticized capitalism and sanctified selfishness, "Your work is the process of achieving your values. Your body is a machine but your mind is its driver. Your work is the purpose of your life, and you must speed past any killer who assumes the right to stop you . . . Any value you might find outside your work, any other loyalty or love, can only be travelers going on their own power in the same direction."[11]

We don't work just to make a living. Increasingly, the world of work provides the meaning of our lives. It becomes an end in itself rather than a means. A decade ago, only twenty-eight percent of us enjoyed the work we did. And yet, according to a Yankelovich survey, eighty percent of us reported that we would go right on working even if we didn't need the money. By the 1980s this profile changed. We are just as attached to our work, but now we are demanding that the workplace provide an outlet for our creativity. Yankelovich reports in 1988 that fifty-two percent of Americans respond "I have an inner need to do the very best job I can, regardless of the pay" and sixty-one percent when asked what makes for the good life say "a job that is interesting."[12]

Something very strange has happened to work and leisure in the last generation. The great promise of emerging technology was that it would finally set men free from slavery and we could flower. As late as the 1960s philosophers, such as Herbert Marcuse, sociologists, and futurists were predicting a coming leisure revolution. We were just around the corner from a twenty-hour work week. Soon we would be preoccupied by arts, games, and erotic dalliance on leisurely afternoons. At worst we would have to learn to cope with "pleasure anxiety" and the threat of leisure.

Exactly the opposite happened. Work is swallowing leisure. The fast lane has become a way of life for young professionals who are giving their all to career. In the 1990s Americans may come more and more to resemble the Japanese—workaholics all, living to work rather than working to live, finding their identity as members of corporate tribes.

Recently the awareness has been growing that work, even good and creative work, may become an addiction that destroys other human values. A Workaholics Anonymous movement has emerged with a twelve-step program for men and women who feel their work lives have gotten out of control. According to a WA recruiting broadside if you answer yes to three or more of the following questions you may be a workaholic:

1. Do you get more excited about your work than about family or anything else?

2. Are there times when you can charge through work and other times when you can't get anything done?

3. Do you take work with you to bed? on weekends? on vacation?

4. Is work the activity you like to do best and talk about most?

5. Do you work more than forty hours a week?

6. Do you turn your hobbies into money-making ventures?

7. Do you take complete responsibility for the outcome of your work efforts?

8. Have your family or friends given up expecting you on time?

9. Do you take on extra work because you are concerned that it won't otherwise get done?

10. Do you underestimate how long a project will take and then rush to complete it?

11. Do you believe that it is okay to work long hours if you love what you are doing?

12. Do you get impatient with people who have other priorities besides work?

13. Are you afraid if you don't work hard you will lose your job or be a failure?

14. Is the future a constant worry for you even when things are going very well?

15. Do you do things energetically and competitively, including play?

16. Do you get irritated when people ask you to stop doing your work to do something else?

17. Have your long hours hurt your family and other relationships?

18. Do you think about work while driving, while falling asleep, or when others are talking?

19. If you are eating alone, do you work or read during your meal?

20. Do you believe that more money will solve the other problems in your life?

Maybe the standards of WA for what constitutes a workaholic are a trifle high, or maybe they're an index of how consuming work has become, but (I confess) according to the above questions, I and most of my friends qualify as workaholics.

Part of the problem is that work, community, and family are getting mixed up and lumped together. Increasingly, Americans live in places where they are anonymous, and seek to find their community at work. Companies, with the help of organizational development consultants, are trying to make the workplace the new home, the new family. The new motto is: humanize the workplace; make it a community; let communication flourish on all levels. The best (or is it the worst?) of companies have become paternalistic or maternalistic, providing their employees with all the comforts and securities of home.

Here is what work looks like in the now and future world of the corporate utopia:

> "So here's the scoop: instead of working at home, it's going to be living at the office. The future is not the 'home office.' It's the 'office home.'
>
> "To be blunt, offices are in many ways nicer places to live. The view out of my office window, for example, is a lot prettier than the view from my bedroom window.
>
> "Inside the office, it's a clean, well-lit place. Somebody comes by each night and tidies up. A trained accountant takes care of my business expenses. We have Macintoshes with sophisticated games. We have a full kitchen and bath facilities.
>
> "In our New York office, we have exercise rooms, aerobics classes, a cafeteria, and day care. Offices are going through the same evolution as malls. Work 'R' Us. . . .
>
> "Home is where you have to do it all for yourself. For creature comforts and economic stability, the office has the

home beat cold. But, of course, that's not what's important about home. It's the emotional contact. Or is it?

"That offices have become communities has been clear in mass culture since *The Mary Tyler Moore Show,* where the real family was the job family. Now for every *Cosby* there's an *L.A. Law . . . Thirtysomething* has got the 80s zeitgeist exactly right. The series gives work and home equal billing.

"I certainly relate to my officemates better than I do to my neighbors. My office friends are interested in most of the same things, have about the same education, and laugh at most of the same jokes."[13]

In short, the workplace is rapidly becoming its own culture that defines who we are. Like minisocieties, professions and corporations create their own ritual and mythology. Doctors share a common story, a history of disease and cure, a consensus about the means of healing with other doctors. Businessmen share the language of profit and loss with other businessmen and acknowledge the same tokens of success. As economic organizations have grown larger than governments, employees render them a type of loyalty previously reserved for God, country, or family.

To determine what happens to men within the economic world we need to look critically at its climate, its ruling mood, its ethos, its aims, and its method. We should no more accept a profession's or a corporation's self-evaluation, its idealistic view of itself (we are a family, a "service" organization, dedicated to the highest ideals of quality, etc.) than we would accept the propaganda of any tribe or nation.

A recent critical study of the climate of corporate culture suggests it may be more like a tyrannical government than a kindly family. Earl Shorris, in a neglected and very important book, suggests that the modern corporation represents a historically new form of tyranny in which we are controlled by accepting the definitions of happiness that keep us in harness for a lifetime. Herewith, in short, his argument:

> "The most insidious of the many kinds of power is the power to define happiness. . . .
>
> "The manager, like the nobleman of earlier times, serves as the exemplary merchant: Since happiness cannot be defined, he approximates his definition through the display of symbols, such as expense account meals, an expensive house, stylish clothing, travel to desirable places, job security, interesting friends, membership in circles of powerful people, advantages for his children, and social position for his entire family. . . .

"In the modern world, a delusion about work and happiness enables people not only to endure oppression but to seek it and to believe that they are happier because of the very work that oppresses them. At the heart of the delusion lies the manager's definition of happiness: sweat and dirty hands signify oppression and a coat and tie signify happiness, freedom and a good life.

"Blue-collar workers . . . resist symbolic oppression. One need only visit an assembly line and observe the styles of dress, speech, and action of the workers to realize the symbolic freedom they enjoy . . . They live where they please, socialize with whomever they please, and generally enjoy complete freedom outside the relatively few hours they spend at their jobs . . . No matter how much money a blue-collar worker earns, he is considered poor; no matter how much he enjoys his work, he is thought to be suffering. In that way, blue-collar wages are kept low and blue-collar workers suffer the indignity of low status.

"The corporation or the bureaucracy . . . becomes a place, the cultural authority, the moral home of a man. The rules of the corporation become the rules of society, the future replaces history, and the organization becomes the family of the floating man . . . By detaching him from the real world of place, the corporation becomes the world for him.

"Men abandoned the power to define happiness for themselves, and having once abandoned that power, do not attempt to regain it. . . ."[14]

The new rhetoric about the workplace as home and family needs to be balanced by an honest evaluation of the more destructive implications of the iron law of profit. Home and family are ends in themselves. They are, or should be, about sharing of love to no purpose. They file no quarterly reports. Business is an activity organized to make a profit. And any activity is shaped by the end it seeks. Certainly business these days wears a velvet glove, comporting itself with a new facade of politeness and enlightened personnel policies, but beneath the glove is the iron fist of competition and warfare.

The recent spate of best-selling books about business that make use of military metaphors tell an important story about economic life and therefore about the climate within which most men spend their days. Listen to the metaphors, the poetry of business as set forth in David Rogers's *Waging Business Warfare* from the jacket copy:

"Become a master of strategy on today's corporate killing-fields—and win the war for success. . . . How to succeed in battle: Believe it: if you're in business, you're at war. Your enemies—your competitors—intend to annihilate you. Just keeping your company alive on the battlefield is going to be a struggle. Winning may be impossible—unless you're a master of military strategy . . . You can be—if you'll follow the examples of the great tacticians of history. Because the same techniques that made Genghis Khan, Hannibal, and Napoleon the incomparable conquerors they were are still working for Chrysler's Lee Iacocca, Procter & Gamble's John Smale, Remington's Victor Kiam and other super-strategists on today's corporate killing-fields . . . Join them at the command post! Mastermind the battle! Clobber the enemy! Win the war!"[15]

Or, maybe to succeed you need to know *The Business Secrets of Attila the Hun*? Or listen to the language of Wall Street: corporate raiders, hostile takeovers, white knights, wolf packs, industrial spies, the underground economy, head-hunting, shark-repellent, golden parachutes, poison pills, making a killing, etc.

When we organize our economic life around military metaphors and words such as *war, battle, strategy, tactics, struggle, contest, competition, winning, enemies, opponents, defenses, security, maneuver, objective, power, command, control, will-power, assault* we have gone a long way toward falling into a paranoid worldview. And when men live within a context where their major function is to do battle—economic or literal—they will be shaped by the logic of the warrior psyche.

The High Price of Success

At the moment the world seems to be divided between those countries that are suffering from failed economies and those that are suffering from successful economies. After a half century of communism the USSR, Eastern Europe, and China are all looking to be saved from the results of stagnation by a change to market economies. Meanwhile, in the U.S., Germany, and Japan we are beginning to realize that our success has created an underclass of homeless and unemployed, and massive pollution of the environment. As the Dow rises to new heights everyone seems to have forgotten the one prophetic insight of Karl Marx: where the economy creates a class of winners it will also create a class of losers, where wealth gravitates easily into the hands of the haves, the fortunes of the have-nots become more desperate.

On the psychological level, the shadow of our success, the flip side of our affluence, is the increasing problem of stress and burnout. Lately, dealing with stress and burnout has become a growth industry. Corporations are losing many of their best men to the "disease" of stress. Every profession seems to have its crisis: physician burnout, teacher burnout, lawyer burnout. Experts in relaxation, nutrition, exercise, and meditation are doing a brisk business.

But finally, stress cannot be dealt with by psychological tricks, because for the most part it is a philosophical rather than a physiological problem, a matter of the wrong worldview. Perhaps the most common variety of stress can best be described as "rustout" rather than burnout. It is a product, not of an excess of fire but of a deficiency of passion. We, human beings, can survive so long as we "make a living," but we do not thrive without a sense of significance that we gain only by creating something we feel is of lasting value—a child, a better mousetrap, a computer, a space shuttle, a book, a farm. When we spend the majority of our time doing work that gives us a paycheck but no sense of meaning we inevitably get bored and depressed. When the requirements of our work do not match our creative potential we rust out. The second kind of burnout is really a type of combat fatigue that is the inevitable result of living for an extended period within an environment that is experienced as a battle zone. If the competition is always pressing you to produce more and faster, if life is a battle, if winning is the only thing, sooner or later you are going to come down with battle fatigue. Like combat veterans returning from Vietnam, businessmen who live for years within an atmosphere of low-intensity warfare begin to exhibit the personality traits of the warrior. They become disillusioned and numb to ethical issues; they think only of survival and grow insensitive to pain. You may relax, breathe deeply, take time for R and R, and remain a warrior. But ultimately the only cure for stress is to leave the battlefield.

The feminist revolution made us aware of how the economic order has discriminated against women, but not of how it cripples the male psyche. In ancient China the feet of upper-class women were broken, bent backwards, and bound to make them more "beautiful." Have the best and brightest men of our time had their souls broken and bent to make them "successful?"

Let's think about the relation between the wounds men suffer, our overidentification with work, and our captivity within the horizons of the economic myth.

Recently, a lament has gone out through the land that men are becoming too tame, if not limp. The poet Robert Bly, who is as near as we have these days to a traveling bard and shaman for men, says we have raised a whole generation of soft men—oh-so-sensitive, but lacking in thunder and lightning. He tells men they must sever the ties with mother, stop looking at themselves through the eyes of women, and recover the "wild man" within themselves.

I suspect that if men lack the lusty pride of self-affirmation, if we say "yes" too often but without passion, if we are burned out without ever having been on fire, it is mostly because we have allowed ourselves to be engulfed by a metabody, a masculine womb—The Corporation. Our fragile, tender, wild, and succulent bodies are being deformed to suit the needs of the body corporate. Climbing the economic or corporate ladder has replaced the hero's journey up Mt. Analogue. Upward mobility has usurped the ascent of the Seven-Story Mountain, the quest to discover the heights and depths of the human psyche.

At what cost to the life of our body and spirit do we purchase corporate and professional success? What sacrifices are we required to make to these upstart economic gods?

Here are some of the secrets they didn't tell you at the Harvard Business School, some of the hidden, largely unconscious, tyrannical, unwritten rules that govern success in professional and corporate life:

Cleanliness is next to prosperity. Sweat is lower class, lower status. Those who shower before work and use deodorant make more than those who shower after work and smell human throughout the day. As a nation we are proud that only three percent of the population has to work on the land—get soiled, be earthy—to feed the other ninety-seven percent.

Look but don't touch. The less contact you have with real stuff—raw material, fertilizer, wood, steel, chemicals, making things that have moving parts—the more money you will make. Lately, as we have lost our edge in manufacturing and production, we have comforted ourselves with the promise that we can prosper by specializing in service and information industries. Oh, so clean.

Prefer abstractions. The further you move up toward the catbird seat, the penthouse, the office with the view of all Manhattan, the more you live among abstractions. In the brave new world of the market you may speculate in hog futures without ever having seen a pig, buy out an airline without knowing how to fly a plane, grow wealthy without having produced anything.

Specialize. The modern economy rewards experts, men and women who are willing to become focused, concentrated, tightly bound, efficient. Or to put the matter more poignantly, we succeed in our professions to the degree that we sacrifice wide-ranging curiosity and fascination with the world at large, and become departmental in our thinking. The professions, like medieval castles, are small kingdoms sealed off from the outer world by walls of jargon. Once initiated by the ritual of graduate school, MBAs, economists, lawyers, and physicians speak only to themselves and theologians speak only to God.

Sit still and stay indoors. The world is run largely by urban, sedentary males. The symbol of power is the chair. The chairman of the board sits and manages. As a general rule those who stay indoors and move the least make the most money. Muscle doesn't pay. Worse yet, anybody who has to work in the sun and rain is likely to make the minimum wage. With the exception of quarterbacks, boxers, and race car drivers, whose bodies are broken for our entertainment, men don't get ahead by moving their bodies.

Live by the clock. Ignore your intimate body time, body rhythms, and conform to the demands of corporate time, work time, professional time. When "time is money," we bend our bodies and minds to the demands of EST (economic standard time). We interrupt our dreams when the alarm rings, report to work at nine, eat when the clock strikes twelve, return to our private lives at five, and retire at sixty-five—ready or not. As a reward we are allowed weekends and holidays for recreation. Conformity to the sacred routine, showing up on time, is more important than creativity. Instead of "taking our time" we respond to deadlines. Most successful men, and lately women, become Type A personalities, speed freaks, addicted to the rush of adrenaline, filled with a sense of urgency, hard driven, goal oriented, and stressed out. The most brutal example of this rule is the hundred-hour week required of physicians in their year of residency. This hazing ritual, like circumcision, drives home the deep mythic message that your body is no longer your own.

Wear the uniform. It wouldn't be so bad if those who earned success and power were proud enough in their manhood to peacock their colors. But no. Success makes drab. The higher you rise in the establishment the more colorless you become, the more you dress like an undertaker or a priest. Bankers, politicians, CEOs wear black, gray, or dark blue, with maybe a bold pinstripe or a daring "power tie." And the necktie? That ultimate symbol of the respectable man has obviously been demonically designed to exile the head from the body and restrain all deep and passionate breath. The more a corporation, institution, or profession requires the sacrifice of the individuality of its members, the more it requires uniform wear. The corp isn't really looking for a few good men. It's looking for a few dedicated Marines, and it knows exactly how to transform boys into uniform men. As monks and military men have known for centuries, once you get into the habit you follow the orders of the superior.

Keep your distance, stay in your place. The hierarchy of power and prestige that governs every profession and corporation establishes the proper distance between people. There are people above you, people below you, and people on your level, and you don't get too close to any of them. Nobody hugs the boss. What is lacking is friendship. I know of no more radical critique of economic life than the observation by Earl Shorris that nowhere in the vast literature of management is there a single chapter on friendship.

Desensitize yourself. Touch, taste, smell—the realm of the senses—receive little homage. What pays off is reason, willpower, planning, discipline, control. There has, of course, recently been a move afoot to bring in potted plants and tasteful art to make corporate environments more humane. But the point of these exercises in aesthetics, like the development of communication skills by practitioners of organizational development, is to increase production. The bottom line is still profit, not pleasure or persons.

Don't trouble yourself with large moral issues. The more the world is governed by experts, specialists, and professionals, the less anybody takes responsibility for the most troubling consequences of our success-failure. Television producers crank out endless cop and killing tales, but refuse to consider their contribution to the climate of violence. Lawyers concern themselves with what is legal, not what is just. Physicians devote themselves to kidneys or hearts of individual patients while the health delivery system leaves masses without medicine. Physicists invent new generations of genocidal weapons which they place in the eager arms of the military. The military hands the responsibility for their use over to politicians. Politicians plead that they have no choice—the enemy makes them do it. Professors publish esoterica while students perish from poor teaching. Foresters, in cahoots with timber companies, clear-cut or manage the forest for sustained yield, but nobody is in charge of oxygen regeneration. Psychologists heal psyches while communities fall apart. Codes of professional ethics are for the most part, like corporate advertisements, high sounding but self-serving.

When we live within the horizons of the economic myth, we begin to consider it honorable for a man to do whatever he must to make a living. Gradually we adopt what Erich Fromm called "a marketing orientation" toward our selves. We put aside our dreams, forget the green promise of our young selves, and begin to tailor our personalities to what the market requires. When we mold ourselves into commodities, practice smiling and charm so we will have "winning personalities," learn to sell ourselves, and practice the silly art of power dressing, we are certain to be haunted by a sense of emptiness.

Men, in our culture, have carried a special burden of unconsciousness, of ignorance of the self. The unexamined life has been worth quite a lot in economic terms. It has enabled us to increase the gross national product yearly. It may not be necessary to be a compulsive extrovert to be financially successful, but it helps. Especially for men, ours is an outer-directed culture that rewards us for remaining strangers to ourselves, unacquainted with feeling, intuition, or the subtleties of sensation and dreams.

Many of the personality characteristics that have traditionally been considered "masculine"—aggression, rationality—are not innate or biological components of maleness but are products of a historical era in which men have been socially assigned the chief roles in warfare and the economic order. As women increasingly enter the quasimilitary world of the economic system they are likely to find themselves governed by the logic of the system. Some feminists, who harbor a secret belief in the innate moral superiority of women, believe that women will change the rules of business and bring the balm of communication and human kindness into the boardroom. To date this has been a vain hope. Women executives have proven themselves the equal of men in every way—including callousness. The difference between the sexes is being eroded as both sexes become defined by work. It is often said that the public world of work is a man's place and that as women enter it they will become increasingly "masculine" and lose their "femininity." To think this way is to miss the most important factor of the economic world. Economic man, the creature who defines itself within the horizons of work and consumption, is not man in any full sense of the word, but a being who has been neutralized, degendered, rendered subservient to the laws of the market. The danger of economics is not that it turns women into men but that it destroys the fullness of both manhood and womanhood.

History is a game of leapfrog in which yesterday's gods

regularly become today's demons, and the rectitude of the fathers becomes the fault of the sons. The Greeks invented the idea of nemesis to show how any single virtue stubbornly maintained gradually changes into a destructive vice. Our success, our industry, our habit of work have produced our economic nemesis. In our current economic crisis we are driving to the poorhouse in new automobiles, spending our inflated dollars for calorie-free food, lamenting our falling productivity in an environment polluted by our industry. Work made modern men great, but now threatens to usurp our souls, to innundate the earth in things and trash, to destroy our capacity to love and wonder. According to an ancient myth, Hephaestus (Vulcan) the blacksmith, the only flawed immortal who worked, was born lame.

Somehow men got so lost in the doing that we forgot to pause and ask, "What is worth doing? What of value are we creating—and destroying—within the economic order?" Work has always been our womb—the fertile void out of which we give birth to our visions. Today we need to stop the world for a while and look carefully at where our industry is taking us. We have a hopeful future only if we stop asking what we can produce and begin to ask what we want to create. Our dignity as men lies not in exhausting ourselves in work but in discovering our vocation.

Remembering Dr. Faust, it might be a good idea to pause and ask ourselves how much of our psyches we will trade for how much profit, power, and prestige. Maybe we should require graduate schools, professional organizations, places of labor, and corporations to put a warning over their doors. Caution: Excessive work may be hazardous to the health of your body and spirit.

I fear that something beautiful, terrible, and complex about work has escaped me. Some part of the mixed blessing I cannot capture in words.

A friend who is a successful entrepreneur asked me, "Are you antibusiness? Business is where I create. It is where the excitement and juice is for me. I can hardly wait to get to my office." My literary agent, Ned Leavitt, tells me: "My work is my art. When I dress in my suit each morning I feel like a knight going forth to battle, and I love to fight hard and win in a hard bargaining session with a publisher and get the best deal for my clients."

I know. I know. I am also one of the work-driven men. And I am lucky to have work that fits skintight over my spirit. I hardly know how to separate work from self. Even when I subtract the long hours, the fatigue, the uncertainties about money, the irritation of having to deal with a million nit-shit details, the long hours in the limbo of jet planes and airports, the compromises I have to make, the sum is overwhelmingly positive. I don't know who I would be without the satisfaction of providing for my family, the occasional intoxication of creativity, the warm companionship of colleagues, the pride in a job well done, and the knowledge that my work has been useful to others.

But there is still something unsaid, something that forces me to ask questions about my life that are, perhaps, tragic: In working so much have I done violence to my being? How often, doing work that is good, have I betrayed what is better in myself and abandoned what is best for those I love? How many hours would have been better spent walking in silence in the woods or wrestling with my children? Two decades ago, near the end of what was a good but troubled marriage, my wife asked me: "Would you be willing to be less efficient?" The question haunts me.

THE RITE OF SEX: MAGIC WANDS AND PRIVATE TOOLS

"The loins are the place of judgment."
—N.O. Brown

The night had finally arrived. We had dinner at a fancy restaurant and talked formally the whole time, almost as if we were strangers, knowing what we were going to do shortly, but not wanting to say anything about it. I drank four cups of coffee that only added to my anxiety and excitement.

As I walked into the office of the motel I put on my most sophisticated face and imagined the way Cary Grant might have handled the situation in *An Affair to Remember*. In my best man-of-the-world voice I requested, "Room for two please, double bed."

I suppose number 64 was a standard motel room, but I remember it as a chamber of mystery, dimly lit around the edges, the bed like an altar, prominently placed in the center and illuminated by a soft light.

The first part was easy; we had done it a hundred times. We looked at each other, kissed, touched, looked, kissed, touched, each time longer, more intimately. But when, I wondered, did we get to the magic moment? All the books I had read warned of the importance of foreplay, lubrication, getting her ready, not hurrying, being considerate, taking her rhythms into account, and I certainly wanted to be a good lover and do it right. She seemed to like the kissing and holding and petting and didn't seem in any hurry to get to the next stage, so I waited. More foreplay. Endless foreplay. Finally the tide seemed about to change and I decided it was time. I decided but "it" didn't. My cock was awash in a flood of lubrication but was timid, hiding, clinging to innocence. Now she was ready but I wasn't, and the books hadn't given me much advice on how to handle this situation. And Cary Grant wasn't any help. It was too soon to think about impotence but not too soon to worry.

"I'm sorry," I said apologetically.

"Sorry about what?" she asked.

"I'm not ready, and I'm embarrassed."

"Don't worry, I'm not in any hurry. I like what we are doing."

A swirl of thoughts and feelings went through my head. Is she telling the truth? Is she frustrated but hiding it? Does she think I am a lousy lover? Thank God, she understands. But does she? How could she? She isn't the one who has to get it up at just the right minute and keep it up until everything comes out right.

We lay quietly in each other's arms for a long time, intimate but distant. I was caught up in myself, in the feeling that I had failed the test of manhood, and she was lost in not knowing what to do. Finally we drifted into a restless sleep.

Sometime in the middle of the night, when darkness was on the face of the deep, and the spirit of God was moving over the waters, I awoke, aroused.

"Sweetheart, are you awake?"

"Yes."

"Are you ready?"

"Yes."

And I entered her, and entered my manhood, and we moved together until the whirlpool sucked us down into the primal deep, and we slept as one body in the sweet darkness.

We woke in the first glistening light of a new day and made love again. Afterward, we laughed and I roared like a lion, and we were suddenly hungry. She went into the bathroom to shower and I lay in bed a while and savored the redolence of the blended essences of our bodies. As I moved out of bed and toward my clothes I caught a sudden glimpse of myself in the full-length mirror on the door and paused to examine myself. To my surprise the mirror reflected the image of a man I had never seen before—

his cock, resting but proud, pulsated with life, his chest swelled with the joy of being, his sinuous muscles were full of power.

At the diner we held hands and looked at each other with new eyes. The slightest touch of our fingers carried the memory of our night of passage beyond innocence. It was the best breakfast I ever ate.

Getting Laid and Keeping Score

War, work, and sex, the triad of male initiation rites, form the pillars of male identity.

Glance through a collection of erotica and pornography from various nations and times and you will be looking at one large phallus after another. Erection after erection, towering, triumphant. Whether they be stone lingam that decorate temples in India, the winged cocks of Roman times, the ancient hairy Japanese members large enough to be carried in wagons, or steel machines of modern porn, the penis is usually portrayed as larger than life. Seldom, except in classical Greek statues, do we see it in repose, nestled content within its own foreskin.

Why the emphasis on size? Why this continual exaggeration? Why the focus on the erection?

The quick and easy answer is that men are horny to the core and naturally celebrate the phallus in its proud stance. Larger-than-life erections are monuments to exuberant masculinity. Sure enough, every man knows those moments when his cock rises, stands tall, and is so full of the primal mystery that it seems a natural object of worship. It has an awesome life of its own and is deserving of hymns of praise.

But every man knows this is only half of the truth.

The slow and difficult answer is that our focus on erection is also a compensation for our feelings that the penis, and therefore the self, is small, unreliable, and shamefully out of control. Rebellious private, it does what it wants, and that includes going AWOL, refusing to stand and deliver, and ignoring the orders issued from general headquarters. It retreats from flowery combat in the erogenous zones as frequently as it engages the enemy. It embarrasses us. So we pretend it is braver than it is, build monuments to its courage, decorate it with garlands, in hope that praise will flatter it into compliance.

But either way—celebration or compensation—there is something obsessive in the male focus on the penis. It is difficult for us to see it in true perspective. It is as if we look at it through both ends of a telescope. Looked at through the "wrong" end of the telescope it appears too small and too far away, a shameful little boy that hangs its head and cannot satisfy the demands of an insatiable female. Through the "right" end of the telescope it is magnified, and is too large and too close. Either way it is out of focus. For reasons that are far from obvious, men's egos are nearly inseparable from their penises. Male identity revolves around the penis in a way that female identity does not revolve around the vagina.

Nobody knows when a boy's penis becomes the pole around which his consciousness revolves. Modern little boys, unrestrained, play with, sing songs to, proudly display erections. Statisticians and psychologists have established that boys, once aroused to sex, think about it on the average of six times an hour on a slow day. Freud, who had an active sex life of only ten years and therefore is not to be trusted on these matters, claimed that the fragile edifice of male identity was built upon the shaky foundations of castration anxiety. Seeing little girls and large mamas, who had nothing where there should have been something, we assumed early there was a species of unfortunate humans who had lost the dignity given by a dangling destiny (possibly victims of primal dads on the rampage). Therefore we became anxious lest the same misfortune befall us. No doubt Freud was a little bit right. Multiply six thoughts per hour by twenty-four hours, by three hundred sixty-five days, by four score and ten years, and it is inevitable that we will have some existential anxieties and thoughts of devouring teeth and dangerous knives mixed in with images of vaginal nests.

Any way you slice it, and for God's sake please don't, considerations of the nature and destiny of the penis are close to a man's heart. Indeed they frequently replace the heart. So much is written about men and sex—laments, advice, cheerleading, political manifestos, empirical studies, titillating accounts of every conceivable way of fitting pegs in holes, etc.—that a Martian might be led to think that the practice of manhood was one long dance around the maypole. Certainly by now we must know a great deal, if not everything, about men and sex. You would think there would be nothing new to say about sex.

But fortunately, the fountain of discovery still spurts and flows. There is yet more news from the erotic frontier. My "news" about male sexuality comes from pondering the fact that it took The Group of Men nearly ten years to begin to be candid about sexual experience. The only subject we have had more difficulty discussing than sex is money. As a result I have become convinced that men's private experience of sex is vastly different from the usual stereotypes, is as complex as women's, and is as filled with longing for intimacy and spiritual meaning.

The shape of the breaking story about male sexuality is not yet clear, but here are some of the possible headlines.

We lie a lot about sex, first to ourselves and then to our partners.

We are more ambivalent than we appear to be.

Tenderhearted omnipotent studs, like unicorns and whores with hearts of gold, only live in Aesop's fables.

Most of us have a difficult time forging a marriage between the heart and the penis. We can't get our tenderness and our potency together.

Some of us only want to have sex with a person we love.

A lot of us thrive sexually only in marriage.

Impotence is a normal part of our sexual cycle.

By and large, our sexuality has been so formed by our roles as warriors and workers that we do not yet know how to separate our sexuality from the mood of performance and conquest. We might well adapt the old Zen koan, "What was your original face?" to make a new koan for modern men: "What was your penis before you were warrior and worker?"

But wait a minute. I am getting ahead of the story. The best way to begin to imagine a more wholehearted and whole-phallic form of male sexuality is to remember how we got to be the way we are. Creating a wholesome hope involves recovering the history of our wounds. Let's go back to the beginning, to our initiation into the mystery of sex. Back to the ungainly adolescent years of "dreaming innocence" when sex was an unopened Christmas package.

A boy's initiation to sex usually takes place somewhere in the psychological arena that is bounded by the wet dream, the locker room, and the back seat of a car.

Wet dreams are possibly the most significant of all the neglected phenomena of sexual initiation. Some men never experience wet dreams, others have them only after they have first had intercourse. But for some, the dream is the trumpet that awakes the latent sleeper. For such men, long before the appearance of the first pubic hair, before the outer body began to be sculpted by the hormones, before fathers, mothers, authorities explained about birds and bees and surrounded them with adult wisdom and dire warnings, the Great Primal Penis conducted the first sexual initiation. Suddenly without warning the sexual apocalypse arrived, and the revelation of the mystery appeared in a dream.

Here is how two men describe their first wet dream:

> "I was making love to a small, beautiful girl, but I wasn't sure what I was doing. And then I was sucked into a large vagina, spiraled through the clouds and ushered into a new universe. It wasn't scary."

> "I didn't know anything about sex but I was beginning to find certain girls beautiful. I kept a picture of Elizabeth Taylor from the newspaper advertisement for *National Velvet* in my wallet. Then one night I dreamt I was making love to her. When I entered her I was simultaneously within the beauty of her face, the depth of her vagina, and the exploding stars. It was the Fourth of July in every cell of my body, skyrockets and all. When I woke I lay very still. I was amazed to find a sticky, milky river flowing from my penis onto the sheets. I had no words, no concepts for what had happened to me. But I knew I had passed over into a great new territory. I had a secret too large to tell, too sacred to share. That was my introduction to sex. The experience was so intense, so psychedelic, so memorable that the first time I actually had sex with a woman I was disappointed that the reality didn't measure up to the dream."

The initiating dream is important because it gives some men a fundamental experience early in life that links the sexual and the mystical, the profane and the sacred. Before we fall into the sadly distorted forms of sexuality that are proscribed for us by our culture, we are sometimes introduced into the possibility of ecstatic sexuality. Our creative imagination makes common cause with our hormones to present us with a vision of sex at its best before we are taught to behave like "real men." As Job said, "God gives us songs in our sleep." Most of us forget these visions and possibilities and adjust to far more crippled forms of sexuality. But at least they are encoded deep within our psyche and can be remembered when they are needed later in our journey toward full manhood.

But enough of dreams for now. It is time for the locker room, for the gross drama that year after year retains top cultural billing in the theater of men's psyches.

Surprisingly, although we are bombarded with sexual stimulus and propaganda on every front, we remain extremely private about our personal sexual experience. Fathers who may have led profligate sex lives still do not talk candidly with their sons about sex. For the most part the sexual mysteries are taught (and usually mistaught) to young boys, not by experienced men, but by slightly older boys. In modern America the locker room has replaced the kiva as the site of initiation.

Most men still remember the atmosphere of the high school locker room—stale sweat, smelly gym clothes, gossip, dirty jokes, and endless variations on sexual mathematics. Talk centers around verbs such as "getting laid, screwing, getting it on, balling, fucking," indicating anonymous action, or on nouns such as "pussy, cunt, cocks, tits and ass," designating parts of the body. If any actual female is named in the conversation it is only to identify her as an "easy lay" or one who "puts out." The range of the conversation runs the gamut from bravado to bragging. Quantity, not quality, counts—notches on the gun. Scoring, or how many times one has done it with how many girls, is a large item. Likewise the tales, which are later to become the justification for rape, in which the hero boasts that "She was asking for it, so I gave it to her." Often the lessons in sex education are illustrated by dog-eared pornographic pictures, cards, or magazines.

Within the locker room there are usually four groups: the self-acknowledged studs and make-out artists; the courtiers who applaud the big men and encourage the telling of the tales; the shy virgins who are embarrassed by locker-room curriculum, and the silent lovers who have girlfriends they both love and respect. I still remember when, as a shy virgin of fifteen, I was definitively put down by a high school hero who demolished me with a line: "I've fucked a lot of women and drunk a lot of whiskey. What have you done lately?" At the time it didn't seem as if "I've thought a lot about my life" was an adequate reply, so I kept quiet.

The evidence suggests that many men never graduate from the locker-room school of sexuality. The smell of old jockstraps and raunchy attitudes still clings to the macho heroes. The frequency of date rape, the sale of girlie magazines, and the popularity of hard porn provide a fairly accurate index of how many men in their chronologically mature years are still caught in the adolescent philosophy that reduces women to objects with desirable parts to be used and abused by men.

Fortunately, most men graduate to a somewhat more advanced stage in the process of sexual initiation—the responsibility of a relationship. In the usual course of events, adolescent experimentation ripens into a relationship that involves sexual commitment. With the progression—becoming lovers, living together, marriage—the arena for the second stage of initiation changes from the backseat or motel room to the shared bedroom. Now a different drama begins in which the locker-room hero is transformed into the man with the magic wand. The man who previously took pride in how many girls he could "get" now finds his pride invested in his performance as a lover. The new test on which his self-esteem depends is whether he can "satisfy" his woman. The question that surrounds his lovemaking is, "Did you come?" and the unasked question beneath that is, "Am I all right?"

Our culture imprints its myths deep within our sexual being. Our first initiation is to fulfill the role of the sexual warrior, to conquer and possess as many women as possible as the proof of potency. Our second initiation is to fulfill the role of sexual worker, to "make love," to perform, to produce the intended result—satisfying the woman.

At this point I hear a chorus of objections. "You don't mean to tell us that a quarter of a century after the sexual revolution and women's liberation that men still feel responsible for women's orgasms! Certainly men and women have both been liberated enough to take responsibility for their own sexual satisfaction. Nobody believes anymore that it is the man's job to satisfy a woman."

Yes and no. The gospel of shared responsibility may have penetrated a quarter inch into the cerebral cortex, but it certainly hasn't made its way into the emotional centers of the limbic brain, to say nothing of having traveled south to the gonads. Liberal rhetoric aside, the vast majority of men still feel it is their responsibility to satisfy a woman sexually. Our heads may be liberated, but our guts are deeply conservative. And how could it be otherwise? One of the first and most crucial lessons little boys learn is: Please your mother, or else! This infantile message remains tattooed somewhere deep within the hidden recesses of our psyches. Listen to the words of a sophisticated airline pilot: "I have read all the stuff on women's liberation, and I know that many women can't come from intercourse alone. But when my wife has to masturbate after we make love I am disappointed and still feel like I have failed somehow. I guess my old male ego still wants her to have an orgasm through intercourse."

I suspect that many men never get far beyond a performance orientation to sexuality even in their marriages. The messages we get from culture—from our parents, teachers, bosses, advertisements, films, TV—tell us that "A man is only as good as his performance," "A man makes it happen," etc. It is psychologically naive to expect that somehow men are supposed to be able to strip themselves of all this conditioning when they leave the office and enter the bedroom. So long as we (openly) judge men by their economic performance and measure their worth by their wealth, we will continue to judge ourselves (secretly) by our imagined success at performing in the bedroom.

Traditionally, the sexual tests of manhood were not genital. A "real" man proved himself by impregnating a woman, protecting her against enemies, and providing for his family. Currently, easily available birth control and the desire for small families or childless marriages have removed the fertility test; unpopular wars and nuclear arms have eroded the conviction that we are being protected by the military; and two-career families have taken away the male role of being the provider. As a consequence, men seem enormously invested in pleasing and performing for women. For many men the erogenous zones seem to have replaced the battlefield as the arena for the testing of manhood.

There is a further stage in male sexual initiation in which sexuality is divorced from conquest or performance. Some men go beyond the norm, leave the locker room and the performance mode of sexuality behind, and integrate their passion and tenderness. But this usually happens in the second half of a man's journey after he has become disillusioned with the perks and pains involved in achieving ordinary manhood.

Sexual Wounds

Growing up male has its compensations. Pleasure is not one of them. The rites that prepare us for assuming power are not well designed to teach us to explore the kaleidoscopic realm of the senses. Men may learn to be self-indulgent—to buy Rolexes and Porsches—since that is the reward of achievement, but few of us qualify as true hedonists. We are too busy with practical things.

Back to the locker room for a moment. Never once as a budding man did I hear another man boast about the long, slow pleasure he experienced in sex, or speak of the beauty of the changing hues of a woman's eyes, of the sweet contentment of lying with a woman after love. For that matter I never heard a man speak of the pleasure a woman took in him other than to boast of how many times he had made some chick come. Perhaps it was because boys are too green to be patient and too pent-up with unspent jism to invest their eros in long-range propositions. But I don't think male feelinglessness is limited to the young. We are too hooked on the proof of our potency to pause to enjoy the flowers.

I have it on good authority that when women get together and talk about their lovers they don't speak much about hardness, speed, or numbers of orgasms. Instead they praise men who touch softly, who receive pleasure as easily as they give it, who are as comfortable in melting into the softness of communion as in thrusting vigorously in the frenzy of climax. My informal poll of women of all political persuasions reveals that they all agree that they would like men to slow down, take their time, enjoy the trip and not worry so much about the outcome. (One suggested that we make the western song "I Want a Man with Slow Hands" the national anthem.) Almost without exception my informants say that women keep trying to degenitalize men's focus and teach them that there are only two erogenous zones— the heart and the skin.

Because we have learned to measure our manhood by things that can be quantified, we have become poor in experiencing the richness of the small daily pleasures that must be savored moment by moment. The greatest underdeveloped nation in the world lies within the psyches of successful men.

Without knowing why, men gradually come to resent women. In a performance-oriented culture we were taught that we earned love by working hard and taking care of women. Until the recent sexual-economic revolution, men were expected to earn and pay, from the time they started dating until they retired. Many men automatically went to work to provide for a wife and family, performed for what they imagined was women's pleasure, and then felt silently resentful because they ended up feeling they gave more than they got. But the real problem is not that women were not willing to give more, but that men were rendered incapable of receiving more by their social conditioning. It is an axiom of a competitive society that it is more powerful to give than to receive.

Men expect such enormous and contradictory things from WOMAN that any mere woman is bound to disappoint us. She is supposed to be paradise regained, the place we can finally lay our burdens down and receive our just rewards for a lifetime of struggle and toil. She is the savior who is supposed to make us whole and reconnect us to our severed feelings.

And the penis is the straight and narrow pathway to paradise, the bridge over troubled waters we traverse to find the missing parts of our severed selves. That is why sex is so important for us. A woman once told me, "I finally understood that for most men the penis is their only 'feminine' part. It is only when they are doing things with it that they allow themselves to feel."

But if WOMAN is the promise of paradise, she is also the place of judgment and the entrance to hell. Since our entrance to the earthly paradise depends on her good graces, we give her the power to judge and reward or punish us. Without acknowledging that we have given her the keys to the kingdom, we nevertheless set out to fulfill the conditions she requires to win her favors. We try to please her. And ever so imperceptibly we come to judge ourselves by the reflection we see of ourselves in her eyes.

The cliché that men are uninterested in relationships simply is not true. A majority of us spend nearly as much of our psychological energy trying to get our relationships with women right as we do on our work. When men get together with their best friends they talk about women all the time. We try to figure out what's wrong with our love affairs or marriages; lament our losses; hope it will be better next time. We are as incurably romantic as women. What we do not easily confess is our dependence on women or our deep disappointments in relationships. Silence is manly, and we are trained to keep our feelings inside. Better a heart attack than speaking openly about a broken heart.

There is a fundamental difference between the male and female imagination. We imagine sex directly and intimacy indirectly, while women imagine intimacy directly and sex indirectly. It is not that men are only interested in sex, but that we have been so conditioned to curtail our natural needs for intimacy that only in sex do we have cultural permission to feel close to another human being. Listen with the third ear and you can hear a sacred intent beneath the facade of even the most vulgar language. Emotionally speaking, men are stutterers who often use sexual language to express their forbidden desires for communion. What else would you expect from a gender that has been trained for generations to be warriors and workers and conditioned not to feel or express but to stand and deliver?

No matter how hard we try we inevitably fail to discover the secret of masculinity in sex. Certainly, there is a part of the mystery of maleness that can only be known through a sexual encounter with a woman. The seminal promise, the song of our genes, can be heard only in the presence of someone who might incarnate our hope in a child. But whether we enter into sex in the mood of sport-fucking or in tender relationship, we will be disappointed if we expect to find the proof of our masculinity there. Sex may bring pleasure or joy, but not identity. In fact, we are able to lose ourselves in loving sexuality only to the degree that we have found the self elsewhere. It takes a very secure person to surrender to another in love.

The end result of our present sexual rites of manhood is that men and women end up misunderstanding and making each other crazy. We are taught to be strangers in the night, talking different languages. We expect impossible things of one another, resent and blame each other for our lack of fulfillment. What is jokingly called the "war between the sexes" is no joke, but the psychological reality that goes on constantly just beneath the masks of civility we have conspired to wear to satisfy our mutual needs. But the divorce statistics, the scarcity of joyful marriages, the frequency of rape are grim testimonies to the sexual wounds that accompany the "normal" rites that initiate us into the roles our society expects men and women to play. To be a contemporary man, or a woman, is to have a fault-line running down the center of our being, and to be less than half a person.

We urgently need new visions of manhood and womanhood.

TAKING
THE MEASURE
OF A MAN

7

THE MEASURING
OF MANHOOD

"A man is measured by the expanse of
the moral horizon he chooses to
inhabit."

—Sandor McNab

The Self-Measuring Animal

The easy part of thinking about men is to point out our
disease, lament how far we have fallen from our former
glory, and announce that we need a new vision. We are
much better at diagnosing pathology than reaching any
commonly accepted definition of health. Clearly, the secular
rites of manhood we have practiced since the industrial revolution are rapidly becoming obsolete, if not deadly. Our task is to
create a new vision of manliness in a culture that no longer
believes in saints, divinely revealed ideals, or absolute values. We
are trapped within modern, masculine madness and can't find an
exit; we live in the urgency of the moment, captive to quarterly
profit reports and the trends of the day, but desperately needing
an opening beyond the present to something that offers us more
hope and dignity.

Currently the most popular way to settle questions of
morality and value seems to be the public opinion poll. Especially in North America we have a naive faith in what we believe

is common wisdom but what all too often turns out to be the lowest common denominator of opinion as it has been formed by mass media. I discovered in a *Psychology Today* survey (see Appendix) that Jesus and Gandhi were most often nominated as ideal men. But inconsistently, those polled said an ideal man would find his primary sense of meaning in self-exploration and personal growth—not in the selflessness of his ideals. This survey, however, was answered by and reflected the biases of a group of people whose ideals had been shaped by an interest in psychology. We could as easily find a different segment of the population that would elevate actors or rock stars to the number one position.

The question this and all polls and surveys raises: So what? Are we to assume that the meaning of being a man is to be settled by opinion polls? *Vox populi, vox dei?* Is there no higher authority than the judgments of the majority, and should we simply adjust our ideals to the constantly shifting winds of fashion? Do we have anything more enduring on which to base our aspirations than *Esquire*'s yearly report on what's "in" and what's "out" or *People* magazine's weekly picks and pans?

Whether or not man is the measure of all things, as Greek philosophers claimed, he is certainly the measurer of all things, most especially himself. We are self-conscious animals, and our stature as men, our grandeur or meanness, is determined by the horizons of our moral universe, by our choice of heroes and authorities, by trying to keep up with Donald Trump, imitate the life-style of Mick Jagger, or follow in the footsteps of the Buddha.

Where, other than to our contemporaries and the pantheon of popular heroes, might we look for models of manhood?

First we must recognize that we do commonly make moral judgments about men and the nature of manhood that go far beyond the biological facts of gender or the public opinion of the idols of the moment. Neither manhood nor womanhood is ever experienced in a social vacuum. Manhood is not an eternal essence that men acquire by their own doing, but a cultural construct that changes. We take our definitions and our assurance that we are men from a community, from the audience before whom we enact the drama of our lives. We see ourselves as others see us. Whether we become manikins or mensches depends in large measure on how small or large, how trivial or profound, how local or universal, how mean or generous, how prejudiced or compassionate is the community within which we live and seek our definitions of our manhood. Men who take their stamp of approval from the Marine Corps will be confirmed in a very different notion of manhood than those who seek the shared identity of the Peace Corps.

Exemplary Men

Practically speaking, the way each of us defines our sense of ideal manhood or womanhood is by establishing a kind of inner Hall of Fame where we applaud heroes and heroines of the moment, and a Hall of Exemplars where we enshrine those ideal men and women who embody our highest, most universal, values.

Our personal halls of fame are made up of our private heroes, saints, and models. Think of your Hall of Fame as a house of mirrors, each of which gives you a glimpse of some aspect of yourself. It may contain people whose names are in the news, men and women you admire because they are beautiful, powerful, talented, smart, wise, or compassionate. But it will also contain a more intimate group of friends, parents, teachers, and lovers who have enriched your lives with their special gifts of care, insight, and understanding. For instance, my Hall of Fame has a room dedicated to great political leaders (Lincoln, Gandhi, and Gorbachev), a room for teachers, living and dead, who have enriched my mind (Kierkegaard, Freud, Tillich, Camus, Wendell Berry), a room for lovers and guardians of my being (Dad, Mother, my wife, Jan, my friend, Jim), a room for men who incarnate some essential virtue (see Chapter II), and a room dedicated to the physical graces, which is filled with various handsome men, beautiful women, athletes, artists, and explorers. Each person's Hall of Fame is made up of a unique cast of characters because it reflects the self's ideal. Tell me whom you admire and I will tell you what kind of a person you aspire to become.

The Hall of Exemplars contains men and women who have been elevated to positions of the highest honor by a consensus of the ages. They are not merely heroes of the moment but are the pathfinders and definers of the human condition, the spiritual elite who reveal some aspect of the human promise. *Exemplars add something to the definition of "man" or "woman."* Our self-understanding as men is a richly layered thing made up of the portraits of these men who first brought to light some *elemental virtue* without which it is now impossible to understand ourselves. You may think of them as the court of conscience, or as the audience that will accept only the best life-drama we can perform.

Unlike average-to-good men, the Exemplars were not captive to the values and visions of their own narrow time and place, but were heralds of things to come, citizens of both the present and the future. By developing some virtue we all potentially possess, they became the distant early warning of the possible, the harbingers of hope. Their lives are our strongest evidence that human beings are spiritual creatures, that we are able to transcend the conditioning of both biology and culture. In older mythology these saints, shamans, philosophers, mystics, artists, statesmen, inventors, etc., were often pictured as radiant beings crowned with halos because they were luminous, "transparent to the Ground of Being" (Tillich), bringers of light.

For example, think about some of the women who have recently been added to the Hall of Exemplars, the extraordinary women who gave birth to the feminist movement—Simone de Beauvoir, Betty Friedan, Gloria Steinem, Adrienne Rich, etc. They have, for all time, added the words "free," "equal," and "powerful" to the definition of "woman." They are the prophets of a new age in the making. Ever since Roman times the predicates "free," "equal," and "powerful" have been included in the definition of manhood. But no matter how much individual women struggled to achieve personal freedom, no matter how powerful exceptional women became, "freedom, equality, and power" were not part of the way ideal womanhood was defined. Woman was so defined by man that we still have little language that allows us to speak of the unique quality of womanly excellence and greatness. There is, for instance, no feminine equivalent to "virtue" (the moral quality that defines a man) that does not refer primarily to the sexual aspect of a woman's being. It may take a generation for women to explore the meaning of "freedom," "equality," and "power," and longer yet to put them into practice, but at least they will never again be absent from the definition of "woman."

The distinction between the Hall of Fame and the Hall of Exemplars becomes clear in the case of celebrities like Elvis Presley or Marilyn Monroe. Elvis has clearly captured a foothold in fame as a musical innovator, but few would point to him as an ideal man or wish to imitate his drug-befuddled style of life. He may have been a great performer and public persona, but he was not an admirable man. In Marilyn Monroe's life and suicide, we see the fatal contradictions that signal the end of the old definitions of women. Great men desired and possessed her. Even in death she remains enshrined in the Hall of Fame as the Goddess of Love. But although we mourn for her, we cannot admire her, because she lacked that inner knowledge of her own freedom, equality, and power that has recently come to define "woman." She felt herself to be barren, and in her suicide she finally destroyed the feminine persona that was worshiped and used by men who were reputed to be the "best and the brightest."

More often than not, we would be uncomfortable living with the exemplars of virtue. Neither Jesus nor Gandhi would be easy houseguests. But like the north star, they provide a reference point by which we may judge the fullness of man's potential. Even when we do not measure ourselves against the standard of these "perfect 10s" (or when we grant ourselves handicap points for having alcoholic fathers or clinging mothers), we bear them in mind as the benchmarks against which actual men and women must be evaluated.

No discussion of the standards by which we measure ourselves would be complete without acknowledging the men we love to hate, the residents of the Hall of Villains. The drama of manhood is a morality play that is never complete without a full cast of antagonists. The underworld of masculinity includes all types, from the charming rogues and silver-tongued devils to the truly detestable fiends and demons, from Rhett Butler to Hitler. The worst villains in the drama—Stalin, Idi Amin, Pol Pot, Ted Bundy—serve to draw the line beneath which we consider we are dealing with "monsters" and not men. Lesser villains provide us with incarnate definitions of a single vice: Ivan Boesky—"greedy," Jimmy Swaggart—"hypocrite," Charles Manson—"insane," Donald Trump—"egocentric," Richard Nixon—"deceitful," Qaddafi—"hateful," etc. All those who dwell within our private and public halls of villains help us to define the moral hierarchy. As nearly everyone's mother used to say: "Never underestimate the importance of a horrible example."

Reflecting on those men we choose to place in our halls of fame and exemplars provides us with one of our best resources for getting leverage on our present state of confusion and creating a new vision of man. To discover who we are and what we want to become, we need to ask ourselves: Who are the historical exemplars we admire? Whom do we admire from more contemporary times? Who are the men now changing our definitions of what it means to be a man?

A BRIEF HISTORY
OF MANHOOD

Look deep into your own being, as you would into an opal, layer upon layer. Under the facade of your modern personality you will find the whole history of man contained in your psyche. Take an archaeological journey into your soul and you will discover the bones of ancient hunters, warriors, wandering philosophers, desert saints, and robber barons. You are the heir of all of the ways men have defined themselves.

When I was learning to drive, my father taught me that if you get stuck in the mud or snow you put the car in reverse and rock it back and forth. Remembering our past is the way we move out of a present that seems to have no exit into a more open and hopeful future. The best way to get a handle on the challenge facing modern men is to look backward to some of the pivotal moments in history when some new elemental virtue came into being and the definition of manhood changed. Most of the famous men of the past are long since forgotten, but the exemplary men are remembered. A few extraordinary men in every age heard the music of the future, responded to an imperative that came from beyond their own time and place, and came to incarnate new virtues.

The exemplars of any age are the vocational men, men who give voice to the future, men who answer an appeal to become and create something new.

The phallus that is so frequently worshiped at various times in the history of world religions is not the biological penis, not the sexual apparatus, not the severed genital of the male. Freud taught us that any Gothic arch or hot dog could be a phallic symbol, but he failed to teach us that the phallus could be the symbol for the whole man. The phallic principle that gives man dignity and is worthy of worship is his ability to rise to the occasion, to answer the call of history. The phallic man is the one who becomes a cocreator of history by daring to stand forth and seed a fertile moment with a new possibility.

Let's take a whirlwind tour through the museum of man and look at some of the most formative images of essential manhood and the conditions that evoked them. These are the predicates that modify "man," key notions by which we have defined ourselves. Each one is added to the next to create a historical overlay.

As we proceed on our tour you will notice that history seems to be governed by a certain kind of dialectic—thesis, antithesis, synthesis. Call it a dance, a seesaw, a divine play (Lela), the divine spirit disporting with itself (Hegel), or an apple-basket turnover. Inevitably, the conditions of a certain age call forth some new virtue. But, after a time, adherence to that virtue becomes counterproductive and its opposite or corrective is called forth. Ivan Illich called this the principle of "paradoxical counterproductivity." In time, educational institutions paralyze our ability to learn, medicine produces as much suffering as it alleviates, and freeways hurry us elsewhere at an ever-diminishing rate of speed. And definitions of virtue and manhood also evolve and change.

Man as Hunter

Where should we begin in recounting the history of the metaphors men have used to define themselves? As we work our way back beyond recorded history we find only a scattering of carved stone and drawings on cave walls. My best educated guess for the first manifesto of man would be a painting on a wall of the cave of Lascaux that was composed by an unknown artist about 15,000 B.C. The drawing pictures a bison with prominent horns, pierced through the entrails by a spear. On the ground beside him lies a man with an obvious erection and beside him a bird and what appears to be a spear or throwing stick.

What does the drawing tell us? Some experts speculate that the man is a shaman in a trance, the bird the symbol of psychic travel, the stick a male sign, the spear a phallus, and the wound in the animal a symbol of the vulva. Maybe yes, maybe no. The interpretation of ancient symbols or modern dreams is a game anyone can play. My hunch is that the most important element in the picture is what appears to be a self-conscious identification of spear and penis. The artist seems to be portraying the earliest philosophy of a hunting people: I hunt; therefore I am.

From the study of the few hunting and gathering societies that have survived into modern times we know that when men live by hunting, a three-way mystical bond grows up between them and the animals upon which they depend. First, the hunter identifies with the animal—the bear, the bison, the eland—that he must kill. The Bushmen, for instance, believe that they were previously springbok, and that their spirit continues to live in the spirit world with the eternal springbok. Many hunters take animal names. Second, the hunter must communicate with the mind of the animal both to understand its way so he can stalk it successfully and to receive its permission to "sacrifice" it. Third, the hunter identifies his manhood both with his totem animal and with the instruments of his craft. The same power that is in the horn of the bison makes him horny. His penis partakes of the power of the spear, the arrow, the gun with which he kills and provides food to the tribe.

I think we will not be too wide of the mark if we consider the first philosopher to be the man who first mythologized the act of hunting. I picture him sitting quietly and observing the ways of animals until he could place himself empathetically inside their minds. By coming into close communion, he both knew and respected the animal he was to kill, and he created a story in which the animal offered its life as a sacrifice to feed humankind. In this way the hunter received the animal's permission and learned the rituals of preparation and thanksgiving that were to surround killing.

I picture our first hunter-artist flushed with success after the hunt. Returning proudly with his kill he must have felt the potency of his act in his loins. Perhaps, like the Bushman, whose penis even when not aroused rests in an up rather than a down position, the hunter felt the animal power as inseparable from his own masculinity. And perhaps he felt the same logic and the same mystery within the intimate act of intercourse. He must have thought something like this: As the spear wounds and kills the animal that sustains life, so the penis wounds the woman who creates life.

It is impossible to know exactly what elemental virtues the early hunters added to our definition of man. The opening scene of the movie *2001* recreates what is widely imagined to be the moment when ape changed to man by grasping a stone that could be used as a tool or weapon. Whenever it happened in the millennia before history, the first virtues that began to distinguish us from our tree-dwelling cousins were the acquisition of language, the ability to use symbols and metaphors to understand the self, the creation of tools, and the ability to bond empathetically with animals. We should not underestimate the triumph and the sophistication of so-called "primitive" hunting and gathering societies. Although we do not know exactly how to translate the wall paintings on the caves at Lascaux or in Chaco canyon it is easy to see that they were a part of a consistent philosophy of life, which produced what today we would categorize as art, ritual, religion, and a way of initiating the young into the wisdom of the community.

As is inevitably the case, virtues are the flip side of vices. As a rule, hunting cultures are robust but fragile. Depending so totally on the bounty of game, they produce no surplus, and thus have little to invest in creating cultural complexity. Because game periodically gets scarce, they must remain nomadic and limit themselves to portable cultural objects.

Man as Planter

Women have mostly been too busy doing the work of the world to have time to write history, and men, like Russian historians, are in the habit of revising the record so they can lay claim to having invented anything of worth. The story of "man as planter" is more than likely a late addition to the story of "woman as planter."

The untold story of the second great period in human evolution probably should be told something like this: One day when the men were away hunting squirrels, and finding very few, the women got tired of the haphazard protein routine and invented mathematics, science, and agriculture so they could keep the larder stocked. It happened this way. Several of the ladies, all of whom had their periods, were sitting around the cave gossiping and speculating about the nature of womanhood and reality, and things like that, when Einsteina said, "We are moon bodies because the tide of our blood flows every twenty-eight nights when the moon is full." "What do you mean, twenty-eight nights?" someone asked. "See here," Einsteina said, and she showed the women a horn on which she had scratched twenty-eight marks. "I mark the beginning of the flow of the blood and the fullness of the moon and the marks are the same." For what was later to be called "several years" the women talked in secret and tried to figure out if there were other things that could be counted, like the occurrence of spring and winter. One day in a festive mood they pushed a wild wheat seed into the ground and took bets on how many numbers would pass before the bud appeared above the ground. Not long after that they found out that if they planted seeds at a particular numbered day after the spring rains, grain would appear as predictably as their periods and the moon.

Thus agriculture was born, along with science—the insight that nature follows the law of numbers—and women began to store grain and create surplus wealth and cities grew and culture thrived and craftsmen learned to make beautiful jewelry for smart women. It wasn't until many years after squirrel stew became an insignificant source of protein that men gave up the archaic role of great hunter, settled down to the business of farming, and claimed it had been their idea all along.

Needless to say, the metaphors grew as fast as the grain. Before you knew it women became Mother Earth, the night, the moon, and the tide-governed waters, the skin-shedding snake, and anything that seemed to be soft, flowing, and fertile. Men claimed Father Sky, the day, the sun, and anything that seemed to be hard, penetrating, and shooting forth. Sex became plowing the field and sowing the seed, or making a marriage between Mother Earth and Father Sky. The force that made the penis rise and the womb swell was thought to be the same as the power that pushed the bud through the fertile earth and ripened the grain. Couples who wanted crop insurance made love in the fields on the night of the full moon just after the seeds were planted.

There is general agreement among cultural historians that the period of the early agricultural revolution was a time of relative harmony. Things womanly, earthy, and fertile were held in high regard and men seem to have understood that their survival depended on celebrating the rhythm and sticking to the order of the seasons and respecting the natural law that was homogenized into things. Priests and priestesses elaborated rituals that ensured the harmonic convergence of woman, man, and nature. If some of these ceremonies involved the bloody rites of animal and human sacrifice, it was only because blood, like seed, was thought to be a necessary investment to keep the cosmic mother regular and fertile. Such unpleasantness aside, the goddess was on earth and all was right with the world. Cities were unfortified and there is no archaeological evidence of large-scale violence.

The great agricultural revolution added the word "cosmic" to the definition of human beings. For many thousands of years "man" was included in the definition of "woman," the feminine had ontological priority over the masculine, and the goddess possessed greater power and dignity than the male gods who were her consorts. Woman and man lived and moved and had their being within the fertile seasonal rhythms of Mother Earth and Father Sky. They were not lonely parts of a happenstance chaos but children of a maternal cosmos. And man was a *husbandman*, a tender of nature and of woman, a maker of hearth, a practitioner of home economics.

But if man was a child of nature he was also expected to remain within her bosom. The myths of planting peoples stressed the continuity of life and the obligation of the individual to conform to the patterns that had been laid down by the original heroes and heroines. The good life, like a ritual, was a socially sanctioned repetition of the ancient ways. Innovation was not encouraged; uniqueness was not a quality for which a man should strive.

Man as Warrior

Why man changed from farmer to warrior is not clear.

The historical facts of the matter are these. About 1700 B.C. warlike tribes of peoples called Aryans, who had mastered the use of iron and horses as weapons, swept from the north into Greece, India, and the Fertile Crescent. They brought with them a fierce loyalty to a single, patriarchal God. In the story we are most familiar with, Yahweh, God of the Hebrews, sanctified war by giving the country of Canaan to his followers and commanding them to kill or enslave its inhabitants, "dash their little ones' heads against stones," and reduce those who remained to carriers of water and cutters of wood. Being a jealous God, He ordered His followers to worship no other deities and not to "bake cakes to the Queen of Heaven" or offer sacrifices to the Baals and fertility spirits. Yahweh, in the manner of oriental kings, thus dethroned and demeaned the Great Mother. Beelzebub (formerly god of the phallus) was proclaimed a devil. The snake, a creature sacred to the goddess, was accused of being an agent of evil, responsible for destroying the harmony among man, nature, and woman. The chosen people were henceforth ordered to be obedient to the will of their Father in heaven and not remain children of Mother Earth. Being created in His image they were to exercise lordship over the birds of the air and the beasts of the field. As a sign that the umbilical cord binding them to nature had been severed, they circumcised the phallus and sacrificed the foreskin to Yahweh. Sexuality, henceforth, was to be governed by tribal morality, by the law that came down from above rather than by the impulse that came up from below. Nature was not to be trusted. Nor were women. In effect, the Judeo-Christian God cast the phallus and the vulva out of the sanctuary and reduced nature to a backdrop against which God's redemptive drama was being played out on the stage of history.

There is another less historical but more psychological way in which we might tell the story of the emergence of warrior cultures. Success inevitably breeds failure. After a few centuries without hunting or hunger, men began to get bored with farming. One hot and dusty day it occurred to some budding military genius that pitchforks could be used as weapons and it was a lot easier to steal your neighbors grain than it was to grow your own. Quicker than you can say "Pentagon," men began to organize standing, marching, marauding armies and to create hierarchical governments and bureaucratic infrastructures to support the troops. To the victors belonged the spoils, especially women. So when the going got tough the tough got going and soon men began to thrive in direct proportion to their ability to sustain a high testosterone level. Evolutionary selection favored the survival of the meanest and those who could most successfully suppress feelings, except of course feelings of superiority, anger, and disciplined willpower.

No matter what explanation we give to the origins of organized violence, clearly warfare changed the arena in which manhood was to be won. For the farmer, life was a struggle between chaos and cosmos; the theater within which manhood was to be exhibited was the natural world. The challenge was to harmonize with the forces of nature sufficiently to survive. The habit of warfare replaced the theater of nature with the theater of politics. Henceforth the drama of manhood was a battle not against chaos but against an enemy of the tribe who had been defined as the incarnation of evil.

In the beginning of the era of the warrior the central figure on the stage was a single warrior, or rather two heroic warriors locked in hand-to-hand combat, as in the *Iliad*, or *Ivanhoe*. But the more sophisticated the tools of warfare became, the more the large, hierarchically organized armies became the moving force in history. By World War I, the machine gun, long-range artillery, and weapons of mass destruction had reduced the individual to an anonymous clog in a military machine. Warfare, which began as a heroic way for an individual to make a name for himself, gradually metamorphosed into conflict without individuality or honor.

Once war became an established social habit, the values of agricultural society were turned upside down. The ethic of cooperation was replaced by an ethic of conquest. The quest for harmony was replaced by the search for control. The dominance of the senses was replaced by the discipline of willpower. The realm of the sacred was no longer to be found in the nearby fields, rivers, and glades, but in the remote heavenly dwelling of the transcendent God. The business of God was more in the realm of politics than agriculture. He was better at commanding his people to go on crusades and sanctifying genocide than he was at dancing round the maypole or growing crops.

In a warrior culture, once the sword had been proclaimed mightier than the plow, the soldier more potent than the farmer, a man's penis and his weapon became fused. As George Patton said, "Them that does the fighting does the fucking." The penis first became a sword and then a gun and the warrior's ritual of manhood became alternately stroking the penis and the rifle while singing the Marine hymn: "This is my rifle, this is my gun. This is for business, this is for fun." In Hebrew the word for penis and weapon is the same, *za'in*. Rape was a privilege of the conquering hero in times of war and a habit hard to break in times of peace. The rule of the warrior psyche was: Woman is a land to be conquered, possessed, and, if necessary, humiliated.

Before we take leave of *homo furens*, the man of war, we need to notice that for all his destructiveness he introduced some of the innovations and elemental virtues we prize most.

The rise of warfare can't be separated from other social and metaphysical changes that accompanied it. If we focus on bloodshed and cruelty, the habit of war might seem only a dark compulsion devoid of virtue. But look for a moment at the whole picture of which war was a part. The habit of warfare was closely bound up with (1) the rise of patriarchy, male metaphors, and power; (2) the emergence of monotheism and the notion of a transcendent male God; (3) the encouragement for man to transcend and exercise dominion over nature rather than passively accept his "fate"; (4) the unification of small tribes into larger national communities which increased the social horizon of the individual; (5) the growth of cities, complex civilizations, hierarchical organization, and aristocratic culture; and finally (6) the emergence of individualism.

When living within the seasons of nature, hunters, gatherers, and farmers were compulsively conservative. Their myths had a single subtext: Do everything the way it has always been done; don't innovate; repeat the patterns of nature. Early tribal and agricultural societies were relatively harmonious because of their emphasis on conformity and continuity. Within tribal societies everyone knew his place, but individuality was not encouraged.

It took the notion of a God who transcended the order of nature, whose power created and controlled nature, to provide the social sanction for the development of individualism. This God, who stands above the fatedness of nature, commands men to stand above nature and society and woman and take charge of his own destiny. Without the historical introduction of the notion of a transcendent God who ordered his subjects to name the animals and to have dominion over the earth, neither individualism nor empirical science and technology would have developed. Life in the garden of the goddess was harmonious but the spirit of history called for man to stand up and take charge. Now, centuries later, after we have been inundated by the tragedy of warfare and sickened by the side effects of irresponsible science and runaway technology, it is easy to forget the triumph of that moment when men rebelled against their fate, threw off their passivity, and declared: Thank you, Mother, but I can do it myself.

As we try to discern a new vocation for men it is well to remember that the emergence of the martial spirit was creative in its time and that warriors cared enough to offer "the supreme sacrifice" to protect those they loved in a less than perfect world. Mars and Eros have always gone hand in hand.

Homo Sapiens

As nearly as we can tell, Socrates was the inventor and first exemplar of reason. He took the agricultural wisdom about the order in nature and the warrior's delight in combat, turned them inside-out, and created the new ideal of the reasonable man—Homo sapiens.

Socrates appears to have been an unusual man in many respects. An ugly man in a culture that worshiped beauty, he came to be loved and admired because of his manner of life. It is reported that from his youth he received warnings and messages from a mysterious inner voice, or daimon, and that he often fell into prolonged, rapt, trance-like states. Legend has it that the Delphic Oracle proclaimed there was no living man wiser than Socrates, but she said that if he were wiser than others it was only because he knew his ignorance and was willing to keep searching for knowledge. Whether in the ecstasy of thought or in a mystical state of revelation, Socrates became convinced that reason (Logos, nous), which he saw as immanent in nature and responsible for the orderly cycle of the seasons and the predictable movement of the stars, was also the most important faculty in man. If only man would follow this outer-inner law, he could bring reason and harmony into his life and into the life of the community. Indeed, the only way a man could acquire virtue was by acquiring knowledge. Socrates defined the good life in a society, not unlike our own, given to war and commerce, as one given to the cultivation of the soul. Of his lifework he says: "So long as I breathe and have the strength to do it, I will not cease philosophizing, exhorting you, indicting whichever of you I happen to meet, telling him in my customary way: Esteemed friend, citizen of Athens, the greatest city in the world, so outstanding in both intelligence and power, aren't you ashamed to care so much to make all the money you can, and to advance your reputation and prestige—while for truth and wisdom and the improvement of your soul you have no care or worry?" (Apology 29d)

But Socrates understood that the warfare that raged without also raged within the psyche. Man stands divided against himself; the psyche is a battleground between "I want" and "I should." The task of reason is to put an end to this inner warfare, to adjudicate the conflict between desire and duty, to bring order out of chaos, to control the rebellious emotions and bring peace within the psyche and the polis.

Socrates's great achievements were his redefinition of the arena where manhood was won and his creating of a new method of achieving it.

In Plato's dialogues, Socrates is examining and exhorting his fellow men to examine the meaning of their lives, whether they are in the marketplace, the senate, at a private party, or on the battlefield. While the dialogues often end inconclusively, seemingly with more confusion than clarity, the Socratic method of the inquiry creates the new definition of virtue. Knowledge and virtue, the highest forms of manhood, which Socrates claims are inseparable, are not discovered in commercial cleverness or courage in battle, but in dialogue, in the public arena, where men join together in conversation to search for the truth.

As important as Socrates's ideas were, it was his example that etched itself indelibly on the ancient imagination. From 399 B.C. until the death of Christ the single event that most clearly defined the ideal man was the manner in which Socrates faced death. That he could courageously drink the hemlock, rather than flee and break the law of his beloved Athens, was the highest proof to the Greek mind that the human spirit was motivated by a reason that transcends time and death. He crystalized the highest vision of how a rational man lived and died within a cosmos governed by a divine Logos and a city (polis) governed by law.

As well as being the exemplar of the reasonable man, Socrates gave us the instrument that remains until this day the only antidote to the habit of warfare—the Socratic dialogue, the simplest and most elegant means for making peace. In dialogue, conflicts may be resolved by a type of intellectual wrestling match, which philosopher Karl Jaspers called a form of "loving combat." That men have differing opinions and interests is inevitable. That they may settle their conflict without violence is the hope of reason.

But what about women? In the story of Homo sapiens they are assigned the dark, Dionysian impulses, the passions that bubble up from the deep and overwhelm reason. Women are the irrational element in the dreams of men who think life should be as orderly as a syllogism.

All of which brings us to Xantippe, the wife of Socrates. Does it surprise you that we know practically nothing about her?

We have only the gossip preserved by the male fraternity of the Platonic Academy, who report that she was a shrew who made Socrates's home life miserable. Plato would have us believe that she did nothing but pester Socrates to stay away from the Agora and get a decent job. Is she only a nagging wife?

Listening with the third ear I hear the silence of Xantippe. Does she feel that she is never important enough to appear in a dialogue? Does she feel that the exemplar of reason does not care to listen to woman's reason? Does she lie in bed on spring mornings wanting to be touched by the man she admires but cannot reach? Does she remember moments years before when she was the first Athenian to fall in love with the hidden beauty of an ugly young man? Does something within her dry up and die when she is forced to admit that Socrates prefers young boys to her mature flesh? Does she wonder why she has learned so much of the life of reason from her man and he has learned so little of the life of the senses from her?

The vices that go hand in hand with the virtues of Homo sapiens can be deduced from Xantippe's untold story. She, like others of her sex in Greece and most women throughout history, was excluded from public life and serious dialogue. She stood outside the communion created by the "loving combat" of the exchange of ideas. To the rational man, woman represents emotion, the life of the senses, and the animal nature he seeks to control. The suspicion that falls on woman casts its shadow on all of the organs and faculties in man that are thought to be womanly or to respond to the appeals of woman. The cock, like a woman, is suspected of being a rebel against reason and is chastised for independent life. Mind must discipline body. Willpower must establish its dominion over emotion. Spirit must triumph over the flesh. Should Homo sapiens succeed in his project of bringing all things, including women, under his control, the world would finally be orderly—and joyless.

Dionysian Man

Whenever reason becomes too imperious in its demands and the sunlit tyranny of seriousness takes over, listen carefully and you will hear the panpipes starting to play in the distance and glimpse the satyrs leering at you from wild places. The return of the repressed. For every Pat Boone a Mick Jagger, for every Ayn Rand an N. O. Brown, for every Norman Rockwell a Picasso, for every philosopher a rogue, for every Labor Day a Mardi Gras. Man will not be defined by reason alone.

The Greek spirit was too wise to be only rational. In an Athens museum, less than a stone's throw from where Socrates practiced the art of dialogue and Aristotle preached the gospel of moderation, you may view vases with paintings that graphically depict every variety of sexual connection—men with women, men with men, women with women in all manner of athletic positions. In this erotic realism and in the artfully carved friezes of the Acropolis, the Greek love of beauty and celebration of the flesh is as obvious as is the suspicion of the body in the writing of the philosophers.

The Greeks ordained that Dionysius, god of wine, drunkenness, and excess, should share the great temple at Delphi with Apollo, god of reason, order, and balance. In the Dionysian festivals, the theater was born. Watching tragic and comic plays the audience could participate vicariously in the excessive emotions of characters whose lives were out of balance and experience catharsis. In the safety of the theater they could satisfy their desires to break free of the bonds of moderation and rational restraint.

The wild man lives just under the surface of the rational man. He has many names, many faces. He is *homo ludens*, the playboy, the *puer aeternis*, Peter Pan. He is the hero of *Zorba the Greek, A Thousand Clowns, The Dead Poets Society*. Since he is given to play, fantasy, sensuality, fun, and games he is frequently accused of being irresponsible, amoral, a dance-away lover, a boy who refuses to grow up. So say the serious ones, the mature guardians of the ego and the priests of the superego.

But when wildness is not included within the life and definition of a man, something crucial is missing from manhood. Zorba said it best: "A man needs a touch of madness, otherwise he will never be free." The shamans of every tribe have always known that man has a dream-body, or what Freud called the libido. If we lose touch with the outrageous, contradictory, excessive life of our dreams we easily become too domesticated by the social order. The playful child and the wise old man live side by side in the psyche. Impose the tyranny of seriousness and both die.

Dionysian man adds "passion" to the definition of manhood. While Apollo counsels "everything in moderation," the wild man advises us that "the path of excess leads to the palace of wisdom" (Blake). He encourages us to "follow our bliss" and explore the deepest desires of our being.

Prophetic Man

The prophets of Israel seemed to appear out of nowhere, speaking in the name of Yahweh (formerly a God of war and territory), proclaiming that henceforth man would be judged by the justice of his conduct. Sometime near 776 B.C. Amos—country bumpkin, sheepherder, hippie—came down out of the hills and stood on the street corner, started preaching, and went to meddling. After winning the applause of his audience for condemning their enemies for their transgressions, he startled everyone by pronouncing the judgment of God on Israel and Judah for oppressing the poor and crushing the needy. "Thus saith the Lord: For three transgressions of Israel, and for four, I will not turn away the punishment thereof; because they sell the righteous for silver, and the poor for a pair of shoes." And what would satisfy God? Not piety or burnt offerings. Rather, "Let justice run down as waters and righteousness as a mighty stream." Or as Amos's contemporary Micah, another prophet, stated, "What does the Lord require of you but to do justice, to love mercy, and to walk humbly with thy God?"

By suggesting that a transcendent God required that man act in a way that transcended the minimal moral demands of his own society, the prophets introduced a radical principle into our thinking about man. Man is more than culture. He cannot be guided only by his tribal conscience. A man loyal only to the voice of his tribal or national conscience may exploit the stranger, destroy the alien, be ruthless to all outsiders, and still feel guiltless. But the prophets claim there is a higher standard of judgment. They establish what Tillich called "a transmoral conscience," a principle that our being is judged by something that transcends the demands of our immediate culture.

A man is a man only when he measures himself against something more universal than the morality of his own time. The task we are now undertaking—to discover normative standards by which we can measure manhood, to explore the vocation of contemporary men and to sketch an outline of a new type of heroic life—is an attempt to translate the insight of the prophets into modern categories. Our dignity and authenticity as men demand that we never allow ourselves to be only products of our own time. A man may dwell in Jerusalem, Berlin, or Washington, but his citizenship is in a commonwealth that transcends his immediate time and locality. Subtract the relationship to transcendence and you lose the essence of man.

Man as Image of God

Throw out the pious Sunday school pictures of Jesus, the tortuous theology of the Church, and one bright image and clear gospel remains. Man is spirit incarnate, at once a citizen of two king-doms—the here and now and the there and then. As an archetype of man, Jesus exemplifies the notion that virtue and divine inspiration can never be separated because man is created in the image and of the substance of God.

The problem of manhood and the consequent tragedy of history, from the Judeo-Christian perspective, is that men mis-identify themselves. They act out the drama of their lives before the audience of their contemporaries rather than before the all-knowing and merciful eye of God. They get mired in the limited perspective of their immediate desires rather than seek harmony with the will of God.

The image of Jesus on the Cross is central to the Christian notion of manhood because it dramatizes the issue of will, a recurring theme in any discussion of manhood. These days popular professional cheerleaders sell seminars that teach how to develop willpower. A century ago Nietzsche was preaching the Zarathustrian gospel of "the will to power." Before that, Socrates assured us that will automatically followed vision and that to know the good was to do it. The genius of Christianity is that it interconnects the heart, the will, and the divine spirit, and links virtue to surrender. The lesson of Gethsemene is that a man is most virile not when he insists upon his autonomous will but when he harmonizes his will with the will of God.

Discussions about manhood in Western culture cannot avoid the figure of Jesus. He is the most frequently used mirror in which generations of Western men—philosophers from Augus-tine to Tillich, evangelists from Paul to Billy Graham, novelists from Renan to Kazantzakis—have seen their own faces reflected. Like the ink blots used in the psychological Rorschach test, Jesus is a historical X on which men project their own self-understand-ing. Every generation discovers a different Jesus—the magical savior, the wonder worker, the mystic, the political rebel, the labor organizer, the capitalist, the communist, the greatest sales-man who ever lived, the protofeminist, the ecologist. As Albert Schweitzer said, men searching for the historical Jesus look into a deep, dark well, see a reflection of themselves, and call it "Lord."

Without debating the question of the person of Jesus or getting our feet mired in ecclesiastical matters and denomina-tional issues, we may liberate a single insight about manhood that continues to be as revolutionary as it was two millennia ago. A man finds fulfillment (spiritual and sexual) only when he turns aside from willfulness and surrenders to something beyond self.

Virility involves life in communion. When we try to discover the principle of manhood within the isolated self, we will end up not fulfilling the self but destroying it. Manhood can be defined only in relational terms. How large and generous we may become depends on the size of the Other we take into ourselves.

The question Christianity, as well as every religious tradition, puts to men and women yesterday and today is: Do I find my fulfillment in asserting my will to power over myself and others, or in surrendering to myself and others in a spirit of empathy and compassion? And if I can only be myself by surrendering, to what, to whom do I surrender?

Man as Power

From the beginning of time, women have been defined by their ability to surrender to the cycles of nature, birth, and death and to submit to the dominion of another—usually a man. But men have more typically discovered the principle of their being in the exercise of power and in the refusal to surrender. From Machiavelli to Nietzsche to the contemporary advocates of power, men have been warned that they must put away womanly things (such as sentiment), and learn how to accumulate and manipulate power if they are to be truly men.

Arguably the very confused notion of "power" has been the central metaphor that has most dominated the psyche of men during the last several centuries. Consider the various kinds of power men sought as the defining characteristic of their existence: muscle power, political power, sexual power (potency), military power, firepower, financial power, the power of knowledge, the power of positive thinking, personal power.

When men define themselves by power they are at once driven by the impossible desire to become replicas of omnipotent gods and are haunted by their repressed knowledge of their semipotence. By definition they are able to feel their manhood only when they have the ability to make things happen, only when they can exert control over events, over themselves, over women. Therefore they are condemned to be forever measuring themselves by something exterior to themselves, by the effects of their actions, by how much change they can implement, how much novelty they can introduce into the slowly evolving history of nature. I did it; I made it happen; I exist.

The drive to establish potency in any of its various forms always shipwrecks on the shoals of finitude. Muscles grow old;

empires collapse; sexual potency waxes and wanes; for the want of a nail a shoe is lost and the kingdom with it; the clean well-lit sphere of knowledge is perpetually shadowed by the cloud of unknowing; money may make the world go round but cannot purchase a man a single day beyond his allotted time; the will is sapped by declining years; thoughts of disease, defeat, and death that we banish from our waking hours return by stealth to trouble our dreams; and the feeling of personal power is notoriously fragile.

Nietzsche, in spite of being the author of *The Will to Power*, and inadvertently the inspiration for the Nazi notion of the superman, saw that when power becomes an obsession it becomes self-defeating. "Power makes stupid," he warned. The global crises of nuclear weaponry, the defeat of the "great power" in Vietnam and Afghanistan, and the creeping deadliness of industrial pollution have brought modern men to the point where they are beginning to contemplate the wisdom of Nietzsche's warning. The quest for power has led to folly.

Scientific-Technological Man

The impulse that grew into what we now call science and technology has been with us since the first caveman or woman domesticated fire and experimented with cooking a dinosaur steak. Because we are small creatures in an immense universe we inevitably contemplate the starry skies above and the marvels under the sun and stand in dumb wonder before the magnificence of the cosmos. And then we begin to tinker, to invent, to seek some measure of control over our lives. Nature calls forth a quest for understanding and control, using human beings as her-his-its agents. The human condition dictates that we will always try to balance contradictory virtues—wonder and curiosity, reverence and irreverence, surrender and rebellion. Caught between mystery and the search for knowledge, men and women must create both religion and science.

In the mythology of most peoples, there is an exemplary hero such as Prometheus who steals the fire from the gods and brings the gifts of technology to man. The Promethean hero—coyote or raven among the American Indians—is inevitably a trickster who defies the rules of jealous gods who prefer mankind to remain in servile ignorance. The mythic imagination tells us that a man must be willing to storm the stronghold of Mother Nature and God the Father, wrestle their secrets from them, and bring them back to the human community. Being a man has always had something to do with being an outlaw, a thief, a heaven-stormer, an enemy of the established order.

In its more modern form, the myth of Prometheus has been recast into the story of the heroes of the scientific and technological revolution. The saga begins with the careful observations of Galileo, Bacon, Newton, and Darwin, and continues with scientists who learned to devise experiments that would "put nature on the rack" and force her to give answers to men's questions. The tools (or weapons?) of the modern heroes—Niels Bohr, Einstein, Heisenberg—were the instruments that allowed them to weigh, measure, quantify, and control nature.

Thus far our tour of the hall of exemplary men has used images of an ancient hunter, a warrior, a prophet, a philosopher. But for the heroes of technology actual museums exist, dedicated to recounting and celebrating the epoch-making deeds of modern Prometheans. Wander through the National Museum of History and Technology, the National Air and Space Museum, or the museum at Los Alamos and you will find a record of the inventions that have given birth to a new age. There you may see the artifacts connected with modern mythic events: the airplane in which Orville and Wilbur Wright—successors to Icarus—finally achieved the dream of human flight; the telegraph by which Thomas Edison usurped the power of Hermes and Mercury to transmit messages over vast distances; Henry Ford's Model T., which put a chariot of the gods in every man's garage; Robert Oppenheimer's nuclear bomb that harnessed the power of the sun and released the power of Hades.

Without a shadow of a doubt, science and technology have finally demonstrated the truth of the religious insight that man was created only a little lower than the angels. What some feminists now disparagingly refer to as "patriarchal technology" has given us a godlike capacity to shape matter and fulfill our dreams. But it has brought its opposite demonic attribute—the ability to destroy life. Millennia before the steam engine, the Greeks noticed that anything carried to excess bears the seeds of its own destruction. Within our century, the spiritual triumph of science and technology has gradually become our nemesis. Our increasing industrial pollution is only the latest version of the vultures that eat the liver of Prometheus as he is chained to the rock of his hubris. The epitaph of our age was pronounced at the very moment of its triumph. As he stood in a control room five miles from the blast immediately following the successful explosion of the first atomic bomb, two passages from the *Bha-*

gavad Gita flashed into Robert Oppenheimer's mind: "If the radiance of a thousand suns were to burst into the sky that would be like the splendor of the mighty One," and "I am become death, the shatterer of worlds." Later as he reflected on the divine-demonic link involved in the creation of the bomb he said, "In some sort of crude sense which no vulgarity, no humor, no overstatement can quite extinguish, the physicists have known sin; and this is a knowledge which they cannot lose."[1]

The story of the advancement of science and technology threatens to have an O. Henry ending. At the moment of our apotheosis, we are being humiliated by our creations. Our machines have turned against us. As weapons and pollution threaten our existence we approach an era in which the practice of science and technology, which has been the dominant source of masculine pride for nearly two centuries, must give way to some new vocation, some new mode of masculine identity.

The Self-Made Man

The elite ideals of any age are always translated into popular terms.

In the founding years of American democracy the image of statesmen and heroes of the republic inspired our notions of true manhood. "Before the late 1800s self-help manuals defined the male in terms of character. The words most used relating to character were: citizenship, duty, democracy, work, building, golden deeds, outdoor life, conquest, honor, reputation, morals, manners, integrity . . . The good man of the eighteenth century was the one who devoted himself to the good of the community while he 'lived a life of piety' and 'mild religion.' "[2]

But as we began to move westward and develop into an industrial nation, we honored our scientists, inventors, and manufacturers and extended the idea of control and fabrication from nature to man himself. The whole notion of *homo faber*, of the man who fabricates both products and himself, was a fitting philosophy for a frontier nation. America, with a wilderness to conquer and a continent to civilize, needed a muscular, pragmatic, action-oriented vision of manhood. In our pioneer years, we idealized rough men, men willing to forge themselves into tools to clear land, build steel mills, and create cattle empires in lonesome country.

By the turn of the nineteenth century, the ideal of manhood had changed dramatically. The key word was now "self."

The good man was bent on "self-improvement." In this, the era of the "self-made man," exercise, discipline, hard work, moderate habits, and true grit were the mark of manhood. Teddy Roosevelt exemplified the virtues of vigor, robust health, and self-discipline that we most admired. The Boy Scouts emerged as a way of forming the raw material of youth into the finished product of manhood through the imposition of the law: "A scout is trustworthy, loyal, helpful, friendly, courteous, kind, obedient, cheerful, thrifty, brave, clean, and reverent." (And he takes a cold shower should he have the kind of indecent thoughts that might otherwise lead to "self-abuse.")

The virtues of a self-made man were a strong ego, unbending character, and a substantial social persona, foursquare and solid as a brick house. At best, the men who fashioned themselves after blueprints of their own making were solid citizens. With their extroverted minds and outgoing personalities they created an era of unprecedented prosperity. Their entrepreneurship and Yankee ingenuity turned the philosophical ideal of "the greatest good for the greatest number" into a practical reality—a mass society in which every man (white man) had his castle, drove an automobile, and purchased luxuries previously enjoyed only by royalty.

But extroversion has its cost. Hard-nosed realism fosters its own brand of illusions. As it turned out, the self-assurance of the self-made man was much like the facade of a western town—a persona behind which a shadow world lay hidden. The bully men who made America great knew who they were; they were not given to self-doubt or wavering opinions. But beneath their robust personalities lay a repressed nether world of emotion, dreams, and forbidden desires. Generations of self-made men ignored or despised the wildness within the self because it could not be brought under the control of the rational mind and the disciplined will. To gain the world they sacrificed their own soulfulness and abandoned the dream-body, the untamed landscapes of the interior life.

And what is worse, the bully men and rough riders created a tyranny of extroverts that continues to haunt American men. We are still tempted to judge ourselves by their standard of masculinity, which dismissed men who were introverted, intuitive, sensitive, and artistic. They imposed a model of manhood in which all who were not "once-born" personalities with sunlight virtues and pragmatic temperaments were considered sissies. The dark secret of self-made men, as Freud was to show us, was that they explored the far corners of the earth and created empires, but were afraid to navigate the corridors of the unconscious.

Psychological Man

In Europe, World War I signaled an end to optimism and the liberal notion that moral progress is woven into the fabric of history. The specter of trench warfare and the great battles of the Somme and Arles in which a million men were slaughtered shattered a generation's faith in reason and progress. The Depression and World War II were needed to open up a serious crack in the American psyche. The revelation of the horrors of the concentration camps and the genocidal mania of the Nazis confirmed our image of ourselves as the saviors of Europe. Not until the momentum of our fury carried us beyond the limits of necessary violence to the use of atomic bombs against civilian populations at Hiroshima and Nagasaki, and, decades later when our blind crusade against communism in Vietnam ended in disaster, did we entertain any moral self-doubt and began to wonder if there was not something irrational, twisted, and evil lurking in the depths of the American psyche.

Within this climate of cultural disillusionment, Freud and the psychoanalytical movement emerged as advocates of a new ideal of manhood. At the time it seemed as if the far corners of the world had been explored (space had not yet been declared the new frontier) and the heroic adventure of war had become tainted. With *Interpretation of Dreams*, Freud pointed the way toward a new adventure, a new version of the heroic journey— the way of the psychonaut, the explorer of the inner world.

These days it is fashionable to bad-mouth Freud. Every psychologist and graduate of a year-long training course in Transactional Analysis or behavior therapy is eager to pronounce psychoanalysis obsolete and to discourse on the sexist sins and tyrannical personality of the master. Everyone in the field of psychology, it seems, has now gone beyond Freud.

Without question Freud was a man of a thousand mistakes, many illusions, and colossal arrogance, and many of his theories are best forgotten. But the vices of great men are usually on the same scale as their virtues. Long after Abraham Maslow, Carl Rogers, and Fritz Perls are relegated to footnotes in the history of psychology, Freud will remain a permanent resident in the Hall of Exemplars. In spite of his shortcomings, he gave us a new definition of courage in the example of his self-analysis.

Delving into his dreams he confronted the forbidden zones of the libido and wrestled with the excessive desires, unacceptable thoughts, and demons that had been banished from the moderate world of the middle class. In that surrealistic underworld lived cruel mothers, seducing fathers, and children who murdered their parents. Incest was the rule and perversion the order of the day. Men were changed into women with penises and women into men with vaginas. Any building or pointed object might stand in place of an erection; any pit or nest might symbolize a vulva. The heads of state were unmasked as fathers in disguise and all women were suspect of being surrogates for absent mothers.

If Freud's phallus-in-wonderland world strikes us as excessively sexual it is largely because those sexual-erotic dimensions of life were especially repressed in his time. Every generation or two, the *content* of the shadow world of the unconscious changes. What was once forbidden becomes commonplace. In 1923, when Salvador Dali made the first surrealistic film, using "bizarre" imagery of the unconscious—an eye being slit by a razor, ants coming out of a hole in a hand—very few people had any idea what he was attempting to do. Today, in an era where everything sexual is permitted and experimentation with hallucinogenic drugs is common, every twelve-year-old who has seen MTV or television commercials knows how to read stream-of-consciousness imagery. The content of Freud's unconscious is now conscious, and therefore, his "heroic" journey into the sexual underworld seems passé to us. The repressions of our time are no longer primarily sexual. Not until we dare to plunge into the content of our contemporary unconsciousness, encounter our corporate and individual shadows, and wrestle with commonly forbidden visions of our selves, can we judge the measure of his courage.

In passing, we may note one clue to the changing character of the unconscious that provides us with an Ariadne's thread to lead us through the maze of the unique journey we must make into our shadow world. In recent years, after having lain dormant for a decade or more, the works of Carl Jung, Freud's contemporary, and Joseph Campbell have suddenly become compelling. Why now? For Jung, the sexual realm was not as embattled and denied (since he had both a wife and a mistress) as the hunger for meaning and spiritual significance. His work, like Campbell's, leads beyond the sexual to the mythic dimension in which we may discover our communion with men and women throughout the ages, with animals, plants, and the divine spirit.

It was Freud's genius and historical destiny to call men back to the psyche, to remind us not to lose ourselves in the world of action. He taught us that healing the wound of manhood involves remembering our fathers and mothers and recollecting the family drama within which our childhood was set. Building upon the foundation Freud laid, modern psychology has given men back their inwardness, their subjectivity, their feelings, and the permission to pay attention to the stories of their lives.

But the cost has been considerable. If therapy has reintroduced some men to their feelings, it seems to have encapsulated them in privacy. Perhaps we have a larger percentage of sensitive men who can communicate about their experience than ever before. But we seem to be missing the cosmopolitan men, the old Stoic ideal of a man whose psyche was linked at once to political action and the natural world around him.

Postmodern Man

Today, the notion of postmodernism is all the rage. Around 1960, we entered an era characterized by a new style of life, art, and identity. While the modern world was shaped by the industrial revolution and mass production, the postmodern era is shaped by the information revolution, the ethic of consumption, fast-changing styles, and lack of commitment to any single perspective. According to Todd Gitlin, "Postmodernism is completely indifferent to the questions of consistency and continuity. It self-consciously splices genres, attitudes, styles. It relishes the blurring or juxtaposition of forms (fiction-nonfiction), stances (straight-ironic), moods (violent-comic), cultural levels (high-low) . . . It neither embraces nor criticizes, but beholds the world blankly, with a knowingness that dissolves feeling and commitment into irony . . . It takes pleasure in the play of surfaces, and derides the search for depth as mere nostalgia."[3]

At best, postmodern man has gone for the gusto, done away with pleasure anxiety, and thrown off the old capitalist tyranny of scarcity-consciousness and postponed gratification. He is no longer trying to improve his soul, develop his willpower, or save himself for some future heaven. He has given up the quest for a single identity, a consistent point of view or triumph over tragedy. His stance is one of irony rather than romance.

At worst, postmodern man is the concupiscent consumer. He might be called a dilettante except that he is too cool to dive into delight. His tastes, life-style, and convictions are formed by fashion. Like the god Proteus, and unlike the substantial self-made men of the last century, he changes shapes at will. His life is organized more around the idea of "taste" than of "right or wrong"; his world is aesthetic rather than moral. You could call him disillusioned except that he has never dared care about anything passionately enough to have developed hope or illusion.

In truth the postmodern man is not so new as he thinks. Kierkegaard described him a century ago as Don Juan, the aesthetic man whose life is a series of one-night stands and fleeting romances. He is a blank page, a tabula rasa, upon which the moment writes its tale. Weightless, he suffers, in the words of Milan Kundera, "the unbearable lightness of being." Unlike the classical "hero with a thousand faces," he avoids the depths and keeps himself satiated with a thousand amusing facades. The mall, the automobile showroom, and the electronic supermarket are his catharsis. If he turns to more "serious" matters he becomes what Trunkpa Rinpoche called a "spiritual materialist." He samples religions and salvation schemes.

With the emergence of postmodern man we reach a point where moral reasoning gives out. Once we abandon the age-old quest for consistency, for forging a single identity, for a unifying vision we are left with no guiding principle except to follow the dictates of the moment. "Taste" replaces "ought," and as the old proverb says, "About taste there is no dispute."

Without an organizing center, postmodern man is lost, wandering in a wilderness of confusing plurality. But, paradoxically, being bereft of set moral landmarks, he is in a unique position to undertake a new journey.

These images, exemplary types, elemental virtues, form the strata of the male psyche. Each had its heyday. Each was a creative response to its time, a vocation called forth by a contemporary need. Each has contributed to the definition of man. Each reached a point of "paradoxical counterproductivity," a moment when it produced a result, the opposite of what it intended.

Together, the responses men made to the circumstances of their times form the history that undergirds our present condition. We listen to these elders whose voices are still within us, not because they give us answers to our questions, but because they give us courage to respond to the vocation of our moment in history.

Virility and Vocation:
Fierce Gentlemen

History is a Zen master.
It presents us with koans,
quandaries, questions, vocations.

If the changing ideals of manhood have always been shaped by historical challenges, we must assume that modern manhood will also be defined by the problems and opportunities emerging today. Virility has always been measured by a man's willingness to hear and respond to the calling of his age. So, before we can begin to paint a portrait of a now and future man, let's sketch the social and political context within which men will live in the last decade of the twentieth century and beyond. What changes in our self-understanding and in our ways of acting are evolving now? What is a manly vocation in the 1990's and what will it be in the next century?

The challenges that face us are clear. Whether we will respond to them is not. For the foreseeable future, men's lives will be caught up in the turbulent confluence of two great mythic systems—one dying, one being born. The old myth perceives reality as constant discord and believes combat, warfare, and economic competition are inevitable; it hopes for clear-cut victories and progress. The new myth perceives life and reality as a unified network of mutually interdependent entities whose well-being is enhanced by cooperation and compassion; it looks forward to a world order not based on warfare, and an economic system that is ecologically viable.

The tragedy of the old rites of manhood is that they made so many of us morally tone-deaf. We have become so tough-minded and tough-hearted, such experts in control and command, that we can hardly hear the crying needs of our time or the first faint strands of melody the future is sounding.

We hear with our hearts, or not at all, and not unless we are willing to be enchanted, inspirited, encouraged, and engaged.

What does history require of men today? What vocation invites our response?

Men in our time are called to deal with the darkness at noon, the failure of our success, the impotence of our power, the waste products of our creativity. The quandaries of our time are war (the shadow of power) and pollution (the shadow of progress). If we solve these koans that history has presented to us, everything will change—the nature of national sovereignty, the economic system, the psyches of men and women. If we do not solve them, the human species may well go the way of the dodo bird. As men, our challenge is to grow beyond the myth of war and the warrior psyche and to create a new form of ecological economics that will preserve the earth household.

Beyond the Myth of War and the Warrior Psyche

The habit of organizing society around the warfare system, and the psyche of men around the necessity to become warriors, is rapidly becoming a historical anachronism, a puzzle we must solve in the near future. In the past, tribal skirmishes and limited war were occasionally necessary and provided a way for men to practice heroic virtues. But with the introduction of total war and nuclear weapons there is no longer a theater of war with civilian spectators where brave men can slay wicked enemies, rescue fair maidens, and protect their families. The warrior's nuclear shield doesn't protect us anymore. We are all huddled together on a worldwide battlefield, brothers and sisters in a nuclear family, one race, indivisible, with destruction and fallout for all.

There is a hollow sound in our battle hymns, a growing sense of ambivalence. It is as if we know we are celebrating the manly virtues and necessary sacrifices of a passing era. Perhaps the last war memorial (the first to be designed by a woman) has been built. The Vietnam War Memorial in Washington, D.C., is the American wailing wall, a place of sorrow and remembrance, a testimony to the futility of war. The mourners come to rub their fingers over a single name on the wall, like blind men and women trying to decipher from the carved letters in the marble some meaning or purpose that will heal the aching void in their hearts where there was once a son, a brother, a father, a lover, a friend. But the message of the monument—where the dead stand not by rank or "importance" but are ordered only by the date on which they gave up their youthful immortality—seems to be: "No more war. No more false glory." No more political histrionics that force men and women to fight and die on foreign battlefields where the line between heroism and dishonor becomes blurred.

The logic of history is leading us to the end of nationally organized violence, although there is no guarantee that we will heed our vocation to end war. It is possible that by default we may choose World Wars III, IV, and numberless covert actions as unconscious means of solving our ecological problems by reducing the population by a billion or so each generation. But any way you play it, the curtain is falling on "The War Game" and the actors are taking off the ritual masks.

It is hard to imagine a utopian world in which nations would not be organized around warfare. But, listen to Albert Camus, certainly one of the most lucid and unsentimental minds of our century: "It would be completely Utopian to wish that men should no longer kill each other . . . But a much sounder Utopia is that which insists that murder be no longer legitimized . . . The choice is simple, Utopia or the war now being prepared by antiquated modes of thought . . . Skeptical though we are (and as I am) realism forces us to this Utopian alternative. When our Utopia has become part of history . . . men will find themselves unable to conceive reality without it. For History is simply man's desperate effort to give body to his most clairvoyant dreams."[4]

At the moment, men's best hope is this "clairvoyant dream." None of us can paint an accurate portrait of the man of tomorrow. Clearly, the challenge we face is to revision ourselves, to imagine a world beyond war, to dream of a new kind of virility, a new breed of heroes who will no longer hone the killing arts and take pride in dueling scars, purple hearts, and battlefield honor.

Certainly men and women in the future may remain warriors, in that they will still need to contend with power. But we face the dilemma that, for the first time in human history, we must learn to manage power without resorting to violence.

The best metaphor for a peaceful way of managing power would combine the images of a wrestling match, a dialogue, a democracy, and a love affair. The Greeks' highest vision of peace was incarnate at the Olympic Games, a contest, or agon, between well-matched and respectful opponents in an arena of ritualized, limited battle. The model for the peaceful arena is the dialogue. By talking together, out of disagreement we create some synthesis beyond our individual views. Dialogue, or conversation, is democracy. "A republic is made up of people locked in civil argument. And the point of the argument is neither to win nor to end the diversity of opinion and power. Peace means keeping the argument going in a civil manner, ad infinitum."[5]

When I visualize peace, I think of fierce men, women, and nations struggling together to define their boundaries and enhance self-respect with love and politics as a playing field, I see rivals facing each other not as incarnations of evil, but as worthy opponents.

No one saw more clearly than Nietzsche, the philosopher who centered his idea of the superman on the idea of power, how the warrior psyche would be changed to the core by the task of forging peace:

> "And perhaps the great day will come when a people, distinguished by wars and victories and by the highest development of a military order and intelligence, and accustomed to make the heaviest sacrifice for these things, will explain of its own free will, 'We break the sword,' and will smash its military establishment down to its lowest foundations. Rendering oneself unarmed when one has been the best armed, out of a height of feeling—that is the means to real peace, which must always rest upon a peace of mind; whereas the so-called 'armed peace' as it now exists in all countries, is the absence of peace of mind . . . Rather perish than hate and fear, and twice rather perish than make oneself hated and feared—this must someday become the highest maxim for every single commonwealth too."[6]

To solve the riddle of war we will have to change our definitions of gender, our deep inner feelings of what it means to be manly and womanly. As light is particle and wave, war is woven of the shadows of men and women, disowned power and repressed love. We need a new quantum politics: Waging nuclear peace requires both woman's liberation and man's liberation; a new understanding of the genderal web that binds us in a hostile system of blind violence.

Beyond Consumptive Economics: Toward an Earth Advocacy

The struggle between the myth of progress and the ecological myth is already raging around us in every community, pitting real estate developers against conservationists, lumbermen against environmentalists, advocates of rapid growth against advocates of no growth. The great paradigm war that is shaping up involves two radically different visions of the future, two views of humanity's place in the surrounding world, and, consequently, two divergent ideals of manhood and womanhood. For the moment, let's name these conflicting worldviews the Progressives and the Radicals. Here, in summary fashion, is how they view the future and therefore the challenge of the present.

THE RADICALS:	THE PROGRESSIVES:
They are ecologically focused. Their horizon is local, bioregional, and planetary. Their loyalty is to home, hearth, and community.	They are economically focused. Their horizon is international, urban, and abstract. Their loyalty is to job, profession, and corporation.
Their organizing metaphor is biological—the link between organism and environment.	Their organizing metaphor is technological—the link between increasingly complex machines and economic growth.
They desire a world governed by respect for all species in the commonwealth of being.	They desire a world governed by economic development of all nations.
Their eros is for the sensual enjoyment of the natural world, for wilderness and garden, for intimacy, friendship, and community.	Their eros is for organizing, entrepreneurship, inventing, increasing data-knowledge, manufacturing, and consuming of products.
They view men and women as mysterious opposites whose different gifts shape all relationships.	They view men and women as essentially identical except for reproductive functions which concern only the private aspects of relationships.

Progressives are still informed by the great myth of progress that has dominated the technologically developed nations since the "death of God" and the beginning of the industrial revolution. Within this mythology, humankind, through its rational capacity and its technological genius, is destined to control the future of evolution. Progress (which is never distinguished from "growth," "change," or "motion") and an ever-increasing gross world product is our destiny and moral imperative. The axioms of the Progressives are: More is better, the latest is the greatest, speed increases efficiency, yesterday's limit is today's challenge, technology will create a world economy and a global village in which all peoples may become satisfied consumers.

Americans in general, and corporations in particular, are bullish on the future because of a hidden assumption that is as old as gnostic dualism—the belief that matter, stuff, nature is something to be transcended and dominated. Our current hope for a glorious future is based on "the information revolution" ushered in by our latest candidate for the messiah, the computer. The microchip—miniaturized mind, moving at the speed of light—heralds a new postindustrial age. We who are the masters of the new technology will not be forced to suffer heavy industry, dirty jobs, or messy raw material. The work of fabricating things from matter will be exported to underdeveloped countries—the backwaters of history—such as Taiwan and Korea where there are pools of cheap labor and governments that do not require environmental impact statements. Like gods of old, we will live with clean hands in the realm of pure abstractions.

Listen to the ancient gnostic promise of freedom from matter as it recently appeared in *Fortune:*

> "The Central Event of the twentieth century is the overthrow of matter . . . The powers of mind are everywhere ascendant over *the brute force of things.* [italics mine] . . . All the *dirt, rock,* and *gunk* [italics mine] that had been ignored for centuries suddenly acquired worth in the age of mass manufacturing. The new industrial revolution . . . is rapidly returning what used to be called 'precious natural resources' to their previous natural condition as dirt, rock, and gunk . . . *To see the world primarily in terms of its waste products is possibly the most perverse vision in the history of science* [italics mine] . . . Overthrowing the superstitions of materialism . . . *modern man is injecting the universe with the germ of his intelligence, the spoor of his mind* [italics mine] . . . Thus the triumph of the computer does not dehumanize the world; it makes our environment more subject to human will."[7]

Please note the emotional tone and metaphors George Gilder uses to characterize nature: *"the brute force of things," "dirt, rock, and gunk," "waste products."* Don't forget to be thankful that, at long last, flocks of daffodils, exaltations of larks, and the fertile humus are going to be "injected" with the "germ" of modern man's intelligence, the spoor of his mind, and subjected to his will. No more dirt, gunk, or brute matter.

What we have here is the ultimate macho vision: a cosmic cocksman in technological drag.

Radicals are informed by the myth of the interdependence of all life forms that is emerging from quantum physics, systems analysis, and the science of ecology. Within this mythology, humankind must learn to limit its growth and its demands on the environment. The axioms that express the radical program for the future are: Less is more, small is beautiful, speed kills, zero population growth, don't consume the earth, appropriate technology, sustainable economics, sustainable agriculture.

In the 1990s and beyond, these competing worldviews will be the battleground and the context within which each of us must decide, once again, what it means to be an honorable man. At the moment it is the best and worst of times. Never have so many had so much; never have so many had so little. Never have we grown at such an exponential and cancerous rate, the gross world product increasing in direct proportion to shrinking forests, expanding deserts, eroding soil. We exist in a situation of cultural schizophrenia, caught between visions of boundless hope and exhausted resources. Full speed ahead—put on the brakes. Expand—conserve and learn to live within limits. What are we to do?

Even the most cockeyed technological optimists have begun to sing faith hymns to Gaia. They concede that "As we become increasingly aware of the fragility of the earth, we will have to treat it more kindly."

"Treat it more kindly?" What does that mean? Kindness is the recognition of kinship. What yet unimaginable philosophical-religious-social-political-genderal-psychological revolution lies curled up in this innocent phrase! What would it require of us to treat air sheds, watersheds, the humus, the myriad species of mammals and plants, to say nothing of beetles and earthworms, as kinfolk?

Is it, for instance, possible within an increasingly urban culture to learn about our kinship with wild creatures and to cherish our elemental humanity, our union with earth, sky, fire, and water? Will generations raised in high rises learn from Walt Disney and *The Wild World of Animals* to love and fight to save the habitats of mountain lions and antelopes? Living in fabricated environments, can we gain a sense of kinship with other members of the commonwealth of living beings by seeing their images flit across our television screens? At what point is it conceivable that we might look at the damage we humankind inflict upon other forms of life, and be willing to give up our highly consumptive style of life? Every time I count the road kills on the highway—dead deer, owls, pheasants, shunks, raccoons, foxes, etc.—and notice the forests and ponds dying from acid rain, I wonder how many other species we will destroy before we might be willing to make the changes in the industrial economy that would be necessary to be more kindly to the earth.

And, to make the problem even more difficult: If we were willing to become citizens of the earth, how would we undertake the magnitude of changes this would require? We can imagine making minor changes—recycling our beer bottles and manufacturing cars that get greater gas mileage. But to date we remain sequestered within a Pollyanna bubble of self-delusion in which our politicians and corporations assure us we can create an ever-expanding economy and still preserve our fragile ecology. The current Dow Jones index notwithstanding, our optimistic expectations for a future technological utopia undimmed by human tears are based on denial and repression of awareness.

Add: Progress + Pollution + Population

Subtract: Plagues and Poverty

Discount (for the sake of argument) chemical war, nuclear winters.

And any way you compute it you still get a threatening and challenging vision of the future.

The future that is beckoning us will demand a total reorientation, a paradigm shift, a new sense of who we are, a postindustrial, posteconomic identity.

The radical vision of the future rests on the belief that the logic that determines either our survival or our destruction is simple:

(1) The new human vocation is to heal the earth.
(2) We can only heal what we love.
(3) We can only love what we know.
(4) We can only know what we touch.

The ecological perspective is not about stopping dams to save a few snail darters, or preserving forests to protect spotted owls. It is not noblesse oblige, doing nice things for "brute" nature, or conserving "dirt, rock, and gunk." It is not providing reservations for quaint creatures such as pandas. Ecology is a new code word for destiny-vocation-identity.

But why is this especially a men's issue? Why not a human issue? Or a women's issue? Women, no less than men, have enjoyed the comforts of the labor-saving and life-extending gifts of industrial civilization. Whenever possible they have been in the front ranks of consumers. Their dedication to the ethic of planned obsolescence and the worship of "style" has been as obsessive as men's. Their love of disposable diapers and pre-packaged convenience foods has contributed a fair share to the mountain of garbage. Women must bear their share of guilt and responsibility for the profligate life. But until very recently, woman was identified with the natural rather than the economic order. No matter how she might participate in a consumer culture, her primal psychological identity was with the biological order. Her bottom line was not profit and loss, but birth and nurturance. Men's identity since the industrial revolution, on the other hand, has been so closely bound up with exploiting natural resources that creation of an earth-honoring ethic will require men to make a fundamental change in our self-understanding. Not just our actions must change. Our identity must also change.

The growing earth and not the economic pseudoworld is the horizon within which virtue must be discovered anew. If the primal sense of belonging to the commonwealth of sentient beings doesn't sink down into our hearts, guts, and balls, if it doesn't change our understanding of what it means to be a man, if it doesn't change whom we admire and what we aspire to become, we will certainly become the destroyers of our homeland.

Whether we are gay or straight, hard or soft, wild or vulnerable, feelingful or thoughtful, are all of secondary concern. When men center their concerns about masculinity on their genitals, on making money, on accumulating power, or even on exploring their "feminine" side, they trivialize manhood.

First and foremost, the vocation of now and future men is to become gentle and earthy. We can have justifiable pride only if we face the monumental issues of changing the social and psychological systems that have brought us to the edge of degradation. How can we stand tall and rejoice in our strength if we do not become earth-honoring? How can we respect ourselves if we do not care enough to husband and pass on the heritage of earth's fullness to our children? If, in the words of the cynical bumper sticker often seen on the motor homes of the retired, "We are spending our children's inheritance," how can we rejoice in our virility? If men fail to respond to the specific challenge of our age, we cannot gain any true sense of phallic power from any athleticism of the penis or any number of possessions.

The dispassionate, postmodern, cool man is the antithesis

of the phallic male—no passion, no standing forth, no risk, no eros, no drive to survive and enrich history. Nor is the "new age" man who is self-absorbed in his own feelings and committed to "personal growth" a candidate for heroism. It is an illusion to believe that the virility men have lost can be recovered by anything except a new vocational passion.

Our loss has been ontological, not psychological. A deficiency in meaning and in being. A refusal to care for what matters, a limpness in the face of the challenge of our history. The challenges seem overwhelming, and we are understandably tempted to retreat into professions and corporations that swallow us, into private pleasures and high consumption. But let's call that what it is: moral cowardice, abdication of responsibility, voluntary myopia. And if we continue on this path we will continue to feel empty and devoid of meaning.

The historical challenge for modern men is clear—to discover a peaceful form of virility and to create an ecological commonwealth, to become fierce gentlemen.

How we can accomplish these monumental changes is unclear. As modern men we have little experience to guide us in the task of becoming earth-stewards and husbandmen. We do not yet know how to take the fierce warrior energies, the drive to conquest and control, that men have honed for centuries, and turn them toward the creation of a more hopeful and careful future. We do not yet know how to restrain our technological compulsion, limit economic growth, or keep population within an ecological balance. We do not yet know how to act purposively and rationally on the natural world in a kindly way. We have not yet developed technological wisdom, technological discipline, technological stewardship. Ecological destruction is not the result of science and technology, but of social decisions that allow scientific and technological institutions to grow in undisciplined ways. We do not yet know how to distinguish progress from growth, development from frantic activity. We have not yet found the courage to calculate the true profit and loss to all species that results from trade, business, and industry. We have not yet created a form of government in which the nonhuman constituency of the land are given an equal voice in decisions that determine the fate of all members of the commonwealth of living beings.

The man who leads us out of this ignorance will be in our sons' Hall of Exemplars.

The exemplary man, the hero, is excited by the unknown. He hears the call and responds, not knowing where the journey will take him or what obstacles he will meet along the way. Cautious men will say that it is foolhardy to begin without a Triptik, a cost analysis, or a feasibility report from a committee of experts and the promise of cooperation from appropriate governmental agencies. But official sanction for radical departures is seldom given. Fortunately, heroes seldom ask permission from the authorities. In their foolishness they do not know the limits of the possible, so they screw up their courage, shoulder their doubts, and start down the path.

A PRIMER
FOR NOW
AND FUTURE
HEROES

—

THE SOULFUL QUEST: PILGRIMAGE INTO SELF

"The search is what anyone would undertake if he were not sunk in the everydayness of his own life . . . To become aware of the possibility of the search is to be onto something. Not to be onto something is to be in despair."

—Walker Percy,
The Moviegoer

"It is precisely the soul that is the traveler; it is of the soul and of the soul alone that we can say with supreme truth that 'being' necessarily means 'being on the way' (en route)."

—Gabriel Marcel,
Homo Viator

Map for a Heroic Journey

The majority of men in any given society undergo the standard rites of passage, earn the insignia of manhood, and are relatively satisfied. In ordinary times, most men and women do not have radical questions about their identity. They have been imprinted, indoctrinated, and governed by stereotypes, role models, heroic images, and commonly accepted ideology. They accept the mythic horizon as the only possible account of "reality" and place their trust in the Great Mother, God the Father, dialectical materialism, democracy, technology and the inevitability of progress. Most people remain relatively unconscious, unaware of the forces that shape their lives.

In every society, however, there are extraordinary men and women who, for a variety of reasons, stand outside the social consensus, shatter the norms, and challenge the status quo. These iconoclasts—prophets, rebels, revolutionaries, reformers, shamans, visionaries, mystics, artists, madmen, geniuses, schizophrenics—trouble the waters and disturb the majority but bring new creative energies into a society. As the pathfinders of new ways of being and seeing, they pay a high personal price. They are often painfully self-conscious and lonely, and are both stranger and stronger than average folk.

In untroubled times, only extraordinary men and women radically question the consensus reality. However, in troubled times the number of people thrown into psychological turmoil and radical questioning increases. And that of course, is our present condition. As overdeveloped nations stand at the end of the industrial age of infinite progress and as underdeveloped nations stand at the beginning of industrialization, enormous numbers of people are becoming reflective about the values and visions by which they will live. Never before has such a large proportion of the world population been so questioning. We have entered a time of great turmoil and creativity; the "normal" majority is becoming increasingly reactionary in an effort to conserve the values of a passing era, and the hero's path is becoming crowded with individuals looking for a way into a more hopeful future.

In the next decades we will see a widening division between two types of men and two visions of manhood as the conflict grows more intense between the traditional Western, patriarchal, technological, conflictual, militaristic worldview and the new quantum, ecological, cooperative worldview. For the moment I will designate them as follows:

HOMESTEADERS	PILGRIMS
Citizens	Questers
Believers	Questioners
Culture-bound	Transcend their time and tribe
Once born	Twice born
Frequently unconscious	Frequently painfully self-conscious

HOMESTEADERS	PILGRIMS
Initiated into and remain within the mythic horizon of their society	Undertake a heroic journey into unknown, tabooed, uncharted territory
May be powerful or weak	Are usually vulnerable and strong
The good they do springs from their practice of civic virtues, adherence to duty, law and order, conserving tradition	The good they do springs from their invention of innovative virtues, prophetic visions, sensitivity to new vocations, creating novelty.
The evil they do springs from obedience and banality	The evil they do springs from overreaching ambition, or hubris
May be candidates for the Hall of Fame as archetypes of accepted heroic types	May be candidates for the Hall of Exemplars for incarnating new ideals and philosophies of life

The next two chapters will map the heroic journey of this newly emerging tribe of spiritual pilgrims. Since no one has ever come this way before it may not be possible to provide more than a tentative outline of the stages and way stations. Our old models of manhood, like the Newtonian models of the universe, no longer fit our expanding knowledge of the way things are. But our situation does have parallels with times past that offer some help.

Joseph Campbell, the great mythologist and cartographer of spiritual landscapes, has described the stages of the journey of "the hero with a thousand faces" as a magnification of the formula represented in the rite of passage: separation—initiation—return. A hero ventures forth from the world of common day into a region of supernatural wonders. He encounters fabulous forces and wins a decisive victory and, finally, returns from this mysterious adventure with the power to bestow boons on his fellow man. If we translate this formula from mythological into psychological terms it can provide us with our best view of the path that lies before us as we struggle in the next years to recreate manhood. Inevitably, any major transformation of the psyche involves a long process of the destructuring of the old self, before there can be any constructing of a new identity. The new pilgrimage for men is a journey of death and rebirth. The journey has two distinct stages:

The Soulful Quest, Chapter 11, is a pilgrimage into the depths of the self. We leave the sunlit world of easy roles and prefabricated tokens of masculinity, penetrate the character armor, get beneath the personality, and plunge into the chaos and pain of the old "masculine" self. This isn't the fun part of the trip. It's spelunking in Plato's cave, feeling our way through the illusions we have mistaken for reality, crawling through the drain sewers where the forbidden "unmanly" feelings dwell, confronting the demons and dark shadows that have held us captive from their underground haunts. In this stage of the journey we must make use of the warrior's fierceness, courage, and aggression to break through the rigidities of old structures of manhood, and explore the dark and taboo "negative" emotions that make up the shadow of modern manhood. The journey itself involves a series of passages: from sunny pragmatism to the dark wisdom of dream time; from having the answers to living the questions; from emotional numbness to manly grief; from cocksureness to potent doubt; from artificial toughness to virile fear; from infantile guilt to mature responsibility; from isolation to loneliness; from false optimism to honest despair; from compulsive action to relaxed waiting, fallowness, and renewal.

In the second stage of the journey, *Homecoming*, Chapter 12, we return to the everyday world with a new sense of self, new virtues, and a new understanding of virility.

From Sunny Pragmatism to the Dark Wisdom of Dream Time

When I first went to a psychotherapist he told me I should be prepared for a complete reversal. "If you want to make significant changes in your self," he warned me, "you have to commit yourself to a period of months or years in which you are willing to allow what happens in your imagination, in your dreams, in your fantasies, in your emotions, in your interactions with your therapist to be more important than what is happening in your 'real' life." He warned me it would be confusing. And it was.

For three years my priorities and perspectives were radically changed. Like Chuang-tze, who dreamt he was a butterfly and then didn't know whether he was a man dreaming he was a butterfly or a butterfly dreaming he was a man, my day and night selves switched positions. The figures who inhabited my dreams became more real to me than those with whom I spent my daylight hours. My father, long dead, came to life again and we did battle. I found the courage to be angry with him for the wounds he had inflicted on me, to defy him, to break his taboos, and finally to crawl so far inside the secret pain of his being that I could forgive and heal him by daring to do what he could not. I raged against my mother-wife-lover-anima, cowered before her primal power, afraid of abandonment and death, until I finally saw the face of womankind shine upon me and her thighs open to welcome me home. Many nights I awoke in terror with the knowledge that I had been running forever from faceless demons, and I returned to sleep with a resolve that next time they appeared I would look them in the eye, demand to know their names, and gain power over them. In dreams I came to know all of the excesses of myself that were so carefully disguised during business hours. No sooner did my moderate, pragmatic, and reasonable self sleep, than my Dionysian self awoke and came out to play. In dreams I left behind every trace of the Eagle Scout ("trustworthy, loyal, helpful, friendly, courteous, kind, obedient, cheerful, friendly, brave, clean, and reverent"). For a thousand nights, I reveled in cruelty, dirt, all manner of sexual excess, "polymorphous perversity," omnipotent power. Every night I underwent protean transformations in which I became simultaneously bird, beast, man, or woman. I and my father, I and my mother, I and my wife-lover-friend, I and my children all became one and switched costumes and roles at will.

By and large, men in the modern world have become trapped in extroversion. Psychological studies have shown that men remember their dreams far less than women, and seldom dream in color. As problem solvers, change agents, engineers responsible for continuing progress, and merchants dedicated to the growth of the gross national product, we have not had the luxury of paying attention to the shadow-dramas that govern the world of dream time. So, inevitably when we come to explore the unknown landscapes of the self we must become acquainted with the creatures that rule the unconscious kingdom of the night. This means that we have to lay aside rational and pragmatic virtues and submit ourselves to the logic of the imagination. As we pass through the looking glass, our values and visions of who we are change; a reversal of figure and ground occurs. Things are not what they seem. Maybe men are not powerful and women weak. Maybe warfare is a shadow-drama and economics a mythic system that ignores our deepest needs. Maybe dreams make the world go round. In the beginning, only this is certain: Unless we allow the free play of the imagination, we can never become realistic again.

From Having the Answers to Living the Questions

A man may begin his pilgrimage in a hundred different ways. The death of a father, mother, wife, friend, or child suddenly opens up an abyss of terror into which everything that felt safe and secure disappears. The Mercedes, the country club, the well-invested portfolio hold no magic against death. Or, you wake up some Monday morning and realize that your job, your wife, your friends bore you, and you have a powerful urge to run away. Or, you travel to Nicaragua and listen to a mother whose son was killed by a CIA-financed Contra and you lose your trust in a president who called them "freedom fighters." Or, you see a picture of a child starving in Ethiopia and you want to give up a successful law practice and get food to the hungry. Or, you get sick and your body suddenly feels old and vulnerable. Or, all that was firm and erect in youth begins to sag, and you can't take "yes" for an answer. Or, one day out of nowhere you realize that you don't know who you are, and none of the cards in your wallet provide the slightest clue to your real identity. Or, your wife leaves a note on the kitchen table that says: "We're finished."

Call it midlife crisis, depression, alienation, the dark night of the soul, the opening of a new path. But honor it. Listen. Respond. In the beginning all you can know is that the old pillars of your identity no longer support the weight of your being. It is time to leave behind the achievements and virtues you have laboriously accumulated during the first part of your life. Good-bye to the stereotyped roles—of rich man, poor man, doctor, lawyer, merchant, chief—of warrior and conquistador.

The first rites of passage are imposed on a boy by society, separating him from the warm, encompassing, and limiting perspective of mother and family and thrusting him into the world of adult responsibility. But rites of initiation into extraordinary manhood must be self-administered. The crisis in a man's life comes when he is separated, or suddenly perceives himself as separated, from the encompassing but limiting perspective of the normal world of adulthood. Then, he must enter into a deeper relationship with himself, become an authority in the nuances of his own experience, define manhood for himself. Our boyhood initiation consisted primarily of internalizing the *answers* that were given us by adult authorities. In Sunday school, civics class, the workplace, the army, we memorized the myths and meanings before we had the experience of life. We pledged allegiance to the official conclusions. The rite that initiates us into extraordinary manhood begins when we start to live with a new and disturbing set of *questions*.

The questions that animate homesteaders are:

What is my duty?
What do my neighbors think of me?
How can I become a success?
How can I gain money, power, prestige?
Do I have the courage to fight for my country?
Can I suffer without whimpering?
How do I provide for my family?

But a man who is a pilgrim, who has lost his way, asks the perennial, mythic questions:

What do I really want?
What brings me joy?
Who am I when I dream?
Why do I feel the way I do?
What do I fear?
Who has wounded me?
Whom have I injured?
How do I deal with guilt?
Do I need to have enemies?
How do I forgive?
Whom and what will I love?
How will I express my sexuality?
Who are my people? My family?
Where is my place?
What is the source of my power? My self-esteem?
What is sacred? Worthy of respect? Inviolable?
For what, or whom, would I sacrifice my time, my energy,
    my health, my life?
What can I do to lessen the quantity of evil in the world?
What are my gifts? What is my vocation?
What must I do to die with a sense of completeness?
What myth have I been (unconsciously) living?
In what measure are my "values" mere prejudices, my
    duties blind commitments to unexamined norms?
What have I sacrificed to win the approval of others? To
    become "successful?"
In what ways have I blinded myself, disowned my power,
    denied my potential?

To be on a quest is nothing more or less than to become an asker of questions. In the Grail legend, the classical tale of male heroism, we are told that when the Knights of the Round Table set out on their quest, each one entered the forest at the place it was darkest and forged a path where none had been before. The inner, psychological meaning of this myth is that full manhood is to be found only when we commit ourselves to a life of questioning.

The mood of our contemporary quest is reflected in Rilke's advice to a young man: "Be patient toward all that is unsolved in your heart and try to love the questions themselves like locked rooms and like books that are written in a foreign tongue. Do not now seek the answers . . . Live the questions."[1]

From Cocksureness to Potent Doubt

If questing and questioning are the essence of manhood, the virile psyche will be very different from the one to which we have become accustomed. To date, the virtues we have expected of good-to-average men have been clarity, decisiveness, will-power, the ability to control feelings, stick-to-itiveness, self-confidence, and a stoic attitude in the face of suffering. But these virtues are incompatible with a life of questing and questioning. How, after all, can we be solid citizens—foursquare and substantial—and be filled with radical questions?

Since the world is an unsolvable mystery whose surface has scarcely been penetrated by our efforts to know and explain, the assumption that we can understand and conquer all is actually a symptom of insecurity and an inability to tolerate ambiguity and darkness. Nothing is less appropriate in our time than the posture of certainty.

Some years ago a writer in *The New York Times*, reporting on the appointment of Alexander Haig as Secretary of State, said he was "a man without self-doubts." A triple heart bypass and no self-doubts? A terrifying thought! I do not want a man without self-doubts to have his finger on the doomsday button. The more power a man holds, the more he should question his deepest convictions, and consider that they may be self-serving rationalizations. Animals act without question or hesitation. Men reflect, deliberate, and suffer the agony of momentous decision. Hannah Arendt said, when she was covering Adolf Eichmann's trial in Jerusalem, what impressed her was the thoughtlessness and banality of this man who had efficiently arranged for Jews to be transported to the death camps. He did his duty, obeyed his superiors, and never asked any searching questions.

Descartes became the first modern man when he rejected the medieval notion that we should subject our reason to the authority of the Church, the guardians of revealed truth. In the solitude of his room in winter, he spent day after day daring to doubt his beliefs, giving us an example of the first steps of the heroic journey. The courage to make the affirmation *Dubito ergo sum*—I doubt, therefore I am—is what separates the men from the boys.

You may be certain that if you want to be a pilgrim, you are going to get lost. The old Boy Scout manual offered some practical wisdom for those who are lost on any quest. First, don't panic. Second, stop doing what you were doing. Third, sit down and calm yourself. Fourth, look for landmarks. Fifth, follow trails or streams that lead downhill or toward open space. A mountain man was once asked if he often got lost. "No," he replied. "I've never been lost. But sometimes for a month or two I didn't know how to get where I was going." Explorers need to know how to be lost comfortably. The adventure of the spirit begins when we stop pretending and performing and accept our confusion and insecurity.

Compare these traditional male self-definitions and visions of the sacred:

I am within Mother Earth; therefore I am. Neolithic man. Sacred place—the fertile earth.

I repeat the archetypical acts of the heroes and gods; therefore I am. Mythic man. Sacred place—the ritual, dance.

I contemplate-reason; therefore I am. Greek man. Sacred place—the orderly dialogue, community, cosmos.

I obey the will of God; therefore I am. Hebrew, Christian, Islamic man. Sacred place—synagogue, church, mosque, the place of revelation.

I fight; therefore I am. The warrior. Sacred place—battlefield, ground consecrated by blood sacrifice.

I make; therefore I am. Industrial man. Sacred place—factory.

I work; therefore I am. Economic man. Sacred object—the almighty dollar, investment.

I possess; therefore I am. Capitalistic man. Sacred place—property.

I consume; therefore I am. Consuming man. Sacred place—the mall.

I am incorporated; therefore I am. Corporate man. Sacred place— the company.

I doubt; therefore I am. Questing man. Sacred path—the pilgrim spirit.

Notice the reversal, the revolution in values. To find the essence of a man's potency in questioning, wondering, and doubting is to claim as a mark of pride what has recently been considered a cause for shame. The stone the builder rejects becomes the foundation for the new temple. The willingness to doubt and question is itself our new sacred ground. The spiritual journey is not about getting somewhere else. It's not about progress or destinations. It is about acquiring a "beginner's mind" (Zen) or the innocent eye. In recognizing our lostness, we have found the seed of a new identity. Our being is becoming, our goal is to begin again.

Here is how my earliest intellectual hero, Søren Kierke-gaard, the Danish "Christian existentialist" philosopher, de-scribes the condition of the authentic man: "And this is the simple truth: that to live is to feel oneself lost. He who accepts it has already begun to find himself, to be on firm ground. Instinctively, as do the shipwrecked, he will look around for something to which to cling; and that tragic, ruthless glance, absolutely sincere because it is a question of his salvation, will cause him to bring order into the chaos of his life. These are the only genuine ideas, the ideas of the shipwrecked. All the rest is rhetoric, posturing, farce."[2]

From Numbness to Manly Grief

When men who have spent their formative years in extroverted action first turn inward toward the unknown territory of the soul, they soon reach the desert—the vast nothingness. Before rebirth comes the painful awareness that we have long been dead. Before feeling comes the dreadful knowledge that we have been anesthetized and are numb.

The popular cliché says that men think and do, women feel and emote. It's a half-truth worth playing with. Most of us learned that real men were supposed to control their feelings. From childhood onward we heard that "men don't cry." We learned to work hard, take a lot of punishment, and not bitch about it. Remember the pride we took in climbing mountains, ignoring the cold, running until we were exhausted, taking hard punches, pushing the limits, driving all night? No pain, no gain. That's the right stuff.

Little did we understand that by doing the manly thing, girding up our loins, pulling in our guts, pushing out our chests, tightening our jaws, and constricting our breathing, we forced most feelings into exile in our unconscious. It is hard to experience a lot of emotion when the body's potential for motion is constricted.

In the early days of encounter groups, when the leader asked me, "What are you feeling *now?*" the most honest response I could give was, "I don't know." Being out of touch with my feelings went with the territory of modern manhood. Like most successful men, I had focused on my goals, and on the means to achieve them. A decade of graduate school had left me hard-driving, highly competitive and strong-willed, and insensitive to the nuances of feeling or emotional versatility. I could identify the major philosophical movements in the nineteenth century more easily than I could tell whether I was feeling anger, grief, anxiety, or fear.

So, when I began the inward journey, I was worried that if I began to peel the onion, strip off layers of my accumulated personality, maybe there would be nothing underneath. Maybe it was better to stay busy and follow "Satchel" Paige's advice: "Don't ever look back because something might be gaining on you."

There are good reasons for this worry. It would be lovely if some chinook wind could pass over our frozen emotions and bring the instant joy of spring. Unfortunately, whatever "negative" feelings have been long repressed, tabooed, or denied must be brought into awareness before the repertoire of more "positive" feelings becomes available. In order to be free, the prison doors must be flung open and the imprisoned feelings invited into the commonwealth of the self.

Since boys are taught not to cry, men must learn to weep. After a man passes through arid numbness, he comes to a tangled jungle of grief and unnamed sorrow. The path to a manly heart runs through the valley of tears.

I was thirty-three years old when I shed my first manly tears. On the day my father died, the dam burst and I lost control of myself. From the first awful phone call until after the funeral I was awash in grief. It was the first time my wife had seen me cry. I soon regained the semblance of control, and, when I was in danger of weeping, left the house and went on long walks. Four years later, I was telling a therapy group about longing for my father to return from his long trips when I was a boy when, without warning, I erupted in an orgasm of grief. Wave upon wave of sobs followed, gathering up all of the pain of my life into a crescendo. I cried for the boy who missed his father's arms, the young professor who already felt old and burdened, and for the man who one day would die and never know why. When I finally stopped crying, I felt empty and embarrassed. What would "they" think of me? Certainly they would not respect me any longer since I had lost my cool. With some trepidation I raised my head and began to look at the room full of people. To my surprise I found that many had tears in their eyes and they looked at me with unbelievable but undeniable tenderness and compassion. More surprising yet, I felt as if I had been purged of some poison. My hard armor of tense muscles softened, I breathed easy and warm springs seemed to be bubbling up from my loins.

Men have much to mourn before they can be reborn.

To begin with, there is the simple sadness that accompanies the awareness of the frailty and fleeting beauty of all passing life. We all carry eternity in our hearts and yet our tenure in time is brief and, finally, tragic. Death interrupts the happiest of lives before all of its promises are fulfilled. The Greeks knew what we have conspired to smother with easy smiles and false optimism—paradoxically, a tragic sense of life yields more joy than warm fuzzies.

Don't ask me to make logical sense of this, but I know it to be a psychological fact that aging and death come as a terrible surprise to men. "Old age is the most unexpected of all the things that can happen to a man," Leon Trotsky said. In his eighties, Joseph Campbell told me, "I don't feel like an old man. I feel like a young man who has something wrong with him." Listen and you will hear men talk about their rebellion against aging. We "do not go gentle into that good night." Perhaps this feeling is uniquely American, a product of a youth-worshiping, obsessively optimistic culture. Or maybe men find it difficult to grow old because we were never allowed to be young.

And then there is the grief over our lost innocence. The world into which most men were initiated and indoctrinated required us prematurely to put away childish things—play, imagination, sensuality, carefree wandering, experimenting with different roles, adventure. By our midtwenties we had manfully shouldered the load of work and family.

A grief close to the surface for men these days is the aching void of the absent father. Many boys lost their fathers to the world of work or because of divorce and desertion. But even if the father was physically present, he was often emotionally inhibited or too tired after work to form a close bond with his children. A friend told me, "My father was a traveling salesman, but even when he was at home he wasn't close to me. All my life I have suffered from uncertainties about my masculinity. I think it is because he never shared himself with me. He didn't tell me what kinds of problems he wrestled with, what he felt, what it meant to him to be a man. I have had to make it all up for myself, and I'm never sure that I have it right." (Unfortunately we can expect even worse in the near future. Sixty percent of children born in 1987 will not be living with or supported by their birth father when they reach adolescence. Single-parent families, usually with the mother present and father absent, account for the raising of fifty percent of today's children).

For many men the path to vital manhood involves first grieving the absence of their fathers and then, if their fathers are living, making a renewed effort to establish a new relationship. A score of grown sons have told me about returning to visit their fathers and for the first time, with fear and trembling, saying, "I love you, I want to know about our life." More often than not, the fathers have responded awkwardly but gratefully to the invitation. They, also, have spent a lifetime missing intimacy with their sons and daughters, but lacked the communication skills to open a dialogue.

When we consider the world around us, it is clear that a day without grief is a day without awareness or compassion. Pick up the mourning newspaper (I meant to write "morning" paper but I will allow the "mistake" to stand), and you find the daily litany of the normal suffering that accompanies the human condition.

Unlike the salesmen of optimism who cheer us up and tell us to look on the bright side, the great explorers of the spirit encourage us to look honestly at suffering. Siddhartha, the young prince who was to become the Buddha, lived within a wealthy ghetto where he did not have to see ugliness, poverty, disease, old age, or death. His quest for enlightenment began when he ventured outside his privileged enclosure and saw an old man, a diseased man, a corpse, and a monk who had dedicated his life to the pursuit of liberation. The first of the noble truths he discovered was that "Life is suffering." We can never be liberated so long as we cling to the illusion that we can turn the world into paradise.

Closer to home, the Christian vision invites us to a joyful participation in the sufferings of the world. As the central heroic drama, the passion of Jesus teaches us that our souls are forged in the crucible of sorrow and trust. Even Albert Camus, who rejected any overt religion, said that we could only discover happiness after we had willingly confronted the absurdity and injustice of the world.

When we refuse to soften, to surrender, to mourn our daily dying, we necessarily live with a high degree of illusion and depression. Freud taught us that the person who will not mourn gets stuck in melancholy. When we secretly harbor the adolescent dream that we may remain youthful and triumphant forever, we are certain to feel, as the ravages of age begin, that we have somehow failed and that our coming death represents a final defeat.

The alternative is to cultivate the bittersweet discipline of mourning and enjoying each passing day. "Blessed are those who mourn, for they shall be comforted."

From Artificial Toughness to Virile Fear

As we push deeper into the interior of a man's psyche, we discover that in back of the facade of toughness and control there is an entire landscape of undifferentiated fears, with all manner of beasts, demons, and ghosts lurking in the shadows. And to win our soul or rescue our self from its entrapment in our personality, we have to do battle with a legion of fears we never knew we had.

How long ago was it that we men forced our fear into exile and condemned it to live in the shadow? Evolution demanded that the male be tough enough to repel the onslaught of saber-toothed tigers, or more recently, corporate raiders. If you want the no-nonsense definition of a man, skip the claim that we are *Homo sapiens* and go directly to "fearless" and its synonyms—undaunted, bold, intrepid, audacious, brave, courageous, valiant, valorous, doughty, daring, adventurous, heroic, gallant, plucky, gritty.

I can hardly remember a time when I wasn't working at being fearless. Can you? It started with seemingly innocent advice and guidance from grown men, big brothers, and sometimes mothers: "Don't be a scaredy-cat. There is nothing to be afraid of." Early on, we learned that fear could be controlled in the same way as grief: Lock your jaw to prevent it from quivering, tighten your chest, and push yourself to the edge of danger to prove yourself. We flirted with fearful things: walking through graveyards at midnight; running through the turf of rival gangs; sneaking into a haunted house; stealing a car; jumping from the cliff high above the swimming hole; taking a dare; going to the whorehouse. And, finally, we went to war—without ever acknowledging the depths of our terror. Every time we resisted yielding to the seduction of fear, we fell more deeply in love with our own image of ourselves as heroes. We are men; we are unafraid. We can do what must be done.

But we paid a terrible price for our conquest of fear, for viewing ourselves as actual or potential heroes.

For starters, we reduced our world to an arena within which courage is constantly demanded, and other virtues—patience, honesty, kindness, contentment, intelligence, wisdom— are not cultivated. Somehow, men have managed, although not without the complicity and cooperation of women, to create a world dominated by competition and warfare. We are in constant danger and must regularly risk our lives in order to ensure our survival. It is as if modern history has become the story of the shoot-out at the O.K. Corral. Better cosmocide than cowardice. Even with *glasnost* and the crumbling of "the communist threat," we are finding it difficult to break our addiction to fear and defensiveness. Somehow courage has become a rogue virtue, a virtue perverted into a vice.

Perhaps the greatest price men have paid for their obsession with fearlessness is to have become tough on the outside but empty within. We are hollow men. The connection between fearlessness and feelinglessness should be obvious. Fear, along with grief, joy, and anger, is one of the primal feelings. And the ability to feel is indivisible. Repress awareness of any one feeling and all feelings are dulled. When we refuse to allow fear we correspondingly lose the ability to wonder. When we repress our grief we blunt our capacity to experience joy. The same nerve endings are required for weeping and dancing, fear and ecstasy. Recently, in making the PBS documentary *Faces of the Enemy*, I interviewed a man in prison facing trial for the brutal murder of a husband, wife, and two children whom he had not known prior to the time of the killing. One of the most chilling moments for me was when he spoke about his total loss of feeling. "If they hang me, they hang me. I'm not afraid to die," he said. "You don't seem to feel much remorse, either," I said. "I don't feel much of anything," he replied.

The consequence of men's phobic avoidance is not that fear is balanced by authentic courage, but that it goes underground and remains hidden. Buried in the male unconscious there is a clandestine emotional network governed by greater and lesser fears. The alternative to being controlled by these unconscious fears is to break the taboo and explore the lush landscape of fears we normally avoid.

From a combination of self-observation, listening to the confessions of my closest men friends, and deducing what lies beneath the male facade, I have started to construct a catalogue of men's fears.

Some fears are primal, unchanging, native to the human condition. According to Buddhism, there are five universal fears: fear of death, fear of pain, fear of insanity, fear of loss of livelihood, and fear of loss of reputation (including fear of public speaking).

Other fears are fashionable in one age and circumstance and absent in others. Traditionally, American men have feared homosexuality so much that we can be said to be a homophobic culture. Real men don't touch each other, except for the ritual NFL pat on the ass after the touchdown. Otherwise someone might think we were effeminate. Rednecks consider "queer-bashing" a sport, and any man with soft emotions or a fey manner is ostracized from the brotherhood of beer buddies. Yet homophobia never made the list of the top ten fears for Socrates, Hadrian, or Michelangelo, or anybody in the ancient world or Renaissance.

Men and women seem to have different styles of fearing. Men's fears focus around loss of what we experience as our independence, and women's around the loss of significant relationships. We most fear engulfment, anything that threatens to rob us of our power and control. Women most fear abandonment, isolation, loss of love. Traditionally, women have been expected to be more fearful than men. But experience and hearsay have convinced me that men are more fearful of death than women. When we get sick and our flesh no longer rises to the dictates of our will, we feel the Reaper, the Raper, coming for us and we panic. Men make lousy patients. Ask any doctor. Disease and disability frighten us more than they do women, who have known from first menstruation and childbirth that mortality is often accompanied by cramping and pain and that we are born in order to lose control. Sickness raises the specter of all that men have been taught to fear: weakness, dependency, passivity.

Recognize yourself? With or without boots and Levi's, most of us aspire (and fail) to be Marlboro men. Our mottos: Don't fence me in; Live free or die; Avoid entangling alliances; Look out for tender traps. Commitment, even when necessary, feels dangerously like engulfment. And vaginas, sweet sanctuaries for wandering warriors, are guarded in dreams by rows of teeth. We fear (and desire) that old black magic drawing us down, down into the sweet embrace of flesh, obscure fusion, lost in sensation, out of control. But after each near surrender we hurry back to the fortress of our independence to escape the threat of engulfment in the feminine. Real men should stand alone. And tall.

Of course, men's self-images and the reality of their lives are radically different, nearly opposite. Few men are autonomous architects of their own values. Rarely do men, like Martin Luther or Martin Luther King, Jr., come to the time of testing and say: "Here I stand. I can do no other." Heroes of conscience are always an endangered species. In matters of morality most of us are passive followers who fear the disapproval of our peers and the wrath of the authorities. Many Vietnam veterans have told me they disapproved of the war and feared the enemy. But more than that they feared being disobedient, being thought cowardly, and letting their comrades down.

Men usually do not talk much about their sexual fears and disappointments. Sex is a big thing for us. And we judge it in more absolute terms than women do. It is either/or. Up or down. And should our erector set fail or collapse in the middle of the job, the most sophisticated of us still suffers a degree of embarrassment. Liberated women a generation ago were confessing in *Ms.* magazine how often they faked orgasm. But no man has yet been able to write an article, "How I Faked an Erection." And no matter how many times women have told us it is the tenderness and sensuality that counts, we still carry around scorecards and rating systems in our minds.

There are two classical approaches to perfecting the art of fearing wisely and learning the virtue of courage: the extroverted adventurer's path of confronting physical danger, and the introverted psychonaut's path of doing battle with the monsters of the psyche and spirit.

For as long as deeds of heroes have been recounted, men have courted danger in far and fearsome places, on peaks, in caves, in deserts, in oceans, on playing fields, and on battlefields.

Something drives us to seek an ordeal against which to measure ourselves. And the majority of our gender seem to be extroverts and literalists who want the fear against which we test ourselves to be physical—a clear and present danger. We want to be taught we are men by something that threatens us with pain and death.

I had been scuba diving for several years when Gif Warner, captain of a salvage boat, asked me to help bring up the bow section of the *African Queen,* which ran aground in 1960 and sank on the Fenwick Island shoals. I was more than a little nervous as we prepared to explore the interior of the ship. Six-foot swells made it hard to get into the water without being smashed between the dive boat and the protruding section of the wreck. But once beneath the surface the wave action ceased and we entered the weightless world. As we entered the cargo hatch, thirty feet down, the groanings and creaking of the wreck played a cacophonous counterpoint to the hissing of our Aqua-lungs. All was well until we started to swim, or rather feel our way, up the narrow, dark passageway that led to the chain locker. What unknown dangers were lurking in liquid blackness? Sharks? Morays? Could the wreck turn over and trap us inside? My mild claustrophobia rapidly gave way to full-blown panic. I turned and started groping my way back toward the outside. Then, just as suddenly, something shifted within me, and I became more afraid of what would become of me if I yielded to my fear than I was of the darkness. I turned around and immediately I could see. There was enough light filtering through cracks in the wreck to see Gif in front of me, emerging from a hatch in the chain locker in a flood of bubbles, beard streaming, looking like Mephistopheles emerging from hell. I laughed with relief. Pushing my fear in front of me, I made my way deeper into the maze of the wreck.

Struggling against a fear occasioned by physical danger leads to an immediate high. As my friend Jim Peterson, ski devil, cycle monster, and playboy adviser, says: "Adrenaline is God's own aphrodisiac." But like all substances from coffee to coke that elevate intensity, it has its dangers. Risk addicts and thrill-seekers get hooked on flirting with danger and death and nothing else makes them feel alive. Confronting a calculated danger in an ordeal may be a useful ritual for learning about courage. But ritual becomes obsession and ceases to yield self-knowledge when it becomes an end in itself. On the path of courage, outward adventure leads us inward, and vice versa.

The way of the psychonaut leads into the jungle of the psyche, into the heart of darkness. It is no less fearsome or fraught with perils than the outer path. As Gerard Manley Hopkins says: "Oh, the mind, mind has mountains; cliffs of fall frightful, sheer, no-man-fathomed. Hold them cheap may who ne'er hung there."[3]

Psychological courage is rarer than its physical counterpoint. Because they have not dared to wrestle with anxiety, fear, hate, anger, pride, greed, longing, grief, loneliness, despair, impotence, and ambivalence, many extroverts bow obediently to authority and established opinion and never claim the territory of their psyche for themselves.

The monsters the psychonaut must confront are named differently in East and West. According to both Hinduism and Buddhism, the enemies of self-knowledge are fear and desire, aversion and attraction. What we must conquer is nothing less than our fear of suffering and death and our attachment to pleasure. Western psychology has named the inner demons shame and guilt—the need for approval and the fear of punishment. The psychonaut dares to explore the inner world of sensation, feeling, thought; to savor experience and come to an original set of personal values and a sense of inner authority and power. Such men and women are not fearless so much as they fear self-betrayal and loss of self more than loss of reputation.

From Guilt and Shame to Responsible Morality

It takes a lot of psychological detective work to discover how much of your life has been motivated by guilt or shame. If anyone had asked me at age forty if I felt guilty or ashamed, I would have denied it indignantly. So would most men. But if an anthropologist from Mars looked at the way I acted, he would have concluded that I was certainly driven by some invisible force. I acted as if I were trying to measure up to some unstated standard of perfection. I worked most of the time but still felt I was falling behind. I constantly compared myself to other men and felt my achievements were inadequate. I was judgmental toward myself and others. I felt I was constantly failing to live up to the expectations of the women in my life.

When a man wends his way down into the secret heart of darkness he finds shadowy figures with burning eyes that seem to accuse him of monstrous crimes and terrible failures. "You should. . . . You should not. . . . You ought to have. . . . You ought not to have. . . . You have broken my commandments. You have failed to live up to my expectations. You will be punished as you deserve. I will leave you alone and helpless and you will die."

Scratch a take-charge guy and you will find a guilty boy. Rub the veneer off a driven man and you will find the shamed child who can never do enough to measure up. Woody Allen notwithstanding, you don't have to be Jewish to feel guilty.

Men are supposed to make it happen. So if it is not happening, or it is going wrong, it is our fault. The psychological consequence of being the gender that has taken charge and assumed the responsibility for ordering and controlling the world is that we unconsciously feel we have failed when things are in a mess. Think of the male psyche as the defendant in Kafka's *The Trial*. We are vaguely charged with an unnamed crime; we feel we are probably guilty, but are not sure what we have done wrong, or left undone.

It is as if a toxic mixture of guilt and shame creates a psychic smog that lingers in the male unconscious, obscures the sun, and cuts us off from our native virility. Our performance anxiety, our ability to be manipulated by women, our unquestioned obedience to authorities, our timid submission to corporate hierarchies, are all manifestations of unconscious guilt and shame. In most men there is a large gap between the bold persona and the inward feeling of shrinking before the threat of an unknown punishment, the fear of being abandoned by the source upon which nurturance depends.

On the path toward freedom we must confront unconscious guilt and shame and discover the degree to which our actions have been preprogrammed by fear of punishment, rejection, and failure.

One of the most startling definitions I have heard in a long time is: "Sin is seeing your life through somebody else's eyes." (Sebastian Moore). In a nutshell, this describes the way in which infantile guilt and shame alienate us from our true self, and it suggests that the path to spiritual maturity involves learning to look at life through our own eyes. Inevitably, when we are young we interpret our lives through the eyes of parents, adults, and authorities. We are little and they are big. We automatically adopt their values, their religion, and their philosophy of life. Our conscience is their conscience. But at some point, we must kick Dad and Mother, priest, pope and president out of our psyche and seize the authority for our own lives. We must become responsible for our own values and visions. On the pilgrim's path each man must become Moses, going on a vision quest to some mountaintop and returning with the ten or twenty commandments that he holds sacred. So long as we obey or break the rules that have been set up for us by the Giants—Parents and other Authorities—we remain good or bad children. Growing into the fullness of our humanity means that we become co-authors of the rules by which we will agree to have our lives judged.

In the annals of heroism, there is a story that has always moved me, about a German private in World War II who was ordered to shoot civilian prisoners. Before the command was given to the firing squad, he stepped forward and said he could not violate his conscience by killing unarmed men and women. His commanding officer then ordered him either to proceed with the execution or to take his place among the prisoners. Without hesitation he switched places and was executed by the obedient soldiers who a moment before had been his companions.

From Isolation to the Awareness of Loneliness

Western culture was built on the notion of the dignity of the individual, and very few philosophies of life have been so often and so justly praised. The virtues of individualism were ratified in practice by the American Revolution and proved to be uniquely suited to a frontier nation.

But recently it has begun to look as if individualism is rapidly leading us into anarchy. What was once our strength is now tearing us apart. We are losing our moral consensus, our sense of community, our willingness to sacrifice for a shared ideal of the future, our understanding of what it is that gives dignity to the life of a man or woman.

As one of the main defining characteristics of manhood, individualism has produced generations of great and isolated men, men who had the courage to stand alone but lacked the awareness of their need for communion. In a capitalistic society, triumphant masculinity is won by beating the competition, being number one. Top dog, top man, top gun. The Olympic gold medal winner ascends the stairs and is crowned. But the top rung on the ladder is very narrow—room for only one.

I asked a senior executive of a major oil company, whose way to the top had involved moving eleven times in nineteen years, if his friends were mostly in his company. "I don't have friends anymore," he said. "After several moves we found it was too painful to say good-bye to our friends, so we stopped getting close to people. When we move to a new town we join the country club and the church and associate with the people we find there. But the only closeness we have is within our family."

The downside of individualism has been the weakening of men's bonds to other men, to women, and to nature. In creating ourselves as unique individuals we have cut ourselves off from others and have increasingly become superior strangers, without community or a cosmos in which we feel ourselves to be at home.

Joseph Campbell tells the story that when D.T. Suzuki, the great Zen teacher, was asked to comment upon Christianity he responded: "God against man. Man against man. Man against woman. Man against nature. Very strange religion."

Contrast our sense of cosmic isolation with the feeling for life of the South African Bushman. "This first man lived in an extraordinary intimacy with nature. There was nowhere that he did not feel he belonged. He had . . . none of that dreadful sense of not belonging, of isolation, of meaninglessness which so devastates the heart of modern men. Wherever he went he belonged and, what was more important, wherever he went he felt that he was known. . . . The trees knew him; the animals knew him as he knew them; the stars knew him. His sense of relationship was so vivid that he could speak of 'our brother the vulture.' He looked up at the stars and he spoke of 'Grandfather Sirus' . . . because this was the highest title of honor which he could bestow."[4]

The journey into self circles downward and inward until we realize that we are trapped within an illusion that has been woven around us since birth—the illusion that we are separate selves. The truth is that we are single selves who exist only within a community of interdependent beings. There is no I without a thou. As we become aware of how isolated we have been we begin to feel our loneliness for the first time and are filled with a longing for reunion. The prodigal son awakes alone in a strange land and begins to dream of going home.

From False Optimism to Honest Despair

By now you must be thinking: "This journey is not fun. It's too sad, too lonely, too frightening, too heavy. When do we get to the good times?"

Not quite yet.

All the maps tell us that on the path to authentic selfhood we must remain for a time in the dark night of the soul, in the winter of our discontent, until we reach the very bottom of despair. Only then do we discover that the seeds of renewal are blindly pushing their way up through the fertile loam toward the yet eclipsed sun. In past times theologians, philosophers, and spiritual pilgrims spoke about this part of the journey as being crucified, dead and buried, losing the ego, being lost in the wasteland or a slough of despond, descending into hell, being consumed by the hungry ghosts, being in the belly of the beast, doing battle with dragons, encountering demons. Nowadays we strip it of poetry and give it clinical names: stress, depression, and burnout. And, predictably, having renamed the phenomenon, we have created a new class of professionals—stress managers, therapists, and burnout consultants—who destroy the spiritual significance it once had.

But beware the once-born psychological cheerleaders, the purveyors of one-minute solutions, who assure you that all you need to do is change your diet, manage your time more efficiently, exercise more, learn to relax on the job, adjust your priorities, communicate better, learn to enjoy stress, or think positively and avoid "negative" emotions. Because stress is not simply a disease; it is a symptom that you are living somebody else's life, marching to a drumbeat that doesn't syncopate with your personal body rhythms, playing a role you didn't create, living a script written by an alien authority. Depression is more than low self-esteem; it is a distant early warning that you are on the wrong path and that something in you is being pressed down, beat on, kept imprisoned, dishonored. Burnout is nature's way of telling you you've been going through the motions but your soul has departed; you're a zombie, a member of the walking dead, a sleepwalker. And false optimism is like administering stimulants to an exhausted nervous system.

When we arrive at the dark pit of despair, we have reached the nadir, the low point in the spiritual journey—the place which is, paradoxically, the womb of the new self. Despair is the grave from which we may be born again.

But before the rebirth the old must die. As men we have habitually if not obsessively practiced the questionable virtue of optimism. We live by upbeat mottoes: "Every problem is an opportunity waiting for a solution. The difficult we do immediately, the impossible takes a little longer. We will overcome." Despair is the shattering of our manly illusion of being in control that comes with the awareness that our stance as conquerors of life is an illusion and that we are not "masters of our fate" and "captains of our souls." Powerful as we are, we can only whistle a brief melody in the eye of the hurricane. The earth quakes when it wills, the stars move in the heavens, and our DNA preprograms much of the biohuman computer of brain and body. If depression is a learned emotion that results from an artificial sense of helplessness, then despair is a primal emotion that is rooted in the honest awareness of our true helplessness to change the cosmic drama.

The descent into despair seems like death. We lose our old masculine identities. It is as if we wake up one day, it's February in our soul, our old self is dead, and there is no new one to take its place. Our habitual satisfactions and goals seem empty. If we can't win at the game of life what's the use in playing? Why should we get out of bed in the morning?

From Compulsive Action to Fallowness and Waiting

In waiting within this despair, in being true to our depression, to our true feelings, we find the doorway between the old world and the new.

In the dark night of the soul, we lose our old identities as conquerors and workers. And naturally enough we get impatient. "Let's get on with it. Enough of this wallowing around in the psychic mud of 'negative emotions.' After all, we don't have a lot of experience that suggests that anything of value is happening unless we are in control. Nothing prepared us to cherish fallow time. The right name for manly restlessness and inability to enjoy fallowness is mistrust. The male wound is ontological distrust, a vote of "no confidence" in the universe.

Women, even the high-powered types, know innately about gestation. From the moment of their first menstruation they learned about the seasonal quality of the body and soul. Through a lifetime of waiting, expecting, courting, conceiving, feeling the quickening in the womb, growing large with child and giving birth, they come to know viscerally that all new life begins deep within, beyond the reaches of the mind. Women trust in process more easily than men, know that we may be inhabited by hope long before we gain clarity. To wait is to trust that something may happen without conscious intention, without willpower.

In the depths of despair we are guided by the wisdom of the serpent. Snakes, those old phallic symbols beloved of the goddess, are always irritable at the end of summer, apt to bite, as their old skins are being shuffled off before rebirth.

T.S. Eliot, in *Four Quartets,* confronts darkness and by waiting in stillness transforms it into light and "dancing." Hear the testimony of another extraordinary man who was acquainted with the darkness:

"Our good is hidden, and so profoundly that it is hidden under its opposite. Thus our life is under death, love of ourselves under hate of ourselves, glory under ignominy, salvation under perdition, justice under sin, strength under infirmity, and universally every one of our affirmations under its negation."—Martin Luther.[5]

Renewal and the Rebirth of Joy

For nearly a week I have been weary, no energy, incapable of action. I wake in the morning and am still not rested. Nevertheless, being a man, I get up and get on with it. I put myself on automatic pilot and go to work. Midday a friend says, "You look tired." The words break the dam of control and the feeling, the fatigue, floods in.

Finally, I sit, wait, and listen, for what I do not know. Feelings of fatigue and sadness mix. But I can't call it depression. There is nothing wrong with me or my life at the moment. To the contrary. My marriage is better than it has ever been, my work is well received. I am physically healthy and have no personal problems. In the waiting silence I feel the overwhelming sadness and despair of my times: the incalculable suffering of peasants in El Salvador, the growing tyranny of governments everywhere, the insanity of war, the creeping deserts and increasing famines of Africa. I feel guilty for the ease and comfort of my life, at the same time knowing there is little I can do beyond small charity and distant compassion. Mixed with this world-sorrow is the simple sadness of my own life growing toward its inevitable end.

And, then, somewhere on the other side of sadness, I hear a deep unhurried symphony: the wind blowing gently across the valley in which I live, the drone of a multitude of bees, the harsh cry of Steller's jays, a woodpecker drumming a syncopated beat on a rotten tree. My spirit burrows deep into the fertile silence, rests, and is refreshed.

Midway in the spiritual journey, at its very nadir, the path quite unexpectedly begins to turn in an upward direction. In the winter of desire the spirit stirs and is reborn, the phallus rises to the occasion. Without warning your mood begins to change. For no particular reason you can detect depression lifts, despair is replaced with an undefinable sense of hope, and enthusiasm returns. Your dreams may be filled with images of flying, light-hearted men and women, new lovers, beautiful landscapes. A gentle mood of metaphysical peace may come over you, and wild thoughts occur: "Maybe I am okay just as I am. Maybe I don't have to do anything to justify my existence. Maybe I don't have to strive anymore." The feeling that accompanies such thoughts is one of profound contentment and deep relaxation. It is as if the bone slipped back into its socket; the prodigal son returned home; the dreamer awakened from a nightmare; the long war ended; the weary traveler laid a burden down; the falsely accused man recovered his innocence.

For what, in the beginning, may be only a fleeting but revolutionary moment, you feel sheer joy in being alive. Not pleasure or satisfaction for a job well done. Not pride in any accomplishment, but simple gratitude for the gift of life. Such moments of grace may overtake you while you are dancing, eating cold cereal, watching a commercial on TV, making love, sitting still and thinking about nothing in particular. It happened to Martin Luther when he was sitting on the toilet. After years of being constipated and compulsive it occurred to him that his life was of ultimate worth not because of any work he accomplished, but because he was accepted by God even as he remained a constipated sinner. No sooner did it occur to him that "I live by the grace of God," than his bowels opened, his anal compulsive personality underwent a conversion, and the Protestant Reformation began.

In the ascending part of the inner journey a new sense of self begins to develop. If I were to paint a psychological portrait of a man before he began his pilgrimage I would use mostly shades of black, white, and gray, to signify poverty of feeling. During the downward plunge into the depths I would add dark blues and vivid reds to suggest grief, depression, and rage. In the final part of the journey I would add all the other colors of the rainbow to the pallet to indicate the return of the entire spectrum of feelings. As the old, rigid male character armor—foreshortened and shallow breathing, constricted chest and tight anal sphincter, adrenal system overstimulated by a fight-flight mentality, defensive modes of thinking—softens, a man's entire body begins to become more sensuous and erotic. He tastes, smells, listens, and touches with greater sensitivity, and is responsive to all of his emotions. Instead of charging through the world focused on his goals, he moves more slowly and takes time to appreciate the beauty that surrounds him. It is as if a man, after living for a long time under the threat of being indicted for an unspecified crime, were to awaken one morning with the assurance of his innocence and a sense that his life has become a celebration.

There is a paradox that marks the end of the inward-turning part of the pilgrim's journey. We cannot forget our self until we have remembered it. We remain a problem to ourselves—self-absorbed, compulsively introspective, and narcissistic—so long as we have no authentic self-love. It is only when we arrive at a deep sense of self-acceptance that we are able to be self-forgetting and spontaneous. As the result of daring to plunge into the depths of himself, a man gains an acceptance of the multiplicity of his being. His newfound sense of gentle strength does not come from any conviction that he can perfect himself, conquer and banish his "negative" emotions, but from the vulnerable knowledge that he contains a kaleidoscope of human virtues and vices.

Emerging from the long journey into the shadow of the self the prodigal son returns to a world that was never his home until he wandered far from it.

HOMECOMING: A SAMPLER
OF HEROIC VIRTUES

The second part of the heroic journey leads out of the self and into the world, version from "me" to "we," from the solitary self to community, from therapy to action in the everyday world. To repeat Joseph Campbell's formula, "The hero comes back from this mysterious adventure with the power to bestow boons on his fellow men."

What virtues would make up the character of the modern heroic man? What kind of moral landscape would he inhabit? What will men look like as they emerge from a heroic journey in which their old identities are lost, their shadows confronted, their hidden fears faced, their forbidden longings honored? Will they be supermen? Soft? Androgynous? Wild? Postmodern aesthetes? Playboys? Self-altering scientists? Cyborgs?

We need to take note of a peculiar problem that arises when we try to sketch a modern hero:

It is easy to make vivid portraits of traditional heroes. They are the stuff from which history, biography, and motion pictures are made—Alexander the Great, Isaac Newton, Lawrence of Arabia, Winston Churchill, George Patton, Albert Einstein, John F. Kennedy, Martin Luther King, Jr., John Lennon, and Paul Newman. The formula for portraying the traditional hero is simple: Draw the hero larger than life. He should stand head and shoulders above other men, and loom even larger in relationship to women. The hero, by definition, is the most visible man. He exercises some kind of extraordinary power over the lives of others. He is a man apart from others.

As nearly as I can tell, the new heroic man is nearly the opposite of the traditional hero. The common virtues of modesty and humility (being of the earth—the humus) were the antithesis of the traditional hero and are the heart of the new hero. This means that the new hero may lack visibility precisely because he has given up the conceit that any man is "larger than life." His courage, the essence of the ecological ethic, is his willingness to fit in, to be a part of the whole, to live in harmonious intercourse with his surroundings. He is not a creature of the spotlight. His life may have great dignity but lack the kind of dramatic largeness of the traditional hero. The path of the old hero was usually strewn with the wreckage of those who had been trampled underfoot in the quest for power. A new, more democratic ideal of heroism seems to be emerging. Even in politics, admiration for the old powermongers, strong men, and iron-willed dictators is being replaced by adulation for a new kind of leader who seeks to empower others—Mikhail Gorbachev, Lech Walesa, Nelson Mandela, and Vaclav Havel.

We could argue that the whole notion of the hero is elitist, chauvinistic, presumptuous, and arrogant in its essence—a wrong ideal that is at the heart of the sickness of our times, of our macho politics, and of our destructive efforts to establish dominion over the earth. In short, the notion of heroism *is* the male pathology. It should be relegated to the historical scrap heap.

But I would argue that the need for heroes is part of the human condition and, therefore, the idea of heroism must periodically be redefined. The moment we admit to ourselves that we are less than we might be, that we are broken, wounded, sinful, neurotic, maladjusted, or alienated, we necessarily begin to try to visualize the opposite condition. Tillich's first question, "What is our disease?" leads us naturally to the second question, "How would we be if we were healthy?" Ideals are the polestars that guide us on our journey from the actual to the possible. And heroes are the incarnation of the ideals—the ideals made flesh and story. We need them because they give shape to our aspirations and put a face on our longing for wholeness. Because we human beings are conscious animals we are, irrevocably, the makers of metaphors, the tellers of stories, and the creators of heroes and villains.

Nevertheless, when I try to visualize a now and future hero I run into difficulty. Much as I would like a vivid portrait of manhood at its best, I find that what I have is not a single hero image but a kind of collage made up of fragments of new and ancient virtues exemplified in the lives of men I admire.

The stories and reflections that follow are parts of an assemblage of heroic virtues, which form a portrait of a new kind of man, an exemplary new brotherhood of humble and virile men. The argument of this chapter is impressionistic, not linear or systematic. Modern manhood is a work in progress. It's too soon to see who we are becoming. We can but catch glimpses of a prodigal man who has taken a journey into the depths of self and a new, heroic life, and how he might act on his return to this familiar and strange world.

The Virtue of Wonder

For me, the great exemplar of wonder was my father. During the six years I was working on my book, *Apology for Wonder*,[6] I thought often about the words I would use in the book's dedication. I think they are still the best introduction I can make of the man who taught me that wonder is the primal manly virtue.

For My Father, J. Alvin Keen (1899–1964)

And how can I say why?
His life was anchored in the great simplicities of earth:
The touch of the lithe bodies of children,
The hue of polished stones,
The astringent sun and antiseptic air of the desert,
The elegant geometry of shells and driftwood long bathed in the sea,
The perfume of early blooming lilacs,
The silent testimony of redwood trees,
The refreshment of all that is beautiful and graceful.
And yet there was the resonance of those elusive
harmonies at which music hints and for which faith
strives.
He lived with a growing ability
To deepen the covenants of friendship,
To admire simplicity and dedication,
To accept limitations and disappointments without
resentment,

To forgive the unacceptable and trust the unknown,
To love without grasping
To be grateful for the gift of life.
In his ambiance I learned that it is a good thing to take
time to wonder.

A trip to anywhere with my father was more of a meander than a straight line. If, on the way to the store, he got the idea that strawberries were in season, he would remember that he knew a farmer a few miles out of town who grew the plumpest, the reddest, the most succulent berries. And off we would go, interrupted only by a spectacular sunset which, of course, we had to pull off the road to appreciate properly. "Look at that, boys," he would say, shaking his head in amazement. "Did you ever see such a sight?" Once on a trip to California he stopped in Monterey to walk on the beach and found so much "gorgeous" driftwood that he couldn't get it in the car. So he did the only sensible thing—he shipped the seats of the car home and kept the driftwood with him. On a trip to Florida he fell in love with the shapes and texture of cypress knees, and before we knew it he had bought seventy-six of them. Another time, it took the best efforts of the entire family to persuade him not to buy a stuffed buffalo head.

To this day I judge men by the standard my father set. The men I enjoy and admire most are those who pause to wonder and remind me to heed the wisdom written on the railroad crossing: Stop. Look. Listen. Walking through a city with a friend who is a historian of architecture, I learn to see the shapes of buildings through his eyes and appreciate the language of space and texture. A friend who is a filmmaker and painter often points out to me the way shadow and light play across a landscape. I also number among my friends several men who are so dedicated to a cause or a profession that they never stop in the middle of a walk or a conversation and say, "Wait a minute, let's look at that Indigo Bunting." They are good men but lacking in an essential virtue. Without wonder, the world of men turns into compulsive activity and self-sealing systems of thought and social organization, and men, at best, become experts and efficient professionals and, at worst, puppets and functionaries of assorted institutions.

The second part of the heroic journey involves a rebirth of wonder because our eyes and our perception of the world change as the result of the disillusioning experiences of the inward journey. A man who penetrates beneath his facade loses the illusion that he is a conqueror of life. He no longer sees the world as an arena for his triumph, or nature as a thing that can be controlled.

It is ancient widsom that true virility is rooted in wonder. The best of men have always sung praises to this fundamental disposition toward life. Plato and Aristotle: "Philosophy begins in wonder." Jesus: "Unless you turn and become like children you will never enter the kingdom of heaven." Kant: "Two things fill the mind with ever new and increasing admiration and awe: the starry heavens above me and the moral law within me." D.H. Lawrence: "The sense of wonder, that is our sixth sense. And it is the natural religious sense." Dag Hammarskjöld: "We die on the day when our lives cease to be illumined by the steady radiance, renewed daily, of a wonder, the source of which is beyond all reason."[7]

To wonder is to open ourselves to the gift of being with a sense of gratitude. Before we can act with integrity, before we can think with respect, we must pause to wonder. Over the last three hundred years men switched their stance from wondering to "knowing." We became know-it-alls, take-charge guys. Do we have the wisdom to be the architects of destiny? Do you trust Lee Iacocca with the future? No question about it, he is a smart man. But is he wise? Maybe what's good for General Motors isn't good for the country, the biosphere, or the future of the planet. To continue the modern masculine habit of using intelligence without wisdom and technology without wonder is a formula for certain disaster.

The virtue of wonder also protects us against the spiritual claustrophobia of living in an overdomesticated world within a narrowly defined self-image. The achievements of science notwithstanding, ultimately neither the world nor the self are knowable. We live within a mystery, at once terrifying and fascinating, that always exceeds our understanding. Any definition of who we are is too limiting. I should approach myself like a country that will always contain unexplored wilderness and unfathomable seas. Who am I? More than I can ever know.

The Virtue of Empathy

There is a virtue difficult to name that marks the lives of those who have returned from the journey into depths of the self. If the first part of the heroic journey is marked by an intense focus on the self—self-exploration, self-remembering, self-analysis, self-criticism—the second part is marked by self-forgetting. A man who has become fully alive is no longer a problem to himself. He has been set free from agonizing self-consciousness and is free to explore and participate in the world beyond the self.

In his manner of living the philosopher Gabriel Marcel exemplified, and in his writing described and gave a name to, this heroic virtue—"*disponibilité*," which he suggested should be translated as "spiritual availability" or "spiritual readiness." It is easiest to understand if we start with its opposite. The unavailable man is encumbered within himself. His preoccupation may take the form of an obsession with money, power, reputation, health, psychoanalysis, or even his "spiritual" journey. Whatever the form, it renders him unavailable to give himself to others or live vibrantly. For the unavailable man, life is a bank account and he always calculates how he spends and gives of himself. The available person is not encumbered by his possessions or his self-image, and hence has the capacity to listen and respond to the appeal made by others on him. Though he must wage a constant battle against the forces within himself and his environment that urge him to assume the stance of a self-sufficient monad, he has ceased to believe that life is limited. He is porous rather than impermeable, animated by trust in the inexhaustibility of being.

Perhaps the notion of "empathy" is as near as modern psychology gets to naming this virtue. A good man does not *have* empathy; he *is* empathic. Since he has given up the illusion that he is self-contained, he naturally flows out to others. The result of coming to know myself—the wounds of shame and guilt, the disappointments of love, the unfulfilled dreams—is that I recognize the same in others. When, each day for a month, a friend of mine who is an extraordinary psychotherapist, phones a man who has been beaten and robbed, it is not because the man is a client, but because he feels the injury as if it were his own. In a sense, he has no choice because, knowing his own passions, his compassion is elicited. Empathic men have stepped out of the hierarchical way of viewing relationships—you are either one up or one down—and have become cobeings. You know immediately when you are with them because they don't talk at you, don't interrupt, don't give advice. They listen and stand beside you, and in their presence you have an uncanny feeling that you have been given the permission to be yourself.

The Virtue of a Heartful Mind

I first heard of Howard Thurman when I was a student at Harvard Divinity School. In 1953 God had not yet died and there was much excitement in the theological world. There were giants— Karl Barth, Reinhold Niebuhr, Rudolf Bultmann, and Paul Tillich. I wandered into Cambridge trailing broken chains, a wild-eyed fugitive just escaped from the prison of fundamentalism. I needed someone with a sharp intellect to help me chisel off the broken shackles. In Tillich I found a "savior" (a word, he reminded us, that came from *salvus*—to make whole or healthy). He showed me how a man could think passionately, deeply, and clearly about the complexities of the human condition. He exhibited a love for reason, an eros for Logos. But my spirit was not satisfied. At Harvard the mind was king, and tyrant. I was already reading the mystics—Johannes Eckehart, Jakob Böhme, and D. H. Lawrence—and wondering how the demands of my mind could be harmonized with the longings of my heart and the desires of my body. About that time word drifted across the Charles River that Boston University had a mystic who was teaching a course called "Spiritual Resources and Disciplines."

The first day of the seminar, Howard Thurman, then Dean of Marsh Chapel, arrived in class—a large black man with three prominent bumps on his forehead and a habit of silence so deep that it quieted everyone with whom he came in contact. He sat on the edge of the table for an eternity or so, not saying a word, looking at the dozen members of the class—I mean *really* looking. Finally, in a slow rich voice, he began to read from Admiral Byrd's account of being alone and near death at the North Pole. When he finished he paused and asked, "If you were alone, a thousand miles from any other person, it was fifty degrees below zero, and you were dying, what would have to have happened to allow you to die with integrity and a sense of completion?" The question dropped down beneath all the manufactured certainties of my mind and exploded in my gut like a depth charge. I knew I was in the presence of a man who thought with his mind, heart, and body stretched to their fullest.

Much of what I am still trying to learn from Howard has to do with rhythm—listening and moving to the unique cadences of my time, my life, my body. More than any man I have ever known, he had the virtue of reverence for his own and other people's rhythms. In speaking he could pause for longer than any man alive, refusing to yield to the pressure to form his words before his thought had reached the point of contact with his experience. When traveling in the United States he always took trains because he felt that airplanes destroyed the rhythms of his spirit. His rule of life, which applied to cooking fish, sipping bourbon, and puffing his pipe, as well as to thinking, was to savor his time. "Simmering" he called it. "When you wake up in the morning," he told me, "*never* get out of bed—simmer. And when you get into bed at night, *never* go to sleep—simmer." I did not know it at the time but years later after considerable psychotherapy I discovered that he had been teaching me the great shamanic art of entering into dream time, of traveling on the "royal road to the unconscious." (Freud)

A metaphor that was central to Thurman's thought was the notion of the journey. Like Gabriel Marcel, he considered the ideas of spirit and pilgrimage inseparable. When I was torn apart by the conflicts of divorce, romance, and purpose, he reminded me that I dare not surrender my complexity for a false peace. "Trust yourself in the deep, uncharted waters," he said. "When there is a storm it is safer in the open sea. If you stay too near the dock you will get beaten to death."

Until the day he died, Howard struggled, trying to understand the paradox that is at the heart of all religious experience— the mysterious marriage of choice and surrender, individual freedom and the acceptance of one's destiny. "To be human," he said, "we must insist on the right to cast our vote. And yet, finally, the individual spirit must be grounded in the impulse to yield—'not my will but Thine.'" During the final year of his illness, Howard was taken to the hospital and was more than once near or beyond the point of clinical death. But he kept coming back to finish some part of his journey. "I kept stripping myself of everything. I got ready to wrestle with God. I didn't want to die without being consulted," he told me. In the last month he tried to tell me about his experience of encountering God. "I was in the place where the decisions about the universe were made, where the stuff of life is informed. And I demanded the right to cast my vote about whether I would live or die." A week before he died we had our last conversation. In some way I could not understand, he had gained a satisfying answer to his question about why he had been born a man. Now he was wrestling with the unique character of his life as a man, seeking the reasons for "the grain in his own wood." "Why," he asked, "was I born a *black* man and you a *white* man? What, in the universal way of things, required me to be this particular person that I am?" As he asked this question he seemed startled by his own audacity. He paused. "I suppose a man can never know this, why he is just who he is," he said. He paused longer and his mood changed, almost to anger. "But why," he asked with whispered rage, "why should the ultimate secret of my life be kept from me?"

For a while we talked about other things, spoke about the friendship we had shared, I left with the understanding that we would meet again and pursue this question together, storm the bastion of the unanswerable. When I returned from a business trip, I learned that Howard had died. Or maybe it would be better to say that he had reached the point in his journey when his body could no longer sustain the adventurous impulses of his spirit. My God, how I miss him. But every time I feel my spirit I know, in some way my mind is too small to understand, that Howard is still my traveling companion.

As we've noted, modern men are, in general, more at home with thinking and action than with feeling. But only with a certain kind of abstract, objective, and impersonal mode of thinking. We are good at scientific investigation, accumulating data, market research, and rational analysis. We are not so good at linking up our minds and our hearts and thinking clearly about the deep experiences and longings of our lives. We are much more apt to ask "How can we do it?" than "What's worthwhile doing?" As Aldous Huxley once said, "Our means are human. Only our ends are ape chosen."[8] We are good at technological modes of thought, but ignorant of the art of meditative thinking. It is only a slight exaggeration to say that we have become machine-minded. Our minds, our hearts, and our genitals often seem to exist in exile from one another. It is not that we think too little—we will certainly not be healed by irrational emotionalism or mindless fanaticism—but that we haven't learned to think in a wholistic manner.

We need to acquire a heartful mind. This seems best done through the cultivated discipline of solitude, and the habit of recollection and autobiographical thinking.

A man gradually becomes poor in spirit and loses any relationship to richness of his own being unless he enters into a love affair with himself—*a ménage à moi*. When I look at the heroic man through the lens of Howard Thurman's life, I see a man happy to be alone. I see him going through a day with a quiet mind, moving gracefully, following the rhythm of the ebb and flow of his energies. Perhaps he begins the day by lingering over a cup of tea, and recollects his dreams or reviews his plans for the upcoming day to make certain that he orders his time to conform to his hierarchy of values. I see a man who, when alone, acts as if he were entertaining a guest of great honor.

To see why solitude is such a crucial virtue in our time, examine for a moment the bloody history of the twentieth century in which men, moved by various ideologies and "isms"— fascism, communism, nationalism, capitalism—have killed hundreds of millions of their fellows. The great moral failure of our time has been the willingness of men and women to become passive members of anonymous masses in mindless conformity. With scarcely a moment's reflection, men and women have handed their freedom of mind and spirit over to ruthless governments and leaders. As Erich Fromm said, we rush to "escape from freedom."

Solitude begins when a man silences the competing voices of the market, the polis, the home, the mass, and listens to the dictates of his own heart. Self-love requires the same commitment of time and energy as any other relationship. I must take time to be with myself, to discover my desires, my rhythms, my tastes, my gifts, my hopes, my wounds. We need solitude to keep the relationship between me, myself, and I alive and growing.

Men practice solitude in many different ways. Some backpack into the wilderness, with or without fishing rods and rifles. Some go to monasteries, churches, or religious retreats. Others take train journeys, isolate themselves in a hotel room in a strange city, or withdraw into their inner world while flying on a crowded 747 from Boston to Austin. You can do it anywhere. A generation ago Virginia Woolf said a woman needs "a room of one's own." It's good advice for men also.

Ten years ago, after remarriage and beginning a second family, I built a small cabin near the house. First I placed in it all the practical things I needed to be comfortable and nurture myself—a wood stove, a small kitchen, a toilet, a bed, a table, an outdoor shower. Next I turned the cabin into a personal sanctuary by bringing into it all the icons and sacred objects I had collected from childhood—objects that carry a part of my story. Cherished pieces of driftwood, rocks picked up at memorable times, Indian rugs my father gave me before he died, a picture painted for me by a friend, a cobalt blue bottle, my desert-island books, etc. Once my cabin was finished I began my practice of solitude. One or two nights a week I prepared my own dinner, ate alone by candlelight, smoked my pipe in front of the fire, sat in the rocker, considered my days, slept by myself, caught my dreams—and vowed to accept myself "for richer or poorer." In my solitude, I listened and had many good conversations with myself. I always returned to my home and family refreshed.

To create a heartful mind I must continuously be unfolding the ongoing story of my life and thinking as an autobiographical self rather than as a neutral observer. In scientific thought it is legitimate to try to be objective, to turn one's self into an anonymous and value-free observer. But when we are wrestling with any decision involving fundamental beliefs and values, we only think well when we are in touch with all the passions of our life. When we must decide whether to marry, to have children, to get an abortion, to divorce, to manufacture chemical weapons, to retire, to put our aging parents in a retirement home, to undergo chemotherapy, we need to get distance from the immediate problem and consider what we should do from the perspective of our entire life. To know how Sam Keen should act (not how "one" or "anyone" should act) I have to review my past and revision my future, place the present moment in the context of my memories and my hopes. I must think as a man who has a story.

If our most pressing personal and political problems could be solved by abstract intelligence, we would be well on the way to happiness and Utopia. Arguably we are in the middle of a knowledge revolution, although maybe it is only a data explosion. But wisdom is, cleary, in short supply.

When we think about the nature of virility, we need to ponder the difference between a smart man and a wise man. It seems that smart men think abstractly; wise men think autobiographically. Smart men remove themselves from the problem about which they are thinking; wise men bring all of their experience to bear. Smart men think quickly, with the conscious mind; wise men slowly simmer and allow the unconscious to play. Smart men live in the moment and believe any problem that can be defined can be solved; wise men recollect the past and respect the perennial limits of the human condition. Smart men are usually young; wise men are usually old.

Norman Maclean's novella, *A River Runs Through It*, is a rare testimony to a kind of beauty a man cannot create until the rough edges of youth have been smoothed by time. Maclean taught literature at the University of Chicago until he retired, and produced his only book when he was seventy-three. Every sentence in his story, which is about fly-fishing and the limits of love, and is a memorial to his brother who was murdered, is a polished stone long tumbled in the sand by the current of a rich life.

"I sat there and forgot and forgot, until what remained was the river that went by and I who watched . . . Eventually the watcher joined the river, and there was only one of us. I believe it was the river . . .

"Not far downstream was a dry channel where the river had run once, and part of the way to come to know a thing is through its death. But years ago I had known the river when it flowed through this now dry channel, so I could enliven its stony remains with the waters of memory. In death it had its pattern, and we can only hope for as much . . . It ran seemingly straight for a while, turned abruptly, then ran smoothly again, then met another obstacle, again was turned sharply and again ran smoothly . . . As the heat mirages on the river in front of me danced with and through each other, I could feel patterns from my own life joining with them. It was here, while waiting for my brother, that I started this story, although, of course, at the time I did not know that stories of life are more often like rivers than books. But I knew a story had begun, perhaps long ago near the sound of water. And I sensed that ahead I would meet something that would never erode so there would be a sharp turn, deep circles, a deposit and quietness.

"The fisherman even has a phrase to describe what he does when he studies the patterns of a river. He says he is 'reading the water,' and perhaps to tell his stories he has to do much the same thing. Then one of his biggest problems is to guess where and at what time of day life lies ready to be taken as a joke. And to guess whether it is going to be a little or a big joke. For all of us, though, it is much easier to read the waters of tragedy."[9]

We need to go one step further in probing the virtue of wisdom and the heartful mind.

We began this book by considering how boys are initiated into and confirmed in their sense of manhood by rites of passage that are administered by the elders of the community. Old men and young men define each other through a process of teaching and learning. To grow old without accumulating wisdom and becoming a mentor is to strip the last half of life of its raison d'être.

Nothing has eroded the dignity of manhood more than the cult of youth that grows out of the ideology of technology, the unspoken intention of engineering a future world that is completely within human control. This involves a war against tradition, age, and death. It also involves the hidden assumption that the most recent knowledge makes past wisdom obsolete. We flatter ourselves by baptizing the latest as the greatest. Within this brave new world old people are a nuisance, an embarrassing reminder that our project of accumulating power is nothing more than building sand castles against a rising tide.

To age gracefully we must aspire to become wise and beautiful elders. For this, men require a revolution in identity in which we measure success by our capacity for compassion rather than by accumulation of power, and virility by the capacity to nurture, husband, and mentor.

Maybe it takes the best part of a lifetime to acquire a heartful mind. It seems to happen only when the fire in the belly has burned down, leaving a bed of glowing embers, amid which the bread of life may be baked. No wonder the ancient Chinese portrayed heroes as seasoned men with gray hair.

The Virtue of Moral Outrage

In 1974, when I first phoned Ernest Becker to see if he would be willing to do a conversation with me for *Psychology Today*,[10] his wife, Marie, told me he had just been taken to the hospital and was in the terminal stage of cancer. The next day she called back to say that Ernest would like to do the conversation if I could get there while he still had strength and clarity. I dropped everything and went immediately to Vancouver. When I walked into the hospital room his first words to me were, "You are catching me in extremis. This is a test of everything I've written about death. And I've got a chance to show how one dies. The attitude one takes. Whether one does it in a dignified, manly way; what kind of thoughts one surrounds it with; how one accepts his death."

In the hours we talked, I learned things I will never forget about the intellectual courage required to think clearly about the nature of evil, and the moral courage needed to confront death in a heroic manner.

During the political high jinks and revolutionary sentiment of the late 1960's, Ernest Becker was *the* professor at Berkeley to a generation of students who listened only to men whose ideas were infused with passion and animated by moral outrage. In *The Denial of Death*, Becker took any reader who could bear the anxiety on a shamanic journey beneath the facade of personality where he revealed the defense mechanisms we "normally" use to construct our "character armor" in an effort to deny the terrifying awareness of our animality, the unpredictability of life, and the inevitability of our death. In *Escape from Evil*, published posthumously, he went further and showed that humanly caused evil results from our attempt to deny our crea-tureliness and overcome our insignificance. He unmasked the glorious claims of nations and the warfare state—the promise to provide us with meaning for our lives by giving us enemies whom we can destroy and thereby prove to ourselves that we are the chosen people of God—and showed them to be a demonic form of heroism. "The horror we regularly visit upon each other comes not from any innate sadism or desire to act cruelly toward others but from our desire to belong to an in-group . . . And to achieve this intimate identification it was necessary to strike at strangers, pull the group together by focusing it on an outside target. . . . It is not our aggressive drives that have taken the greatest toll in history, but rather unselfish devotion, hyperde-pendency combined with suggestibility."[11]

By identifying the false heroism of political claims of absolute righteousness—any crime is justified so long as it is for the fatherland, the motherland, the revolution, democracy, the people of God—Becker raised the question of authentic heroism. "The most exalted type of heroism involves feelings that one has lived to some purpose that transcends one." Both his writing and his life force us to ask how we can achieve a sense that we are used for divine purposes, without falling into dangerous forms of self-righteousness.

In my pantheon of heroes the best of men are, like Ernest Becker, spiritual warriors who are alive with moral outrage and who enter the arena to wrestle with the mystery of evil in one of its many disguises. Fierce men, rich in considered judgment, who still have thunder and lightning in them; not dispassionate spectators, or cynics. Any day of the week give me the "hot" Bill Moyers who takes risks, calls presidents liars, and gives vent to prophetic anger at secret wars and hidden government, rather than the "cool" McNeil-Lehrer who nicely report the news and lead discussions on every perspective that is fashionable within the Beltway.

One of the most troubling symptoms of our time is the absence of moral outrage in the American public. The ongoing revelations that the CIA conducted covert wars, arranged assas-sinations, trained many of the Salvadoran military responsible for death squads, was implicated in the deaths of thousands of Indonesians, and gave the South African government information that led to the arrest of Nelson Mandela, continue to be greeted with a yawn. It is as if some invisible solvent has been leeching away our capacity for indignation. When I was first in the USSR in the pre-*glasnost* era I had a sense that free speech was forbidden. On returning to the U.S., I was struck with how our newspapers could print any story of corruption in high places but very little action resulted.

The hero's path in the world is bound to be filled with conflict. A man who has not been morally anesthetized cannot have his eyes opened to unnecessary suffering, disease, and injustice without feeling outrage and hearing the call to arms. From deep in the gut a sense of desecration forms itself into a judgment and grows into an impulse to act. "Goddamn it, it is wrong for governments to spend billions on weapons while children starve! Goddamn it, it is wrong for us to pursue 'progress' at the cost of destroying ten thousand species a year, the wetlands, the forests and the watersheds! Goddamn it, it is wrong for a hundred million people to be homeless, living on sidewalks, in garbage dumps and alleys!"

The sense of vocation that is central to a heroic male identity arises when we are outraged about some specific instance of evil and become warriors in defense of the sacred. If our minds are heartful, we must be outraged by the cruelty in the world, and realize that it is our vocation to become protectors of the powerless and healers of the broken.

To live in this wonderful-terrible moment of history and keep compassion and virility alive, a man must gird up his loins and decide where to enter the struggle against surplus suffering, injustice, poverty, pollution, and the rising tide of population. Suffering is a part of the human condition. In the best of all possible worlds there would still be disease, accident, tragedy, disappointment, loneliness, death. And we require all the spiritual wisdom we can accumulate to accept injuries and losses that we are powerless to change. But above and beyond the essential suffering is the surplus suffering that results from psychological, economic, and political structures that we do have the power to change. The "just war" of the spirit is against the sources of surplus suffering, against the impulses of greed and insensitivity within the self, against those ideologies, institutions, corporations, bureaucracies, and governments that most clearly are responsible for the desecration of the earth. In this effort, the new hero must reclaim and redirect the energies and virtues of the warrior psyche—fierceness, fortitude, daring, courage, cunning, the strategic use of power—that were once used in the defense of tribe and nation.

In the struggle to preserve a sense of the sacredness of life, as in all "holy wars," identifying the enemy is a morally hazardous activity. Self-righteousness easily creeps into our judgments. It is easy to condemn the owners of coffee plantations who exploit the Indians while we are enjoying our café au lait, or rant and rail against pollution as we continue to drive to the corner store. To guard against self-righteousness, the spiritual warrior must practice the discipline of perpetual repentance. I must constantly remind myself that I am a part of the problem I am trying to solve, I am also the enemy against whom I must fight, I incarnate the evil I am called to do battle against. The demons of greed, cruelty, and fear must be fought within and without. The heart that has become hardened and careless is both individual and corporate, both mine and my enemy's. The prophetic outrage that sets the spiritual warrior in conflict with institutional incarnations of evil also sets him in conflict with his own greed and insensitivity. A man who does not know how to wage a just battle, first with himself and then with others, has no values worth defending, no ideals worth aspiring to, no awareness of the disease of which he might be healed. And no mensch worships the status quo.

When we become spiritual warriors, it must be with the knowledge that the battle is never to be won either intellectually or politically. The existentialist philosopher Karl Jaspers once said that "evil is the rock on which every system shipwrecks." There is no answer, no theodicy, no way of understanding that eliminates the insult evil poses to the human spirit. We are not in a world that satisfies our demand for moral explanations. The best approach I know is the one suggested by Albert Camus in *Resistance, Rebellion and Death:* "We are faced with evil. And, as for me, I feel rather as Augustine did before becoming a Christian when he said: 'I tried to find the source of evil and I got nowhere.' But it is also true that I, and a few others, know what must be done, if not to reduce evil, at least not to add to it. Perhaps we cannot prevent this world from being a world in which children are tortured. But we can reduce the number of tortured children."[12]

The Virtue of Right Livelihood

Jim Autry, once a figher pilot and still a poet haunted by the memories of rain on a tin roof in Mississippi, has practiced right livelihood for thirty years within the Meredith Corporation. His job title is President of the Magazine Group, and daily he dresses for battle in the standard coat and tie of his profession, but his vocation is the art of compassion within the corporate community. In *For Love and Profit*, he preaches what he has long practiced: "Good management is a calling, a life-engagement that, if done properly, combines technical and administrative skills with vision, compassion, honesty, and trust to create an environment in which people can grow personally, can feel fulfilled, can contribute to the common good, and can share in the psychic and financial rewards of a job well done . . . Management is, in fact, a sacred trust in which the well-being of other people is put in your care during most of their waking hours."

Here is a taste of the manager-poet at his work:

> "What the Personnel Handbooks Never Tell You. They leave a lot out of the personnel handbooks./ Dying for instance. /You can find funeral leave / but you can't find dying./ You can't find what to do/ when a guy you've worked with since you both/ were pups/ looks you in the eye/ and says something about hope and chemotherapy./ No phrases,/ no triplicate forms,/ no rating systems./ Seminars won't do it / and it's too late for a new policy on sabbaticals./ They don't tell you about eye contact/ and how easily it slips away/ when a woman who lost a breast/ says, 'They didn't get it all.'/You can find essays on motivation/ but the business schools/ don't teach what the good manager says/ to keep people taking up the slack/ while someone steals a little more time/ at the hospital./ There's no help from those tapes/ you pop into the player/ while you drive or jog./ They'd never get the voice right./ And this poem won't help either./ You just have to figure it out for yourself,/ and don't ever expect to do it well."[13]

There is no easy formula for determining right and wrong livelihood, but it is essential to keep the question alive. To return the sense of dignity and honor to manhood, we have to stop pretending that we can make a living at something that is trivial or destructive and still have a sense of legitimate self-worth. A society in which vocation and job are separated for most people gradually creates an economy that is often devoid of spirit, one that frequently fills our pocketbooks at the cost of emptying our souls.

What kinds of jobs, occupations and ways of making a living are compatible with the quest for spiritual integration? Most people would agree that a man who chooses to be an arms merchant, a heroin dealer, a mercenary, or a pimp destroys any authentic sense of spiritual vocation. But if some cases are black and white, most are gray. What about a Montana farmer who grows a crop of marijuana to make payments on his family farm? A Kentucky farmer who grows tobacco? A corporate raider who buys and destroys a company to gain its assets? A savings and loan executive who profits while those who trusted him lose their savings? A manufacturer of agricultural chemicals who sells questionable pesticides? A scientist who works on star wars or plutonium triggers?

Should I become a physician, an appropriate technologist, a forester, a priest, a union organizer, a peace activist? What can I do to make a difference? The cry of the needy, the homeless, the hurt is thunderous and eternal, beyond my ability to respond. Isn't the very idea of being a healer grandiose and presumptuous? A fool's errand? If I care am I not, like Don Quixote, setting myself up for an assault on an impossible objective? How do I scale down the task so that I am not impotent?

For a moment, turn a deaf ear to all cries and appeals and listen to the voice of your own being. Who are you? What are your gifts? What gives you the greatest joy? What have you to offer? Begin the search for your unique vocation by heeding the advice of some wise men. "Follow your bliss," said Joseph Campbell. "To thine own self be true," wrote Shakespeare. The search for what we have to contribute to life begins when we explore our unique selves.

A young man came to therapy complaining that each time he tried to take the examinations for his Ph.D. in sociology he got diarrhea and had to leave. The therapist asked him, "How do you feel about becoming a professor of sociology?" "Shitty," the man replied. "Then why are you doing it?" the therapist asked. "Because my father is a professor and has always planned for me to be a professor and I can't disappoint him." "What do you want to do?" the therapist asked. "I have always wanted to work in the theater as a set designer, but I don't know whether I have the talent to make a go of it." "It seems to me you have to make a choice," the therapist replied. "Either you can become a professor and feel shitty and be disappointed in yourself. Or you can try set designing, disappoint your father, and feel good about yourself. It is too soon to say whether you have a gift for theater. But you will never know if you don't try."

It is quite possible that this young man might spend three years in the theater and discover it was his passion but that he couldn't make a living at it. He might then decide to become a professor and follow his theatrical vocation in his spare time. Many people, perhaps most, have a discontinuity between their vocation and their occupation. You may find your deepest sense of fulfillment in trekking in the wilderness or in teaching "Great Books" courses in the local prison, and make your living by programming computers. So long as your occupation does no violence to your vocation there is no spiritual harm done by separating the two. Indeed, in a society where many people are condemned to trivial and deadening jobs, it is often necessary to find a way to express vocational gifts apart from work. It is crucial to find a way to incarnate our care.

The Virtue of Enjoyment

Etty Hillesum, a Dutch Jew, went voluntarily and died in a Nazi concentration camp because she felt "a camp needs a poet, one who experiences life there, even there, as a bard and is able to sing about it." The following is her diary entry as she watches the Nazi net tighten around the Jews.

> *June 27, 1942.* The latest news is that all Jews will be transported out of Holland through Drenthe Province and then on to Poland . . . And yet I don't think life is meaningless. And God is not accountable to us for the senseless harm we cause one another. We are accountable to Him! . . . And yet I find life beautiful and meaningful. From minute to minute . . .
>
> Sun on the balcony and a light breeze through the jasmine . . . I shall linger another ten minutes with the jasmine, and then . . . to see the friend . . . who can still suddenly present me with an aspect so new that I catch my breath with surprise. How exotic the jasmine looks, so delicate and dazzling against the mud-brown walls. I can't take in how beautiful this jasmine is. But there is no need to. It is enough simply to believe in miracles in the twentieth century. And I do, even though the lice will be eating me up in Poland before long."[14]

In the life of the spirit, paradox is the rule: Yin loves yang, the opposites coincide, the diseased parts form a graceful whole. One metaphor balances another: The moral warrior joins hands with the amoral celebrant, the prophet and the sensualist walk together. In considering the whole and holiness of life, we must at once hold before our eyes visions of horror and wonder, cruelty and kindness. As you read this sentence somewhere in the world everything lovely and terrible is happening: Lovers are shuddering in orgasm, babies are being born, men are torturing the innocent, growing flowers, writing poems, burning rain forests, building hospitals, and so on.

If our eyes fall only on what is terrible, we become hypnotized by evil and either turn aside in despair because it is overwhelming, or become fanatical warriors. Focusing on suffering is depressing and debilitating. Righteous warriors and compulsive do-gooders burn out and give those around them heartburn. As a friend who lived with a crusader for social causes said, "It is a lot easier to be a saint than to live with one."

How can we remain in the humanizing struggle against evil without becoming moralistic, depressed, and burned out?

Look at the checkerboard, blink your eyes, and the pattern changes. Now it is red squares against a black background rather than vice versa. Suffering and joy are like one of those trick "gestalt" pictures that is a double entendre—one moment it is a goblet and the other the faces of two women, or a picture of a woman looking "vainly" in a mirror that becomes an old crone when you change your focus. One of the disciplines of spiritual life is the practice of shifting perspectives, turning the diamond to see each of its facets, holding to the complexities of the paradox. Look into the concave surface of the fun-house mirror and you see horror and suffering; look into the convex surface and you see beauty and joy.

To get through the world alive we have to care until our hearts break and cram our lives full of enjoyment. Both/and, not either/or. The great trinity of virtues—joy, gratitude, and care—is inseparable. Only enjoyment and gratitude for our lives create a spontaneous impulse to care for others.

If I were asked to diagnose the spiritual disease of modern men I would not concentrate on symptoms such as our lust for power, our insatiable hunger for gadgets, or our habit of repressing women and the poor. I would, rather, focus on our lack of joy. Most of the men I know are decent, serious, and hard-working, and would like to make the world a better place. What they are not is juicy, sensual, and fun. The most successful among us are far too busy to waste time on simple pleasures like jasmine and friendship. We have too many important things to do to appreciate the stream of delights that flows constantly through our nerve endings. As one of my most hard-working, world-saving friends said to me, only half in jest, "I don't enjoy pleasure anymore."

If I were prescribing a cure for men, I would suggest a regimen that would restrict our daily diet of excess abstractions and revive our rapidly atrophying senses. Bird watching, talking with children, visiting friends, preparing feasts, making love, fiddling in the garden, playing ball in the streets, listening to music, reading, walking, sitting quietly and doing nothing would be encouraged. I think it likely that we will gain the desire and wisdom to create a more compassionate society only when we learn to take our time and find passionate enjoyment in elemental pleasures. Feel the sweetness of your body and you will empathize with a trapped red fox or a migrant worker poisoned by agricultural pesticides. We feel outrage, and respond to the vocation to protect against desecration, only when we have previously sensed the deep-down sacredness of our own flesh.

The Virtue of Friendship

I first met Jim Donaldson in 1968 when I arrived in California on sabbatical leave to search for the New Age, which at the time was only a rumor in Kentucky. Jim was on the barricades. As the organizer of a radical experiment called the New Adult Community he was the driving force in a group of deserters from the middle class who were going to end political, economic, and sexual oppression, and bring The Establishment of Los Angeles tumbling to the ground. He organized radical protests, meetings with the Black Panthers, the underground railroad to Canada for war refusers, and many other events which are, no doubt, well described in the files of the FBI.

The first thing that struck me about Jim, besides his impassioned words, was his eyes. Searching, penetrating, looking at and through you to some point beyond the moment where, it seemed, he could see a clear image of the ideal and potential you. He was a visionary. He could be charming but never merely polite, and nothing—sex, money, or friendship—stood in the way of his pursuit of a just society. He was, however, generous to the core. He always appeared with a gift—a bottle of wine, a book he felt you needed to read, a poem he had written for your birthday.

As Jim and I came to know each other better we began to analyze and criticize each other more freely. I found his passionate commitment winsome but his ideology rigid and his manner downright manipulative. He found my political views naive, and my life-style compromised by too much comfort and security. If I was too detached, too timid, too sexually repressed, too patriarchal, he was too angry, too intolerant, too judgmental, too careless of the fragile bonds of marriage and the family. Back and forth we went in dialogue and disagreement. No quarter asked, none given. Sometimes we drew blood and retreated from each other for months until the wounds healed. It was not easy for either of us to abide what the other saw.

The years passed, and with them the utopian mood of the sixties. My first marriage ended in divorce in part because Jim forced me to look at many of the unspoken hostilities and destructive compromises that had turned wedlock from a hearth into a prison. Jim abandoned the thankless task of reforming Los Angeles and took to the wilds of the Methow Valley in Washington to grow organic garlic and raise hell with real estate developers and polluters of the watersheds. I remarried and, on a trip to visit Jim, ended up buying a small farm far enough away from his to avoid being enlisted in his swarm of projects and just causes but close enough to visit after the chores were done. Jim kept me informed about what toxic sprays the forest service was using, the situation in El Salvador, the nefarious activities of multinational corporations, how to doctor my horse, and what political actions were necessary to keep our creek from being polluted. Several times a week he would appear in the late afternoon bringing vegetables from his garden, and we would walk or ride in the hills or swim in the river and then our whole family, of which he was by then an integral member, would sit around the kitchen table, fix dinner, eat, and talk. And talk.

Even more years passed. Jim and I both moved away from the Methow and we no longer live in geographical proximity. But the intimacy between us has remained. No matter what happens, our friendship has given us a kind of living immortality. So long as either of us lives we will never be anonymous, unknown, or unsung. Our stories are intertwined in the DNA of our friendship.

Friendship may be the surest source of satisfaction in a fickle world, better than sex, money, or power. The Greeks valued it above romance or reputation and gave it an honored place in the pantheon of love.

Friendship, *philia*, brotherly love, the affection that exists only between equals, is at once the most modest and rugged of the modes of love. It is quiet as an afternoon conversation, but strong enough to survive the acids of time. And while it draws us into our emotional depths it demands no romantic frenzy. No howling at the moon, no explosions of contradictory feelings. No jealousy. Friendship creates gentle men and women. It depends upon nothing so fragile as a pretty face or fancy figures in a bank account, or so irrational as the thick sinews of blood and kin. It is based upon the simplest of the heart's syllogisms: I like you; you like me; therefore we are friends. And while we can imagine a satisfying life without the juicy overflow of sexual love or the sweet burdens of family, we know intuitively that without a friend the best of lives would be too lonely to bear.

Yet, these days friendship is an endangered species. Friendship doesn't thrive in a social ecology that stresses speed, constant preoccupation, and competition between men. It requires slow time. Like great whiskey, it must be seasoned in wood, steeped in patience, and long simmered. No instant intimacy or one-night stands. The cadence of friendship is measured in decade-long rhythms. An enduring friendship is years in the seeding, tended through wet and dry times, not uprooted. Friendship does not have much truck with efficiency or appointment books. It is all about hanging out together over a cold beer in a bar, or bait-casting in a swift stream. It is about being there to listen and help when a friend's life falls apart.

"Normal" American men are homophobic, afraid of close friendships with other men. The moment we begin to feel warmly toward another man, the "homosexual" panic button gets pressed. It makes us nervous to see French or Italian men strolling down the street arm in arm. Must be queer! From a cross-cultural perspective it is we who are odd; close male friendship is the norm in most societies and is usually considered a more important source of intimacy than romantic relationships. The celebrated friendships of David and Jonathan or Achilles and Patroclus reflect a valuation more typical than the American pattern of acquaintanceship or a quick slap on the butt after making a touchdown. In most nontechnological cultures, friendship makes the world go round, not money or sex.

A predictable result of our homophobia is that men become overdependent on women to fulfill their need for intimacy, and swallow the romantic myth hook, line, and sinker. We grow up expecting that some magic day it will happen. We will find the one special woman who will take away our loneliness and heal our alienation. The two of us will fall in love and be all things to each other: lovers, companions, helpmates, and best friends. And then we are disappointed and feel betrayed when it doesn't happen. But any single relationship that is expected to fulfill every need will become claustrophobic, cloying, and swampy.

We need same-sex friends because there are types of validation and acceptance that we receive only from our gender-mates. There is much about our experience as men that can only be shared with, and understood by, other men. There are stories we can tell only to those who have wrestled in the dark with the same demons and been wounded by the same angels. Only men understand the secret fears that go with the territory of masculinity.

Friends alone share the consolation of knowing and being known. Most of our days are spent among polite strangers, colleagues, and casual acquaintances with whom we interact in role-governed ways. We wear masks, playing the part we are expected to play—doctor, lawyer, merchant, chief, father, lover, banker, thief. Only with our best friends can we get off the stage, stop the show, quit performing, and allow ourselves to be seen as we are. Friendship may be the best antidote for the alienation that is the inevitable result of corporate and professional styles of life.

The Virtue of Communion

A dozen of us, more or less, have met every Wednesday night for a dozen years. An odd lot of white men, predominantly "straight" and mostly married, divorced, or trying to be one or the other. We include a lawyer, a filmmaker, a fisherman, two doctors, a psychotherapist, a landscape architect, a foundation director, a businessman, a teacher, an IRS hit man, a writer.

The group began in desperation and loneliness. Years ago, two of us met by chance at a coffee shop and fell to talking about the women in our lives, our failed romances and broken marriages. War stories. Before we knew it a cup of coffee had stretched into a long afternoon, and between the caffeine and the conversation we were wrapped in a warm cocoon that felt suspiciously like the missing intimacy we had been searching for with women. "We should do this more often," he said. "Let's do. I know another guy I think would like to join us," I replied. "Yeah, I know one too. Why don't we meet next Wednesday night at your house." And thus began our men's group.

Over the years, outsiders have observed the profound effect the group has had on its members. A cocaine addict for two decades kicks his habit. A man on the verge of suicide, heavily medicated by his psychotherapist, stops the medication, fires his therapist and is filled with hope. A son, defeated by shame because he could never live up to the expectations of his powerful father, stands tall and creates a business that fulfills his own dream. A husband who is reduced to jelly by his wife's anger stands his ground and learns the art of loving combat. A dance-away lover makes a commitment to an appropriate woman. An arrogant and intimidating man softens. The marriages of all the men get better, except for two men who desert the group—divorcés who fell back into consuming romance and marriage and thought they could find all the intimacy they needed within the arms of their new women.

"What's the secret? Is this some kind of twelve-step program like AA? What do you guys do that is so powerful?" people ask us. The superficial answer is that we don't do anything except talk about the things that matter the most to us, and listen to each other. We laugh a lot. We challenge each other. But a more profound answer is that almost by accident we discovered the missing ingredient that is as necessary to the health of the male psyche as vitamin C is to the health of the body—the virtue of community. Medicine. What I found was that men in our culture share a common experience of growing up male and as a result I no longer feel alone in my struggle. I know that the difficulties about which I have written in this book—ambivalence toward women, the wounds of the warrior psyche, the unending burden of work and performance—are not the result of my personal failure but are the consequences of the kind of society and gender system men and women have conspired to create in our time.

Within the community of men, I have learned that men's loneliness is a measurement of the degree to which we have ignored the fundamental truth of interdependence. In devoting ourselves to getting, spending, and being entertained, we simply forget that we inevitably feel alienated when we do not live within a circle of friends, within the arms of the family, within the conversation of a community. There is no way we can recover a secure sense of manhood without rediscovering the bonds that unite us to others and reaffirming our fidelity to the "We" that is an essential part of "I." To pretend that a man standing tall and alone is virile is to base our view of manhood on a metaphysic of separation that has been shown to be an illusion by almost every advance of the physical and social sciences of our era.

If the pollsters and social scientists who read the data about now and future men are correct, men are in severe psychological danger because of their failure to attend to their need for belonging. According to Jim Fowles,[15] American men may become even more individualistic and isolated in the 1990's, based on present attitudinal trends: 1) a renewed ethic of achievement and independence and a much wider male endorsement of hard work and resoluteness; 2) a greater self-orientation and less group-orientation; 3) growth in attention to exercise and health—related to the intensifying focus on self; 4) a more go-it-alone life—men are increasingly divorced, childless, and living alone. And he concludes that men will be more emotionally isolated than at the present.

What the polls do not reveal is that men isolated from real community form pseudocommunities to fulfill their needs for belonging. But in pseudocommunities men become even more lonely because their sweet individuality is not cherished and they are accepted only if they conform to some tyrannical norm. Just this minute while my mind was simmering I punched the word "men" into Word Finder™ on my computer to see what synonyms were listed. Herewith the list (and the problem of contemporary men in a nutshell). "Men": army, battalion, brigade, company, force, gang, power, soldiers, troops. Evidently the anonymous man (or woman?) who compiled this dictionary could only conceive of men in the plural being united in a manner requiring a sacrifice of individuality and involving the potential for violence. Why, I wonder, did this list of synonyms for "men" not include: brotherhood, guild, fraternity, friends, fellows, team members, comrades? It never seems to have occurred to our Word Finder that men might bond together for kindly reasons in a manner in which the individuality of each member is cherished by the group!

The second part of the heroic journey takes place within the bonds of community, when the solitary seeker returns to the fraternity. Before we can make the large changes in our political and economic systems that are necessary to adapt to the unique challenges of the next era, men need to begin to build a new consensus that can only come out of conversation. The old male bonding rituals—sports, war, business, woman bashing, drinking, hunting—are no longer sufficient or appropriate. We need to break through the conspiracy of silence that surrounded our fathers and condemned them to loneliness, and create a new subculture composed of a million minicommunities of men who talk about what matters to them.

A man without a friend, a family, or a community is an abstraction on the way to becoming a heartless functionary.

The Virtue of Husbanding

We asked a friend where we could find good apricots to dry for winter. "Go see Raff St. Louie down by Chelan," she said. "He grows the best. He's organic to the core, won't spray and won't pick until his 'cots are tree ripe and he has a variety that has a pit as sweet as an almond."

We approached across high tableland with neat farms and green pastures watered by rainbird sprinklers spewing out eighteen gallons a minute. On the right a mile down the lane was a square of brown that seemed from the distance to be a minidust bowl. In the middle stood a house that looked like a rural version of a Charles Addams mansion—once grand, decorated with flourishes of Victorian woodwork, but now fraying at the edges. The roof was papered with cardboard boxes smashed flat and held against the wind by boards nailed in a haphazard design. The only green visible was a large willow tree whose branches cascaded onto the dusty ground like emerald rain. The front porch was stacked with apple boxes. Crowding around the house and extending for a couple of acres in back were apple trees, almost gray, their normal greenness covered with a patina of dust.

We knocked and waited. After what seemed a long time the door opened and out came a small hawk of a man in his sixties with fierce eyes and a navy watch cap pulled low. It was ninety-two degrees in the shade and his clothes blended harmoniously with the land—olive drab infused with dust.

"What do you want?" he challenged.

"Lorianne told us you had some organic apricots."

"Well, I don't have any yet. Won't pick 'em until they are tree-ripe, soft, and sweet. Not even for Lorianne. I suppose you want the ones with the sweet pits? I'm the only one around here that's got any of 'em. They might be ready next week." Once started, Raff kept on talking without a pause like many old people who are starved for the sound of voices. "You know, those 'cots you get in the store aren't worth a damn. Picked green. And they spray 'em with so much poison they don't even taste like fruit anymore. A man come up here the other day from the county agricultural service—*service*, my ass—and said he wanted to look around. I told him he better just stay in his car, cause this was my land and wasn't anybody going to be looking around unless I invited him. And he said that somebody complained that I wasn't spraying my apricots and apples and the bugs were going to contaminate my neighbors' orchards, and if I didn't spray them they would do it and send me the bill. Well, shit. I told him that nobody's going to spray my trees so long as my finger can pull the trigger of my rifle. Well, he hasn't showed up, and I don't think he will. I'll tell you something else. The apple tree he doesn't like to be wet all the time, he's not like this willow. She likes to have her feet wet. I don't go watering my apple trees every week like everybody else around here. I water 'em three or four times a season and then dust-mulch 'em, and I don't pick until after the frost. I've been farming this land for thirty years doing it this way and I've got the sweetest apples around." With a pause for breath he continued, "No, I don't have any sweet 'cots now. But I tell you what: I do have one tree of seed 'cots up by the chicken house that comes on early and you're welcome to pick as many of them as you want."

"I guess we will do that," I replied. "We'll come back and pay you for what we pick."

"Pay me? I said you could have 'em. You're friends of Lorianne."

A week later we returned and before we started to pick the fruit Raff continued our lessons in 'cots and dry-land farming. Taking us over to a large tree he picked a handful of apricots and handed them to us. The flavor was ambrosial, delicate as sunshine, firm as a nubile breast, unlike any apricot I had known, canned or fresh. "Now, crack that pit and eat the seed and you'll taste something you never tasted before," he said. It was essence of almond, apricot, and apple seed all rolled into one.

The talk of land and farming wove us together as we began to pick the ripe apricots. "You live alone, Raff?" I asked.

"Yes, except for those damn cats. I swore I would never have a cat. Too damn much trouble. And they get the birds. Then one night about four years ago some bastard dumped a little kitten out of his car over by my barn. Well, I heard this noise and after a couple of days I saw this kitten, and I said: 'I ain't feeding you, you ain't none of my business.' Couple more days passed and I saw that little kitten wobbling around so weak she couldn't hardly stand up. And I knew she was going to die." Raff's eyes began to tear up and he stopped for a moment to get back in control of himself. "So I got a saucer of milk and gave it to her, and I've had cats ever since. I just couldn't let her die."

"Raff," I asked, "how would I go about getting one of these sweet-pit apricot trees? Could I grow it from a seed?"

"No, that won't work. You've got to bud 'em to another tree. Come here, I'll show you," he said walking around to the back of the house with us in tow. Taking out his knife he cut a small branch from the sweet-pit tree and trimmed the bud off. Then, showing us as he talked: "You have to be careful to slice the bud off just under the cambrian layer. That way the juice is flowing. Then you slice a little nest on the limb of another tree and slide the bud in, like this, all the way down so the sap starts flowing into the bud immediately. Then you take a rubber band and bind it up tight to keep the air out. Now, I'll cut you off some buds and put 'em in a wet newspaper and you graft 'em as soon as you get home."

And that is how I found out about budding, got a sweet-pit apricot tree, and learned how fluid and earthy an old man can be in a dry and dusty place.

I have argued earlier that the ecological perspective provides the horizon within which modern men must come to understand themselves. But what can this mean for urban men? We can't go back to an agricultural economy. Few of us would want to spend our lifetime like Raff, nurturing an orchard and coming to know a small piece of land. No reading of social trends suggests the movement to cities will be reversed by a new wave of ruralization. Increasingly, men's lives are spent within urban environments, within buildings, seated at a desk, a conference table, a computer, or before a television. And the personality types that are most likely to get ahead in a competitive economy are those who are most adapted to dealing with abstractions.

And herein lies a danger and a dilemma. The most likely scenario for the future promises to be hazardous both to men's spiritual health and to the health of the natural environment.

There is no dignity for now and future men unless we assume our proper and necessary role as earth fathers and protectors of our place. As men, our vocation has something to do with being guardians of the future. When by the profligate use of our resources, our carelessness, our commitment to quarterly profit reports and immediate satisfactions, we squander the future that belongs to our children, we forfeit the right to consider ourselves honorable men. If we spawn children and do not care for them our virility is reduced to a biological cock-spasm.

I know of no single honorific that defines a man so much as the verb "to husband." The verb is at once genderal and nongenital. A husbandman may or may not plow and sow crops, but he certainly must take care of the place with which he has been entrusted. To husband is to practice the art of stewardship, to oversee, to make judicious use of things, and to conserve for the future. The image is as central to gay men, bachelors, and widowers living in high-rise apartments as to married or landed householders. Psychologically, the husbandman is a man who has made a decision to be in place, to make commitments, to forge bonds, to put down roots, to translate the feeling of empathy and compassion into an action of caring.

At the moment it is not where we live but how we live that prevents us from being husbandmen. The story is told about Flannery O'Connor, a novelist from a small southern town, who came to New York City to receive a prize for one of her books. At a literary cocktail party in her honor, she watched and listened to the assembled cognoscenti and was overheard to say, "These people aren't from anywhere." Our habit of constant movement, of severing of roots with place and people, and our consumer life-style keep us from belonging somewhere. Our quest for upward mobility keeps us moving on, every five years on the average, until we don't belong anywhere and can't go home again. We buy and sell property but are seldom landed or earthy. Most of us can't name the birds, plants, and trees that surround us, or predict from the fat on the squirrels how long the winter will be. Only a handful, mostly women, remember the lore of healing plants.

Nothing in the notion of husbanding limits the practice of this virtue to rural men. Certainly, we must husband the fields, forests, rivers, and air sheds and nurture them so that they will be productive and refreshing for centuries to come. But we can do this only by also designing and inhabiting our cities in more responsible ways. To husband the earth we need to create a new type of green city with public spaces and gardens, and political participation that invites people to make the city their place. Whether in the country, the city, or the suburbs, men must be grounded in a place. We must come to know our dwelling place, to care for it, to tend it over the years in such tangible ways that, like Raff St. Louie's orchard, it will cease to be an "it" and become a "thou," a living presence with which we live in an intimate relationship. The only way we can heal the wounds we have created in the psyche, the polis, the cosmos is by re-creating a marriage between person and place. That stuff and material that has since the industrial revolution been seen as George Gilder's "dirt, rock, and gunk" must once again become flesh of our flesh and bone of our bone.

After being on the road (less traveled) for a long time, the hero must finally have the courage to come home again and dwell in a single place, tend it, and make it rich with the treasure he has accumulated on his pilgrimage.

The Virtue of Wildness

The old fire road runs through the pines for several miles, winding its way around the shoulders of the mountain. The footing is good, so I let my horse step up from a trot into a slow gallop. But once the fire in her blood is lit, the wind fans her flame and she stretches her legs and burns the miles. I am riding with only a bareback pad, and the faster she runs the easier it is to find the still point behind her withers where I can sit motionless and become one with her motion, horse and man a single centaur. The road dips and passes through a swampy place. Aspens replace the pines, the underbrush is thick, and the roadway is muddy. I rein my mare down to a walk. She doesn't like it, but once or twice I have seen bears eating berries in this thicket and I don't want to surprise one in the middle of a meal. A half mile later the road climbs slowly back into the pines and runs along the top of the ridge, gradually narrowing until it becomes a footpath and then petering out completely, leaving me in the middle of a medium dense forest. I have never been here before, but I calculate that if I follow the ridge for a mile or so it should drop down and bring me out on the floor of the valley a mile below my home.

I approach a place where the ridge ends and the best path seems to be down a narrow canyon. Well into the canyon, picking my way through the brush, I notice a large ponderosa pine looming up ahead. Just as we reach the clearing, a mother bear and two cubs run in front of us and scamper up the tree. I dismount and stand quietly for a few moments to calm my horse, although western lore to the contrary, she seems not to be excited by the presence of bear. Best to be cautious, so I start to lead her around the tree, when suddenly I hear a loud bellowing roar and turn my head and see a large bear on the hill above me. Oh, my God, it was three cubs that ran up the tree! The mother bear was keeping guard, and here we are in the worst possible position—between her and her cubs, and no place to run. Raw fear telegraphs messages of "Emergency!" to every cell in my body. Should I jump on my horse and make a run for it? Send my horse running and try to climb a nearby tree? Yell and throw stones? Deep against the rising tide of panic, a quiet man I scarcely know instinctively takes command of the situation and orders me to continue walking calmly and slowly between the tree and the mother bear. I follow orders, and a hundred yards and a hundred years later I turn and see the mother bear disappearing into the brush in the opposite direction, leaving her cubs high in the ponderosa. I mount my horse and we ride down the mountain faster than we should, the trees and brush parting in front of us as if by magic. Some alchemy begins to transform the fear in my blood into a wild joy. Beyond all understanding, the man, the horse, and the bear have moved together within a preestablished harmony—wild creatures, tamed by bonds we cannot name.

In the beginning and the end, human beings are creatures of the wild. Within the parentheses of the city, and during the brief years of vigor between the helplessness of childhood and the helplessness of old age, we live within a space and time we domesticate by harnessing our cleverness and our will to control. But, finally, nature has its way with us and we are destined to return to that vastness beyond ourselves that we do not control.

Recently many men have become aware that they are overdomesticated and have lost a certain quality of wildness that is essential to manhood. Among men who identify themselves as belonging to a men's movement many have taken up drumming and dancing and have adopted native American rituals in an effort to recover their lost fierceness. These symbolic measures are helpful, but they may foster the illusion that we can discover our essential wildness solely within our psyches or within a new type of fraternity.

Wildness, first and foremost, comes from identification with the literal wilderness—rugged mountains, virgin forests, barren tundras, the habitat of untamed grizzlies, undomesticated wolves, fierce mountain lions. Wildness is no metaphor whose meaning we may learn when we are comfortably housed within a city or enclosed within the boundaries of the civilized psyche. We need large expanses of untouched wilderness to remind ourselves of the abiding fundamental truth of the human condition: We are only a single species within a commonwealth of sentient beings. When we forget this, we first kill off our coinhabitants and then destroy our own habitat.

Nor does the modern city provide the kinds of initiatory ordeals young men need. Sports, drugs, and gang membership replace the confrontation with the vast wilderness with its strange animals and unpredictable dangers. When a roving gang of adolescents attacked, savagely beat, and raped a woman jogging in Central Park in New York City, the newspapers reported that it was their custom to go "wilding." When we lose the natural wildness our need to test our wits easily gets perverted into violence against a socially designated enemy. There are still lessons best learned from meeting a bear on a trail or facing a storm at sea alone in a small boat.

After nearly a century of urban living, men's dreams still testify that we belong in the wilderness. We dream of breaking free and escaping to "a man's place" under the open sky, a place where physical strength counts and clocks do not dictate the rhythms of the day. It is hardly accidental that the Marlboro man is the most successful advertising image of all time. Urban, sedentary, housed men are still haunted by a longing for the outdoors, for being at home on the range, going on expeditions to remote places, living near to the land. The perennial presence of the cowboy within the pantheon of American heroes is evidence of men's psychological need for wilderness.

For twenty years I have been doing workshops on personal mythology, in which I ask participants to draw a picture of an environment in which they would ideally like to live. About ninety-five percent place themselves in rural settings, beside the sea, a lake, in mountains, or deserts.

The more we succeed in reducing the world to a controlled environment, the more we long for the wilderness. The preservation of wilderness is as necessary for our spirits to breathe fully and soar beyond the vistas of cement canyons and suburban patios as it is for the replenishment of oxygen and the survival of loons and bald eagles. We need a place where we can see life organized and vital without the imposition of our will, a place that is hushed, holy, and teeming with meaning and beauty that has not been fabricated or "improved" by human hands. Wendell Berry says it best: "Now it is only in the wild places that a man can sense the rarity of being a man. In the crowded places he is more and more closed in by the feeling that he is ordinary—and that he is, on the average, expendable. . . . You can best serve civilization by being against what usually passes for it."[16]

Our stance of scientific objectivity toward nature is useful but dangerous unless it is corrected by an attitude that is beautifully expressed in Chief Seattle's words: "We know the sap which courses through the trees as we know the blood that courses through our veins. We are part of the earth and it is part of us. The perfumed flowers are our sisters. The bear, the deer, the great eagle, these are our brothers . . . The earth does not belong to man, man belongs to the earth. All things are connected like the blood which unites us all. Man did not weave the web of life, he is merely a strand in it. Whatever he does to the web, he does to himself."[17]

So long as human life remains on the planet, we will live in relationship to three realities: the land we cultivate, the cities we fabricate, and the wilderness in which we dwell with all the other creatures in the commonwealth of earthly life.

*   *   *

These fragments I have collected for a portrait of now and future man at his best are only pieces of the puzzle, but one conclusion emerges from looking at them. Good men are not products of an instant. There is no Shake 'n Bake identity, no microwave masculinity, no easy formula for authentic manhood. We can't create ourselves overnight by willpower, guts, and hard work. Reinhold Neibuhr once said, "Nothing worth doing can be accomplished in a single lifetime." At the center of my vision of manhood there is no lone man standing tall against the sunset, but a blended figure composed of a grandfather, a father, and a son. The boundaries between them are porous, and strong impulses of care, wisdom, and delight pass across the synapses of the generations. Good and heroic men are generations in the making—cradled in the hearts and initiated in the arms of fathers who were cradled in the hearts and initiated in the arms of their fathers.

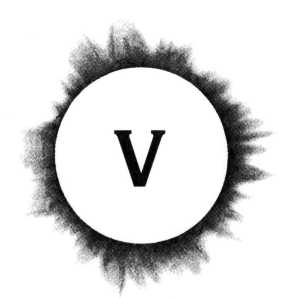

MEN AND WOMEN: COMING TOGETHER

LOVE: INTRODUCTION
TO A DANCE WITH
THREE MOVEMENTS

Men and women of goodwill are suffering from battle fatigue, but don't know how to stop the enmity between the sexes. The genderal consensus that was in place for centuries has imploded, and we are still in shock. Within a generation we have been bombarded by enormous changes—the pill, the sexual revolution, militant feminism, gay liberation, the economic and political emergence of women.

Lately the battle seems to be dwindling in intensity, and there is a hint of peace in the wind. Adam and Eve are winding down their propaganda campaigns, ceasing to throw apples and insults at each other, and are showing signs of wanting to return to being lovers. *Glasnost* and *perestroika* exist between the sexual superpowers. Our longing to be in each other's arms is growing stronger than our need to have a target for our hostility. We would like to come together again.

But how? How do we, who are veterans of so much combat in the erogenous zones, learn to love in a new way?

The first serious impediments to the growth of authentic

love between the sexes is the sentimental, romantic way we think about love.

Most often we talk about love as if it were all "Yes!" Two people in unbroken intimacy. Close. Intimate. Never having to say you're sorry. A warm fuzzy. The popular metaphors for love suggest liquidity: being swept away; waves of pleasure; softening; streaming; orgasm; egos dissolving; two becoming one; the right chemistry that produces fusion. Or we think of it as a state of permanent peace: opening up; vulnerability; lowering of defenses; surrender of separateness; an end to politics and power. In this sentimental view, love is the opposite of conflict. You are either loving or fighting, but not both. Carl Jung said, "Where there is love there is not power. Where there is power there is not love." In love there should be no boundary disputes, no personalities struggling.

I suggest the romantic notion of love is really a description of a harmful codependency.

Authentic love is a dance with three movements: solo, counterpoint, and coming together; it embraces solitude, conflict, and intimacy. Leave any one of the three movements out and you destroy the dance. In a love relationship, people stand alone and apart from one another, enter into respectful struggle with each other, and rejoice in their interdependence. In love, "No" is married to "Yes," elemental forces like flint and steel meeting but not mixing; an encounter in which I and thou stand firm.

True love is the only just and holy war. Two friends pledge loyal opposition to one another. I vow that I will defend the integrity of my separate being and respect the integrity of your being. We will meet only as equals; I will present myself to you in the fullness of my being and will expect the same of you. I will not cower, apologize, or condescend. Our covenant will be to love one another justly and powerfully; to establish and cherish inviolable boundaries; to respect our separate sanctuaries. We will remain joined in the sweet agony of dialogue, the contest of conversation, the dialectic of love until we arrive at a synthesis.

Thus far I have concentrated on exploring men's solo dance, on the assumption that a man needs to define himself apart from his relationships to women before he can discover in a woman a unique person whom he can love as a beautiful and flawed individual. Every prodigal son must leave his motherland (and every daughter her fatherland) before returning to enter fully into the dance of mature love. I have focused on constructing a map of a man's pilgrimage and tried to hear the first echoes of the new historical vocation that challenges the now and future hero. I have tried to keep the questions Howard Thurman put to me in my time of confusion in the right order, and focus on the nature of men's journey.

Now it is time to turn our attention to the other two movements in the dance of love, to return to womankind, to listen, speak "yes" and "no" and join hands once again. Time to move from solo to counterpoint, to coming together.

COUNTERPOINT:
LOVING COMBAT

Fierceness: Standing Firm and the Gift of Anger

Sometimes what looks like a fight is only the fierceness of love. At the moment, the honest struggle going on between men and women is less comfortable but more loving than the old false peace. We have moved from a condition of silent hostility, buried resentment, and covert low-intensity warfare to open conflict. So, the first thing we need to do is acknowledge the strong, strange interchange that is taking place between us. We are wrestling together, changing roles in the hay, engaging in honest intercourse, yessing and k(no)wing each other. And contact is the first condition of love.

Perhaps there is nothing more important for men to learn in their relationships with women than the difference between fierceness and violence. Fierceness is an expression of inner strength; violence is an expression of frustrated, unconscious impotence. One of the shadows that hangs over the male psyche, that makes authentic love between the sexes difficult, is men's predisposition to feel undifferentiated guilt in the presence of women and to resort to violence to deal with their impotence.

Until a man determines where he has injured and demeaned women, and learns to distinguish between appropriate
adult responsibility and guilt and inappropriate feelings of infantile guilt and shame, he cannot exorcise the unconscious image
of the demanding WOMAN before whom he perpetually stands
accused of being inadequate and guilty and begin to have loving
relationships with flesh-and-blood women. Until men can stand
firmly and say "No" to women (who being fully human are
wrong about half the time) they cannot say a wholehearted "Yes."
Marion Woodman, a Jungian analyst, writes, "The great danger
in our society is that a woman can believe that she has become
the independent Ms. when in fact she is merely animus possessed . . . In order for the real Ms. to emerge, the full feminine
has to be differentiated and integrated in relation to the mature
masculine. If she does work on herself, then, God willing, she
may meet a man who has the guts to put a bullet right through
the heart of her King Kong animus. Whether he does that with
anger or with unrelenting courage and faith depends on his
nature, her nature, and the nature of their relationship."[1]

Equality between men and women means that what is
true for the goose is true for the gander. In liberating themselves,
women undammed ancient rivers of anger and pain that swept
away much that lay in the path of the flood—the unjust and the
just. As men liberate themselves, they must also expect the
swamp of hostility to erupt into a deluge of uncomfortable
emotion that will certainly include torrents of rage and sorrow.

To say the least, it was not pleasant for men when women,
struggling for liberation, began to speak their bitterness. Every
man was branded a "chauvinist" and placed in the docket and
charged with being an oppressor. Not surprisingly, most men
reacted defensively. A few were capable of sensing the wound
beneath the attack, but most were so terrified by women's anger
they retreated. It has taken a quarter of a century for men of
goodwill to begin to sort out the charges made against us; to
plead guilty when we are guilty and refuse to accept unjustly
directed rage.

But we also have been injured by the gender system into
which we were born. We also have been battered and crippled as
we groped our way through the dark night of the unconscious
social roles we were indoctrinated to play. Struggling to fulfill a
thousand impossible expectations—to be competitive and gentle,
ruthless and tender, efficient and sensual, to take care of women
and treat them as equals—men have accumulated a sizable

burden of frustration and rage. We also have bitterness we must speak.

For men and women to love each other, we must learn to respect each other's anger. Presently, like porcupines trying to make love, we circle and try to avoid the barbs. We are so terrified of the residue of accumulated anger that has been generated by the battle between the sexes that we settle for superficial contact rather than risk expressing our deepest "negative" feelings and start a new round of warfare. But when we do not express our anger, we simmer in silent hostility and make ineffective love and war at the same time. We hone our defenses against each other at the same time we talk about peace. Not a very whole-hearted or hopeful way to live!

Men (and women) should be forewarned that, in the process of sorting out our experience, we will provoke female anger—both righteous and unrighteous. There is no reason to assume that as we begin to speak our bitterness it will be automatically wise, or that our anger will be appropriately directed. Some of the discoveries men make as they explore their intimate experience of manhood will be pleasing to women, others will not. As a rule, women cheer us when we become more sensitive to the nuances of feeling, when we surrender our compulsion to control. But women are no more anxious to hear about our anger and pain than we were about theirs.

As we move tentatively toward reconciliation it is helpful to remember that anger is a necessary part of the dance of love. Think of clean anger as the voice of the wise serpent on the early American flag who says, "Don't tread on me." Without anger we have no fire, no thunder and lightning to defend the sanctuary of the self. No anger = no boundaries = no passion. Good men and good women have fire in the belly. We are fierce. Don't mess with us if you are looking for somebody who will always be "nice" to you. ("Nice" gets you a C+ in life.) We don't always smile, talk in a soft voice, or engage in indiscriminate hugs. In the loving struggle between the sexes we thrust and parry.

Honor your anger. But before you express it, sort out the righteous from the unrighteous. Immediately after a storm, the water runs muddy; rage is indiscriminate. It takes time to discriminate, for the mud to settle. But once the stream runs clear, express your outrage against any who have violated your being. Give the person you intend to love the gift of discriminating anger.

Ideological Feminism—No! Prophetic Feminism—Yes!

Any man who hasn't spent the last twenty-five years watching Rambo movies or lobbying for the NRA has noticed by now that feminism has profoundly changed our cultural climate. Feminism isn't a passing storm; it is a permanent shift in the weather patterns. A generation of men have been inundated by feminist analysis, rhetoric, demands, and political programs. The women we most admire, fear, and struggle with are feminists. Many men were intimidated by feminism and chose to ignore its challenge. Others passively acquiesced to it, or uncritically accepted it, surviving on a spoon-fed diet of blame and guilt. What the majority of men have not done is confront the feminist analysis and worldview and sort out the healing treasures from the toxic trash. It is time to do it.

"Feminism" is a label that names a kaleidoscope, the many-faceted responses of a multitude of women wrestling with the question of self-definition, seeking social changes that will give greater justice, power, and dignity to women. There is no way to summarize the richness and plurality of this blossoming as women struggle to re-create the world closer to their hearts' desires. But for the purpose of locating one of the most important perceived threats to manhood, we need to make a rough and ready distinction between the best and worst of feminism, between feminism as a prophetic protest and feminism as an ideology.

Prophetic feminism is a model for the changes men are beginning to experience.

Ideological feminism is a continuation of a pattern of genderal enmity and scapegoating that men have traditionally practiced against women.

The distinction between prophetic and ideological feminism is largely a matter of mood, tone of voice, focus, emphasis, feeling-tone.

As a prophetic movement, feminism has been a perennial cry of the agony of women, a vision of what women may become and a celebration of the feminine. Since the beginnings of recorded "his-story" there has been a largely untold "her-story" of exceptional women who transcended the deadening status quo and came alive to the special pain and indignities that accompany the womanly condition. Remarkable women from Sappho to Joan of Arc to Isak Dinesen to Beryl Markham to Simone de Beauvoir were aware of the neglected and usually forbidden possibilities that slept curled within the feminine spirit. But not until a quarter of a century ago, with the publication of Betty Friedan's *The Feminine Mystique*, did the scattered voices become a chorus and a self-conscious woman's liberation movement become a politically potent force.

Among the enlightening perspectives and prophetic insights of the women's movement:

> Western culture has been dominated by patriarchy—rule by the men, of the men, and for the men.
>
> Patriarchy is rooted in hierarchy, obsession with power, control, and government by violence.
>
> Warfare, rape, and ecological destruction of "Mother" nature are rooted in patriarchal habits of thought and modes of social organization.
>
> Misogyny and gynophobia—a devaluation of all things considered "feminine"—form the subtext of Western "his-tory."
>
> A feminist vision demands sexual, artistic, economic, and political equality. (Military?) It further demands that men assume an equal share in the private sphere—the creation of hearth and the rearing of children.

For more than twenty years, a powerful community of feminist activists has worked to secure economic and legal justice for women, the right to equal access to the professions, to government-sponsored child care, to choice on matters of health, birth control, and abortion, among other issues. Feminist theorists have revisioned history, philosophy, language, and the arts in an effort to recover women's contribution to the intellectual life of Western culture.

Because it was born out of a painful awareness of the indignities and political disenfranchisement of women, prophetic feminism has remained aware of the wounding nature of the system itself—wounding to both men and women. It has remained proactive rather than reactive. The voice of prophetic women says: "We don't like the way this world is put together. It hurts. It demeans. It doesn't accommodate our gifts, or allow us to exercise our power. And we are going to change it."

Ideological feminism, by contrast, is animated by a spirit of a resentment, the tactic of blame, and the desire for vindictive triumph over men that comes out of the dogmatic assumption that women are the innocent victims of a male conspiracy.

Perhaps the best rule of thumb to use in detecting ideological feminism is to pay close attention to the ideas, moral sentiments, arguments, and mythic history that cluster around the notion of "patriarchy." "Patriarchy" is the devil term, the code word for the evil empire of men, the masculine conspiracy that has dominated human history since the time of the fall. All of the great agonies of our time are attributed to the great Satan of patriarchy. The rule of men is solely responsible for poverty, injustice, violence, warfare, technomania, pollution, and the exploitation of the Third World.

For instance, Betty Reardon argues that the war system is nothing more than the enforcement of patriarchy and that "patriarchy is the central core of the conceptual structure that determines virtually all human enterprise, both public and private."[2] Having established the single cause, the prime mover of history, the sermon continues in the spirit of Jonathan Edwards's "Sinners in the Hands of an Angry God." "Ecological destruction is, at its base, misogynist . . . it is simply another result of the masculine drive to control and dominate the feminine . . . The rape of the earth is the most apt metaphor for this defilement, a process that has led to the capacity to bring about the death of the ravaged planet. The fate of the Earth would thus parallel the fate of those millions of rape victims who have been murdered as a culmination of the initial crime."

I submit that honest men and women alike should object to such inflammatory language, circular reasoning, and self-serving logic. The threat of the desecration of the earth is too immediate an agony to be used in partisan warfare between the sexes. Without denying the guilt of men and the type of thinking that has traditionally been designated as "masculine" (scientific-technological-abstract) are we to excuse womankind from complicity and active participation in the spoiling of the environment? Go to any mall and watch the frenzied buying of the latest fashions, any landfill and see the mountain of disposable diapers and trash, any thrift store and count the discarded items of serviceable but no longer "stylish" clothes and appliances and it will be obvious that womankind is as compulsive a consumer as mankind. The disease of affluence that leads to the wasting of the earth infects women no less than men! While the majority of the world's population lives in involuntary poverty neither men nor women in "overdeveloped" countries have rushed to adopt an ethic of voluntary simplicity!

If contemporary men were to undertake a global repentance for everything that has happened in Western culture, should we, for instance, repent of the Renaissance or only the

Crusades; for inventing the printing press or only the atomic bomb? No one should take seriously the broadside attacks on patriarchal technology and the guilt trips that accompany them when they are launched by feminists who use computers, ride on airplanes, publish books (not handwritten), use telephones, televisions, record players, washing machines, hair dryers, and, if necessary, CAT scans. There is a bittersweet truth in Gloria Steinem's joke, spoken about the revolution in East Germany when watching the flood of people passing through the Berlin wall to see their relatives in the West and to purchase videos and consumer goods: "It was the first feminist revolution. There was no violence. And then everyone went shopping." There is an existential and moral fallacy involved in seeking to transfer all the blame for pollution onto the shoulders of men. The issue is not genderal. We all have dirty hands. How and whether we can envision a satisfying future, without the multiplication of technologies that increasingly threaten to pollute us out of existence, is one of the great koans and challenges of the present moment. It certainly will not be solved by simplistic sexist moralism.

The language that equates the destruction of the environment with "rape," sexual ravagement, and murder of victims of rape is a transparent device to indict men for the sins of both genders. By trying to shift all blame to men, Reardon implicitly claims a false innocence for women, and by trying to avoid all responsibility, she inadvertently reduces women to a position of impotence and victimhood.

The mythology of ideological feminism goes something like this: Once upon a gentle time we all dwelt harmoniously within the garden of the goddess. In those days life was organized around feminine values—cooperation, sensitivity, nurturance, sharing. Power flowed along matriarchal lines, and reverence for all things living was celebrated in worship of the goddess whose body was Mother Earth. And there was peace and goodwill and partnership among people. Then, beginning sometime between 4000 and 2000 B.C., from the North came the thundering hoof-beats of the patriarchal invaders, barbarian hordes of horsemen armed with swords sweeping into the peaceful agrarian, matrifo-cal cultures of India, Old Europe, Asia. They brought with them fierce and vengeful male gods—Zeus, Yahweh, and Allah—a warrior ethic, the habit of holy war, and a masculine mind that was henceforth to divide and conquer everything in its path—empires, women, and the atom. And the most disastrous of masculine inventions was technology itself, which gradually allowed men to conquer and destroy nature herself.

In short, recorded his-story has been one long tale of decline, until the rebirth of feminism, which remains our only hope for salvation. As Charlene Spretnak says, "How could anyone possibly propose that our present, i.e., patriarchal, culture with its ever-increasing alienation, materialism, suicidal destruction of nature, and sexist corruption is inherently superior to earlier cultures that were harmonious (e.g., citizens of goddess-oriented Crete and Old Europe enjoyed millennia of peace in unfortified towns) and egalitarian."[3] According to this limited view, our only hope for the future is in the rebirth of the goddess and the triumph of feminine values. To quote one of the more radically forthright of the ideological feminists: "At least three further requirements supplement the strategies of environmentalists if we are to create and preserve a less violent world. I) Every culture must begin to affirm a female future. II) Species responsibility must be returned to women in every culture. III) The proportion of men must be reduced to and maintained at approximately 10 percent of the human race."[4]

The following is a list of the characteristics of women and men, culled from articles in feminist anthologies that specifically identify themselves as dealing with "nonviolence" and "spirituality."[5]

Women developed agriculture.	Men invented war and technology.
Women worship nurturing, ecological goddesses.	Men worship destructive, divisive gods.
Women are life-worshipers—servants of Eros.	Men are death-worshipers—servants of Thanatos.
Women are naturally peaceful.	Men are naturally aggressive.
Women cooperate.	Men compete.
Women are empathic.	Men are insensitive.
Women are person-oriented.	Men are thing-oriented.
Women are egalitarian.	Men are hierarchical.
Women share power.	Men manipulate and dominate.
Women are the saviors.	Men are the problem.

In my recent book and PBS documentary *Faces of the Enemy*, I made a study of the archetypical images of the hostile imagination. By the analysis of political propaganda of many nations, I showed that when any people wishes to dehumanize and sanction the conquest, domination, or destruction of another people they inevitably revert to a certain standard repertoire of images and metaphors. In constructing the face of the enemy we always portray him as: aggressor, atheist, barbarian, liar, feelingless automaton, sadist, and rapist; as greedy, beastly, death-oriented, and conspiratorial. It is distressing to recognize how many of these epitaphs have been pressed into service by ideological feminists in the recent war between the sexes. As these feminists reconstruct history, the reign of "patriarchy," which is to say all of modern history, is the story of an invasion by barbarian hordes (male), the worship of false gods (male), the practice of a profane technology, and the destruction by a spiritually inferior class (men) of their spiritual superiors but political inferiors, and the rape of all things feminine.

This type of demonic theory of history renders men responsible for all of the ills of society, and women innocent. If there is warfare it is because men are naturally hostile and warlike, not because when tribes and peoples come into conflict it is the males who have historically been conditioned, trained, and expected to fulfill the role of warrior. If there is environmental pollution it is not because it is the inevitable result of the urban-technological-industrial life-style that modern people have chosen, but because of patriarchal technology. (One of the saddest examples of this tendency to blame comes from the dedication of a recent book on the goddess, in which one of the authors says of her son who was tragically killed in an automobile accident that he was killed by "patriarchal technology.") And if there is injustice in society it is not because some men and some women are insensitive to the sufferings of others but because white male oppressors dominate all women and people of color. Should a Margaret Thatcher, Indira Gandhi, Imelda Marcos exhibit signs of the pathology of power, an ideological feminist will hasten to explain that she has been colonized by patriarchal attitudes. And if Jesus or Gandhi exhibit heroic compassion it is because they, unaccountably, have learned to practice "feminine" virtues.

We also need to question the historical romanticism of feminist ideology. It is always a good idea to be suspicious of nostalgic histories that look back to golden ages, because they hide an inquisitorial program for the future. Be careful what you "remember" because it will give shape to your hopes and dreams. Feminists are right to point out that identifying God as he, as father, sanctioned the domination of women by men. If God is male, then clearly men are more divine than women, more spiritual, more ordained to rule. There is no reason to suspect that reversing the gender and worshiping the goddess will produce anything except another program for genderal supremacy.

When God was a woman—Isis, Ishtar, Artemis, Diana,

Kali, Demeter—she was a terrible mother, as bloody as God the father. By a logic built into the metaphor of childbirth, the goddess required human sacrifice as the price for making the earth fertile. As Monica Sjoo and Barbara Mor write,

> "The ancient people believed that the fetus was entirely formed and fed from the mother's blood—and this was why women didn't menstruate during their pregnancies. . . . Expanding on the perceived power of menstrual blood, it was believed that the Mother as earth body needed strengthening and renewal through blood sacrifice; as her blood created creatures, so the blood of creatures was cycled back to her. What was taken from her by humans in the form of harvest had to be returned in human or animal sacrifice. . . ."[6]

Not unlike the male deities for whom "war was the father of all things," the Mother Goddess taught that all living things were sustained by death, and that blood was the fertilizer of life. If Nature is the goddess we must claim her dark and demonic sides, and not merely her nurturing qualities. She births and kills us. Kali—goddess of creation and destruction in Hindu mythology— was represented as having a plethora of breasts and necklace of skulls. To the millions of victims it could hardly have mattered whether they were sacrificed to the god of war or the Mother Goddess. Nor do we have any reason to believe that the temples of Crete built for the goddess were constructed by union labor. Slavery, forced labor, injustice are not modern or "patriarchal" inventions.

To point to goddess-worshiping societies as models for moderns is a bit like encouraging kids from the Bronx to emulate Grizzly Adams or Daniel Boone. In most premodern cultures the experience of the rhythm of the seasons and the cooperation with "Mother" earth was the daily bread, visceral sanity, and tangible hope all rolled into one. Nobody in those cultures "believed" in the goddess. The assumption of the motherliness of being was homogenized into every atom of their experience. It was the way things "really" were. Now, centuries later, with "Satanic mills" (William Blake) belching out smoke, with three percent of a population growing the food for the other ninety-seven percent, "getting and spending we lay waste our powers: little we see in Nature that is ours" (Wordsworth). "Soiled" has come to mean "dirty," and most of us are so far from the visceral reality of growing things, from digging and planting, tending, waiting, and harvesting that to counsel us to adopt the metaphor of the goddess is a counsel of shallow hope. To remember a time when we were hunters, gatherers, and planters points to the distance of our exile. But we are no prodigal sons and daughters who may return to our mother's bosom, because we have neither the desire nor the ability. To do so we would have to leave behind our machines, shining chariots and magic theaters. True enough, "small is beautiful." But we have fallen in love with what is large, fast, and convenient, and we are in too much of a hurry to wait for anything to grow. To make the goddess organic to our experience, we would have to plant ourselves once again in some habitat and stay put for enough generations to relearn the wisdom of composting, and the secrets of sowing by the moon and harvesting the apples the day after they had been sweetened by the frost. I wish fervently for a community of more earthy cohabitation, a body politic that would reverence and take more of its pleasures, and therefore its metaphors, from the humus. But unless that happens it is much more likely that we will experience ourselves as created in the image of the computer (with DNA as genetic "information," mind as cybernetic feedback, and psyche as biosocial programs) than in the image of the Mother. The lace on that dark veil through which we catch our only fleeting glimpse of what is ultimate is woven from the metaphors that describe those things we value most.

Feminine theological metaphors—the goddess, Mother Nature—were creative in their time. They helped men and women feel on a familiar standing with their world and adjust to the seasonal rhythms of the natural world. But they were replaced by masculine theological metaphors—God the Father, God the Son—at a period in history when men and women began to rebel against servitude to nature. The transcendent, male God sanctioned the development of individualism and the technological impulse to seize control and have dominion over the earth.

Nearing the year 2000, both of these genderal theological metaphors have outlived their usefulness. I suggest that the time has come to cease using genderal metaphors for God or nature. It is more confusing than helpful to speak now of God as "Father" or the Earth as "Mother." We need to find metaphors that do not build a genderal claim of superiority into our way of theological thinking and spiritual practice.

Another consequence of the simplistic effort to assign responsibility for violence to men and peace to women is to confirm the very stereotypes of women that feminists have otherwise been fighting against. Two Canadian psychologists, Lori McElroy and Tana Dineen, point out that: "A major objective of the feminist movement has been to challenge gender-stereo-typed divisions in our society. Yet, although we have been quick to reject stereotypes that view women as man's inferior, we seem now reluctant to challenge stereotypes emerging in the peace movement that view woman as man's superior. This assumed superiority of women is evident in the image of woman as peacemaker and man as warmonger . . . If as women we would stop identifying solely with our biological function, we could start identifying with the human species and begin to accept some responsibility as part of the cause as well as part of the cure for the state the world is in."[7]

Prophetic feminists can see the loopholes in ideological feminists' argument that all women belong to a disenfranchised and oppressed "class." Early on, many feminists borrowed the categories oppressed minorities and colonial peoples used in their fight against racism and imperialism to press their case against "the patriarchy." All men, by definition, became guilty of sexism and all women, by definition, were victims. By includ-ing all women in the same oppressed "class," Eva Perón and Rosa Banks were seated side by side in the back of the same bus.

The notion that women are a class or a repressed minority like migrant workers, blacks, Indians in America, or Jews in Germany, trivializes the pain involved in class structure and the systematic abuse suffered by ethnic minorities. The injustices that go with class and race are too severe to be confused with the gender problem. All upper classes are composed of equal num-bers of men and women. The fruits of exploitation are enjoyed equally by men, women, and children of the upper classes as the outrages of exploitation are borne equally by men and women and children of the lower classes. Both class and ethnic minori-ties suffer real oppression.

There is one certain mark of oppression. Oppressors have greater access to comfort and health care, and thus live longer than their victims. In technologically developed nations since early in the twentieth century, women have outlived men by an average of eight years. Blacks, as an oppressed minority, have shorter life expectancies than WASPs. It is an insult to the oppressed of the world to have rich and powerful women included within the congregation of the downtrodden merely because they are female.

To the degree that any of us have inherited or unequal power, money, talent, etc. and have profited from the system we share greater responsibility and guilt than the disenfranchised and the powerless. Wealthy and powerful men are more responsible than poor and powerless men. The same holds for women.

The first step in giving up the easy comforts of ideology is to get down and get dirty—together.

For starters, men need to listen to feminist ideology with a sense of irony and repentance. Ever since Adam, men have been blaming their problems on women. Women have been systematically accused of being temptresses, seducers, powerful contaminants. And if they were viewed as the weaker sex they were nevertheless blamed whenever a scapegoat was needed.

But the cause of reclaiming female dignity and achieving greater economic justice for women will not be well served by sexist ideology. In this direction lies a dead end. A switch in the dialectics of blame from women to men only keeps the old game alive and ensures that the battle between the sexes will continue. We need to find new ways of thinking about men and women, and about the painful and marvelous ways in which we have related and may relate to each other.

Goethe once said that most sects were right in what they affirm and wrong in what they deny. Feminists of all sorts are right to be outraged by the dehumanization, destruction, and desecration caused by the modern corporate-industrial-warfare system. They are also right to indict men for their role in creating and maintaining this system, and right to insist on masculine guilt. They, however, are disastrously wrong in excusing women from responsibility and culpability for the destructive aspects of a cultural system that can only be created and perpetuated by consensual interaction of men and women (especially the men and women of the elite, powerful, privileged, and ruling classes). So long as we do not break out of the ideological way of dealing with human alienation by assigning blame to the other—the enemy, the devil, a special class, a gender—we perpetuate a diagnosis that leads us to treat the disease in a way that makes it worse rather than better.

The rhetoric that pronounces men responsible and women innocent belies everything we know about psychological dynamics and the interaction between persons in a system. Perhaps the greatest single advance in psychological and social theory in the last fifty years has been the emergence of systems-thinking. Group therapy, family therapy, the Alcoholics Anonymous movement are all based upon the discovery that power, responsibility, action, blame are shared by all participants within a system. In intimate systems, such as a family or a sexual relationship, all parties play dovetailed roles. The bumps on her head fit the holes in his head. An alcoholic wife requires an enabling husband, a rebellious teenager requires a family that avoids its problems by designating him the patient, the woman "who loves too much" requires a "dance-away lover." In short, the relationships of persons within intimate systems are codependent.

Unfortunately, this seminal insight has not yet been applied to the relationship of men, women, and warfare. At the present time, in the genderal system, men seem to be the identified patients and women the innocent parties. But, in fact, we are all still playing set roles in an economic-warfare system we have conspired to create. That the claim of victimization is an accurate description of the complexity of the relationships between men and women is a matter needing much analysis and discussion.

When ideological feminists place men in the docket and charge them with crimes against humanity there are three relevant questions: 1. Is the accuser really innocent or should she be a codefendant? 2. Was the accused in full possession of his faculties when the crime was committed, i.e., was there "diminished capacity" and therefore diminished responsibility in either or both of the genders in question? 3. Can we establish that the defendants—men—were conscious (therefore responsible and guilty) conspirators and that the accusers—women—were unconscious (therefore innocent) victims?

One of the phrases that has paralyzed moral discussion in the last generation is: "Don't blame the victim." But without noticing it, we created a kind of philosophical sanctuary of victimhood into which both the truly innocent and the guilty could retreat. Henceforth anyone worthy or unworthy could claim "victimhood" and diminished responsibility. The syllogism went as follows: Don't blame the victims; I am a victim; therefore, don't blame me. Any person, ethnic group, gender, or class in society could project the blame for their condition elsewhere. Alcoholism, workalcoholism, drug addiction, sex addiction, compulsive gambling, stealing, prejudice, child abuse all became conditions that were designated as "diseases" of which people were victims.

All ideology paralyzes moral reasoning. The task of reasonable men and women, and courts of law, is to try to weigh innocence and guilt on a scale that ranges from zero to one hundred percent depending upon the degree of freedom, insight, and range of opportunities that exist. Severely mentally retarded persons are judged to have little moral responsibility for their actions; abused children who become parents and abuse their children are judged to have slightly more responsibility; public officials who are graduates of Ivy League universities are judged to be almost completely morally responsible for their actions.

We have, as Joen Fagen says, "undergone a massive social shift. Several hundred years from now . . . we will recognize that the most significant event of the last half of the twentieth century has been the emergence of the victim. This began with women and blacks, spread to gays, and rape victims, and children of alcoholics and Vietnam veterans. . . . We are about to be flooded with pain, with the stories, the details of abuse of men, women, and children that have not been told. . . ."[8]

In this atmosphere, the only ones left to be responsible and therefore guilty were the heterosexual, WASP, male establishment. It was only a matter of time before the accused also began to feel themselves as victims. In both trivial and profound ways, men have begun to claim victim status and have ceased to swallow the blame imputed to them by feminists and minorities. The privileged and powerful have begun to feel the wound that comes with the territory—the stress, burnout, alienation, emptiness, that results from striving and the resentment by others of their success. As men become aware that they also inherited their status and were assigned their social roles before they appeared on the scene, they are also beginning to feel victimized.

And a backlash has grown. Men are angry because they resent being blamed for everything that has gone wrong since Adam ate the apple. Yes, we felt guilty because we went to useless wars (but what right do women who were in no danger of draft or combat have to criticize?) Yes, we feel guilty because we created technologies that proved to be polluting (but didn't women, the poor, and the underdeveloped nations crave all those dishwashers, TVs, new cars, labor-saving devices?) Yes, we feel guilty because we were born white, middle-class, and on the fast track to power and prestige (but haven't the women we married encouraged us to succeed and provide?) Men learned in the last decade that they were guilty by definition. It has never been clear what they were supposed to do to atone for their guilt. Change the system overnight? Call off the march toward the high-tech future? Give up power, prestige, and positions?

It's easy enough to scoff at majority men's awareness of wounds and feelings of victimhood, to suspect them of crocodile tears. But I suggest something far more interesting than hypocrisy is happening when men begin to feel the pain and poverty of their positions. When the powerful begin to feel their impotence, when the masters begin to feel their captivity, we have reached a point where we are finally becoming conscious that the social system we have all conspired to create is victimizing us all. Men have begun to feel their unique form of the pain of victimization that has led to other liberation movements among women and minorities. Until recently, we have all been unconsciously playing assigned roles in a drama that we were not aware of having created. THE SYSTEM is running us all.

Is no one responsible? No one guilty? No one to blame? Are we fated to play predestined roles in a techno-economic-social system that is stuck on automatic pilot?

Fate is changed into destiny by awareness. The first act of freedom is the willingness to see how we have been enslaved. The system binds us only in the degree that we choose to remain unconscious.

At the moment, sensitive women and men are both somewhat depressed by the overwhelming complexity and seeming intractability of the techno-economic-gender system that is oppressing our psyches and destroying our ecosphere. But our depression can turn into a sense of empowerment when we begin to look carefully at the way men and women interact in a codependent way to maintain the system. When both sexes feel the fatedness of our separate but equal existence, when we both feel the rage and impotence of being victims, the scales inevitably begin to tip and we begin to feel the other half of the truth— our freedom and potency to change. Only unconsciously chosen systems have the face of fate.

We have this advantage over the ancients. They thought their fate was written in the stars, that they were determined by natural forces over which they had no control. We sometimes flirt with the notion that a selfish gene or an excess of testosterone dooms us to a brutish future, but by and large, we have come to believe in human freedom. We know that the surplus suffering of men and women of all colors comes from a social system that is a human construction. If we do not change our economic-political-social-genderal system, then the fault will lie "not in our stars but in ourselves, that we are underlings." The fault will not be with woman because she gave us the apple, nor with man because he created technology, but with all of us because we preferred the easy way of remaining victims and blaming others for our condition. Our hope lies in taking on the difficult task of dismantling the social system that has made men the way they are and women the way they are. We are free. Whether we exercise this freedom or wallow in blame and victimhood is also a matter of choice.

Ending the Blame Game

To end the painful dynamics that cripple both men and women, we must first lay bare the pathology of the "normal" relationship between the sexes and understand the rules that bind us as antagonists in a genderal blame game. Here is a review of the rules we need to become conscious of, in order to break them and reconstruct our relationships:

Rule 1. Antagonists in warfare and the gender game are made artificially alien to one another. Strangers are turned into enemies. Differences are viewed as deviations.

The gender game begins with an artificial separation of masculine and feminine qualities, an act of intellectual and psychological fascism that forces the complex beauty of actual men and women into the two-column goose-step of "masculine" and "feminine" attributes.

Rule 2. The definition of men and women in the gender game has been created by a process of exclusion and negation. We are not-they.

Manliness and womanliness are both defined by a process of decision, and denial. Each gender is assigned half of the possible range of human virtues and vices. To be manly is to be unwomanly; therefore misogynistic. To be womanly is to be unmanly; therefore misanthropic. We do not know what human beings would be like if encouraged to develop their innate promise without the systematic crippling effect of the gender game. Every man and every woman is half of a crippled whole.

Rule 3. In the antagonistic gender game, the players may switch positions (one-up, one-down, sadist-masochist) from time to time.

Rule 4. The game requires the players to remain unconscious of their roles. Blind passion is the logic of history. We go to war blindly. Only mature love is fully conscious.

Rule 5. Since the players must remain unconscious for the game to continue, cultural institutions must inform each new generation in a way that will create an unconscious compliance with the roles. The rites of passage that confirm boys and girls in the appropriate manly and womanly virtues are rituals that inculcate belief and obedience, not reflection. If the roles are questioned the game is disturbed.

Rule 6. Blame is a central propaganda strategy in all forms of warfare, including the battle between the genders. It is used to deny responsibility and guilt and to take refuge in surplus impotence. "It's not my fault. We couldn't help it. They did it to us."

Rule 7. A game keeps all players equally secure in their roles but rewards each differently. In the traditional man-woman game, the payoffs were as follows:

Men got the feeling of power.	Women got the power of feeling.
Men got the privilege of public action.	Women got the privilege of private being.
Men got responsibility and the guilt that goes with action.	Women got innocence and the shame that goes with passivity.
Men got the illusion of control.	Women got the illusion of security.

Rule 8. From within the horizons of the gender game, one player will be defined as active, powerful, and sadistic, and the other as passive, impotent, and masochistic.

Rule 9. Only from beyond the horizons of the gender game can both players be seen as cocreators of the social system that supports the game. The interactions between the active-aggressive (traditionally male) and the passive-aggressive (traditionally female) partners in the game are symmetrical and equally "powerful." The battle tactics and repressive power of the passive-aggressive or masochistic partner are no less manipulative for being covert rather than overt. Control can be exerted from either the top or the bottom. Both players are also equally impotent, insofar as their roles are unconscious or free, insofar as their roles become conscious.

Rule 10. The game ends when either player jumps out of the horizon of the game and begins to examine the social system that keeps both genders defined in a hostile-dependent, mutually exclusive, competitive way.

The blame game that binds the sexes in antagonistic interaction seems too intricate and ancient to end. It colors and distorts the very fabric of man-woman relationships in our culture. How is it possible to break a habit that is so deeply ingrained?

Fritz Perls, one of the founders of Gestalt psychology, had a paradoxical theory of change. He suggested that the first step in making major changes in personality happens when we stop trying to change. In the beginning *do* nothing. Observe. Watch your conduct, your feelings, your interactions with the objective eye of a scientist. Study the ways you blame others or allow others to blame you. Do you most often play the role of the blamer or the blamee? Notice the different kinds of power and payoffs that go with each role, how self-righteous you feel when you transfer the blame to somebody else, how innocent you feel when you are only the victim. Explore the dynamics of guilt and shame. How do you manipulate others by making them feel guilty? What do you like about being the dominator? The dominated?

The second step is taking responsibility for your habitual roles, feelings, actions, and values. Other people cannot make you feel inappropriately guilty without your complicity. By becoming the observer of your conduct and the arbiter of your values you reclaim the responsibility and power to judge your own life. The only way out of the infantile blame-guilt game is by the assumption of mature responsibility.

The fastest path to ending the blame game is a committed relationship in which two people agree to work together at the process of becoming conscious and compassionate. Helpmates may intentionally interrupt routines and switch positions for a time. Reverse the missionary position. She may become dominant and he submissive. Or vice versa. He may experiment with being a househusband and she the breadwinner. Together they may playfully exaggerate their gender—typical ways of behaving until they become comical—he Tarzan, she Jane—and each begins to acquire the knowledge of the opposite. In Greek mythology, Teiresias, a blind sage, was said to be especially wise because he had once been changed into a woman for seven years and therefore knew the ways of both sexes. A conscious love between man and woman is the royal road to wisdom and compassion.

When we do break the blame game, where does it leave us?

We are still in the same mess that prophetic feminists and radical men have described. The world is dangerous, threatened, and wounding. There can be no question but that the historical humiliation of women, the demeaning, the cruelty reported by feminists is a fact. But men's suffering from gender roles is also a fact. We can make a rough measure of the difference in the sufferings of master and slave, conqueror and conquered, elite and underclass on the scales of justice. But on what scale can we weigh the pains and pleasures that attend the differing life-experience of men and women? And where would we find a weigh-master whose judgment was gender-neutral? (If you were going to be reincarnated and were considering only how much pleasure you would experience in your next lifetime, would you choose to return as a man or a woman?)

The healing of the relationship between the sexes will not begin until men and women cease to use their suffering as a justification for their hostility. It serves no useful purpose to argue about who suffers most. Before we can begin again together, we must repent separately. In the beginning we need simply to listen to each other's stories, the histories of wounds. Then we must examine the social-economic-political system that has turned the mystery of man and woman into the alienation between the genders. And, finally, we must grieve together. Only repentance, mourning, and forgiveness will open our hearts to each other and give us the power to begin again.

BECOMING TOGETHER

Intimacy: How Close Is Close Enough?

Every culture has a different notion of the proper distance that should be maintained between the sexes, how close husbands should be to their wives, how close fathers should be to their sons and daughters, how close brothers should be to their sisters. In some tribes, men lived together in a men's house and visited their wives only rarely. Among the Sambia in New Guinea, where boys were taken away from their mothers, were initiated into men's society, and practiced homosexual rituals until marriage, men and women were considered to be enemies who should have little to do with each other. The most common view of men and women in world mythology, however, is that they are incarnations of separate but equal masculine and feminine cosmic principles—the yin and yang of things—that dovetail in all forms of creation.

Until recently, modern men and women embraced the romantic myth that celebrated the differences between the sexes but held out the hope of an eventual ecstatic union—two hearts beating as one. Together (with baby makes three), they made up the private world of the family in which all needs for "intimacy" were to be satisfied.

Beginning sometime in the 1960s a new sexual myth began to inform American society—the unisex myth. Fueled by the movement of women from the home into the job market, the old rigid definitions of gender crumbled. Sporting their newly acquired habit of aggression, credit cards, and birth control pills, women discovered they could do most anything a man could do. (In theory at least. In practice the old-boy network dragged its feet.) It wasn't long before a host of psychologists and social theorists were suggesting that almost all the differences we associated with gender were socially constructed. Feminists insisted that a little girl given a screwdriver to play with is as likely as a little boy to become a mechanic. With enough behavioral rewards and reinforcements, and a political system committed to full equality, we could condition men and women to be indistinguishable (except for the obvious "biological" equipment which has no deep "psychological" or characterological significance). A generation of hippie men tuned in, turned on, dropped out, became softer, and wore long hair. Among the more affluent, unisex haircuts and boutiques became the rage. Across town in the financial district, the new working woman practiced her opposite but equal style of unisex. She bought a briefcase, and began power-dressing in the "masculine" subdued gray, blue, and pin-striped suits that were the uniform of the upwardly mobile executive.

In the world of psychology, some believed that the unisex myth was manifesting Carl Jung's belief in the androgyny of men and women. In Jungian analysis, to become whole, men must discover their feminine side—their "anima," or soul. To become whole, women must explore their "animus," or worldly and aggressive side. In his spiritual journey, a man turns inward, to the feminine essence of his soul-anima, and explores the womanly feelings he has previously rejected. A woman, in turn, plunges into the rejected masculine fierceness and aggression necessary for her to act effectively in the world. The end of the process is that each man and woman must first consummate an inner marriage between the masculine and the feminine before he or she can relate realistically to a member of the opposite sex.

In passing I should note that I find the whole notion of the marriage within the psyche between "masculine" and "feminine" qualities as confusing as the use of genderal language about God. In my own experience, I can locate nothing that feels "feminine" about holding my daughter in my arms, allowing myself to be comforted, weeping for the pain of the world, or exercising my intuition. Nor do I feel "masculine" when I am chopping wood or riding my horse down a steep mountain trail. I am as much a man when I am being tender as when I am fierce, as much when I am surrendering to a current of feeling as when I am aggressively trying to bring some order into chaos. Pasting simplistic labels—"masculine," "feminine"—on the feelings and modes of perception and action is like trying to make people goose-step in orderly ranks. Good men and women alike can be characterized as compassionate, aggressive, nurturing, powerful, intuitive, reasonable, playful, wise, erotic, or loyal. With the single exception of bearing children, a good man can do anything a good woman can and vice versa. Likewise men and women share equally in the capacity for greed, cruelty, violence, and the desire to dominate those who are less powerful than themselves.

There is an obvious difference between men and women, but that has no relationship to the supposed differences between "masculine" and "feminine." In my judgment, we would gain much clarity if we ceased using the words "masculine" and "feminine" except to refer to the stereotypes of the genders that have been historically predominant. Far better to remain with the real mystery of man and woman than the false mystification of the masculine and the feminine. As nearly as I can tell, I, being a man, have nothing feminine about me. For me, feeling proud of being a man involves practicing the virtues of repentance, compassion, patience, carefulness, etc. My virility is inseparable from opening out, receiving, embracing.

A large part of the appeal of the unisex myth was that it encouraged the hope that if we were essentially similar, then perhaps we could end the war between the sexes and see each other as allies. What remains appealing about the idea is that, if we are androgynes, then we already bear the other within ourselves. The stranger is only the unclaimed part of the self. The gulf that seems to separate the sexes is an illusion, and we can now be close without threatening each other. With artificial role divisions erased, men are free to become househusbands and women to be breadwinners. The notion of "fathering" or "mothering" can be replaced by the gender-neutral notion of "parenting." If there is no intrinsic disposition that is connected to our gender, for all practical purposes men and women are not only equal but the same.

Now, however, the unisex myth seems to be losing even more points on the Dow Jones Mythic Index for a number of reasons.

Psychologists report a new sexual disease among the affluent: Two-Careers-No-Sex. Ten years ago therapists reported "the new impotence"—men's fears in the face of the new aggressive feminists. The new complaint is: No desire. Men and women on the fast track pour their eros into their careers.

As men and women both engage in careers, for the first time, the hidden tyrannical logic of economic competition with its drive for "growth" is becoming clear. Women who gave up marriage and home (although not romance or sex) for success are having second thoughts. On Broadway, *The Heidi Chronicles* traces the loneliness and dissatisfaction that accompanied one woman's choice of a professional life. A joke in a recent magazine shows a harried woman sitting at an executive desk, placing a call to Gloria Steinem and saying, "Remind me what was so bad about staying home with the kids."

Both women and men are becoming disenchanted with the unisex ideal and are reclaiming the uniqueness of the sexes and exploring the differences between the genders. Frills are "in" for women, and the rugged Ralph Lauren urban cowboy look is "in" for men. Financially successful women are exploring *Goddesses in Everywoman* with Jean Bolen,[9] and men are flocking to hear poet Robert Bly talk about recovering "the wild man." Without losing their hard-earned rights to economic equality, women are questioning whether they want to devote their lives to the career track. Many professional women and men are deciding to sacrifice their careers to enrich their private lives: demanding flextime, job-sharing, maternity and paternity leave, sabbaticals for pursuing personal enthusiasms.

In looking at men and women we may choose to stress the similarities or the differences between them. Are we alike enough that we may understand each other's intimate experience. Or are we so different that we can only listen to the other—respectful strangers meeting within a sanctuary where plurality is cherished? Does the best hope for love arise out of perceiving the distance between men and women as near or far? H.L. Mencken once said that the person who coined the term "near beer" was a very poor judge of distance. I suspect the same error in judgment in the effort to eliminate the distance between men and women.

Modes of Being Together

Needless to say, all relationships between men and women are not intimate. There are many modes of relationships, and each

may be authentic and satisfying so long as the goals and limits
are understood and agreed upon by all concerned. Confusion and
injury result when we do not understand the logic that governs
our different ways of being with each other. He wants sex and
she romance. Or vice versa. She expects friendship and he expects
only collegiality. In the ascending order of completeness, intensity, and wholeheartedness of passion the relationships are:

1. In work relationships, a function (that happens to be performed by a male) is coordinated with a function (that happens to be performed by a female). By definition, the
   instrumental relationships that govern economically oriented
   activities do not and cannot involve the fullness of gender or
   personhood. Neither men nor women can "humanize" (or
   "feminize") business and professional relationships sufficiently to include the full promise of manhood or womanhood.

2. In political relationships, a citizen (who happens to be male)
   joins with a citizen (who happens to be female) to exert power
   to secure a more just arrangement of the affairs of the body
   politic. Now and forever, men and women need to make
   common cause as citizens to ensure that justice remain blind
   with regard to race, color, sex, and creed.

3. In strictly sexual relationships a male body and a female body
   come together to achieve mutual satisfaction of sensory
   needs. Insofar as possible, (emotional, personal, and spiritual
   elements are not involved). The danger is that sex divorced
   from personal care easily becomes destructive of the fullness
   of both men's and women's sexuality. The playboy ethic in
   which a body (beautiful) meets a body (beautiful) leaves the
   spirit of a man and woman untouched and alienated.

4. In romance, a masculine persona and a feminine persona,
   each incomplete in itself, come together hoping to find emotional, sexual, and spiritual completion in the other. Romance depends on maintaining beautiful or pleasing facades.
   In romance, the socially created genderal selves meet; the
   pseudomasculine man meets the pseudofeminine woman and
   they live happily ever after, for better (but not worse), richer
   (but not poorer), and in health (but not sickness).

5. In friendship, two persons who happen to be of the opposite
   sex are drawn together for no reason other than mutual liking
   and enjoyment of each other's company. Although it may
   contain erotic tension, friendship is essentially "platonic."
   The moment friends become lovers the dynamics of their
   relationship change. At the present moment in history,

friendship between men and women is one of the great untapped resources for renewing the world.

6. In marriage, an individual man and woman join, for better and for worse, to create an arena within which they may individuate together and explore their wholeness with each other.

7. In seminal relationships, a man and woman join to create a child and an encompassing hearth.

8. In vocational relationships, a man and woman respond to, and are animated by, a common vocation and vision that situates their life together within a horizon that is larger than their hearth or immediate community.

Of these possible modes of relationship, those dealing with the full mystery of intimacy and sexuality, marriage, the creation of hearth and the common vocation of healing the earth, are most in need of exploration by men and women coming together again. And to these we now turn.

The Mystery of Man and Woman

Once we have stripped away all the false mystification of gender, an authentic mystery of gender remains. Beneath the facade of socially constructed differences between men and women, there is a genuine mystery of biological and ontological differences.

Gabriel Marcel proposed a distinction between problem and mystery that is helpful in thinking about gender. A problem involves questions that can be solved because the observer can gain objective distance, pose crucial experiments, and verify hypotheses. We know how to discover whether there is life on Mars or whether the AIDS virus responds to a specific medicine. A mystery at first appears to be merely a problem that is difficult to solve. Am I free, or is my life predetermined? What are the essential—noncultural—differences between men and women? A little reflection shows that in a genuine mystery the distinction between subject and object breaks down. A mystery is something in which I am involved. If, for instance, I ask: Should I commit myself to this marriage? or, Is there any meaning in life? there is no objective, scientific standpoint I can occupy to answer such questions. I cannot separate myself from my life— my will, my values, my sense of meaning, my gender—in order to get a definitive, verifiable answer to any of these questions.

There are more and less intelligent ways to explore and clarify the mystery of our lives but we cannot reduce the great mythic questions—"Where did I come from? What should I do? For what may I hope? What is a heroic man? What is a heroic woman?"—to problems that can be solved.

The question of gender is penultimately a problem, but ultimately a mystery. The social sciences can tell us how different societies structure gender roles, how they define heroes and heroines, how they educate, condition, and initiate boys into the status of manhood and girls into the condition of womanhood. In this sense we can strip away the false mystification that surrounds gender. But underneath the stereotypes lies a true mystery. God did not make persons,—chairpersons, mailpersons, or spokespersons—only men and women. Peel away the layers of the social conditioning and there remains the prime fact of the duality of men and women. Throughout the eons of history we move toward becoming fully human only through a sexual dance of men and women. Each sex is one side of a Möbius strip, a fragment necessary to create a whole.

The mystery of our sexual being is not something that can be settled by science. It is who we are and where we come from. It is deeper than our ability to abstract and objectify. We know more about it than we can ever explain or articulate. Every theory is more simplistic than the facts. Anthropology, sociology, psychology, etc., can show us how we self-limit and give social definition to the genders, how we form and deform. But it can never reduce the preconscious, presocial duality of the sexes to an adequate explanation.

There is a contemporary mind-set that wants to reduce gender to a problem we can solve, an inconvenience we can overcome, a mistake we can, finally, set right. The battle flag of this movement carries the slogan: "Biology is not destiny." Its hope is that, with proper social and biological engineering, women can be "liberated" from bondage to their wombs and from the degrading work of raising children.

Science fiction writers have best seen the logical consequence of this project to free human beings from "bondage" to biology. When gender becomes a problem to be solved rather than a mystery to be reverenced, science and technology can be counted on to produce a solution that will encourage human beings to become more like machines, computers, robots. As we engineer our way out of the bondage to gender, the values of the marketplace replace those of the family and efficiency triumphs over compassion. The encompassing arms of the mother and the muscular arms of the father are replaced by incubators and the care of professional, anonymous child-handlers. In due course, a world without gender makes obsolete those names we have invested with a numinous power only a little less than God's— Mother and Father. The unfortunate by-product of such a technologically rationalized, centrally planned, economically oriented society is that it destroys all the forms of love—friendship, erotic love, and worshipful—that make our lives sweet.

So, what's the difference between a man and a woman? I can't say, but that doesn't mean that I can't recognize the difference. A genuine mystery is protected by silence that remains after analysis and explanation. We approach the mystery of our being by respectful listening, by recollecting our experience, by cherishing paradox and, above all, by loving what we cannot reduce to understanding.

There is a way for man and woman to come together that does not depend on correct explanations, a language in which we celebrate the communion of opposites—in love and sex. When we penetrate to the deepest level of our experience of gender, we inevitably come to a point where the language of sexuality and spirituality mingle. Since the beginning of recorded human history, the phallus and vulva have been metaphors for the sacred. Carnal knowledge and spiritual awareness, the mystery of sexuality and the mystery of being, have been joined tongue in groove. Sexuality teaches us about the sacred, and vice versa.

> "They try to say what you are, spiritual or sexual?
> They wonder about Solomon and all his wives.
> In the body of the world, they say, there is a Soul
> and you are *that*
> But we have ways within each other
> that will never be said by anyone."

> "At night we fall into each other with such grace.
> When it's light, you throw me back
> like you do your hair.

> Your eyes now drunk with God
> mine with looking at you,
> one drunkard takes care of another."
> —Rumi, *Open Secret*[10]

The sexual and the sacred both shatter the categories of our understanding. After thirteen pages of careful reasoning about how we may give names to God, Thomas Aquinas concludes, "But finally we remain joined to Him as to one unknown." In the same way, man and woman are joined to each other as beings unknown, and we commune within a mystery that encompasses us. The love between us is a coming together and a going apart in which the fragments we are as sexual beings move together within the economy of an unseen whole.

Love increases the mystery of the self and the other. In love we learn to respect and adore what is beyond understanding, grasping, or explanation. Together we play our separate parts in the drama of creation. Strangers in the night, opposites joined in a passionate dance, keeping step to an echo of a distant harmony we must strain to hear. Moving toward and away from each other; two becoming one becoming two becoming one, ad infinitum.

Paean to Marriage: The Conjunction of the Opposites

Marriage is: an aphrodisiac for the mature; a great yoga; a discipline of incarnate love; a task that stretches a man and a woman to the fullest; a drama in which a man and woman must gradually divest themselves of their archetypes and stereotypes and come to love each other as perfectly flawed individuals.

As a spiritual path, a dance of individuation and communion, marriage begins on the far side of romance.

If you consider marriage a lifelong romance, you are certain to be disillusioned. The shallowest of complaints is that marriage destroys romance. Of course it does. Marriage is designed to allow two people to fall out of love and into reality.

In romance two people plant a seed in a common pot, fertilize it, water it, turn it toward the sun, rejoice when it buds and blossoms. When it flowers they believe it will last forever. But the greater the passion, the more the affair hastens toward its predestined climax. The plant is stifled by its own growth; it becomes rootbound. To continue to flourish it needs more room to grow. The time for decision arrives. Does the couple invest in a larger pot and transplant what has begun to flower between them, or do they abandon the plant and begin again? One way leads toward the deepening commitments of marriage, the other toward an addiction to romance that requires the changing of partners whenever passion, excitement, and intensity fade.

Recently I cleared a flat place by the stream that had been overgrown with thimbleberries and small alders. After cutting the underbrush, I pulled up plants and roots and cultivated the soil until it was fine and soft. I planted clover, watered it, and waited. Within a week the clover sprouted. Two weeks later thimbleberries charged out like bullies in a schoolyard. Impossible! I had destroyed their entire root system, ground them up into little pieces. I pulled up the offending youngsters by the ears and found that each had sprouted from a disconnected fragment of the original, and that the separate plants were already reaching out to form an interconnected network.

Love may blossom in romance, but in marriage we return to our deep psychic roots that are mysteriously alive no matter how many times they have been severed. Many of us—separated and alienated from our families of origin, divorced, veterans of many love affairs—are surprised when we approach intimacy and commitment to find infantile feelings, needs, expectations we had exiled or repressed come flooding back.

Why does marriage and the threat-promise of intimacy put our souls in a pressure cooker?

Romance is all "yes" and heavy breathing—an affair built around the illusion of unbroken affirmation. Marriage is "yes" and "no" and "maybe"—a relationship of trust that is steeped in the primal ambivalence of love and hate.

> Dear Jananne. I love and hate you: find you desirable and terrible, satisfying and maddening, a helpmate and a saboteur. I was rich and wounded in history long before I knew you. You are a nectarine grafted onto an apricot branch grafted onto peach root stock that goes deep into the ground of my being. In you I taste generations of women who have nurtured and injured me— my ex-wife, past lovers, my mother, my grandmother. One moment I am encompassed in your earth-mothering arms, tendered and warmed. A moment later I look into your face and see bloody Kali ready to devour me. I know you as a woman who can take up a flute and improve on the music of the spheres, and an hour later play the shrill bitch. Light-bringer and shadow monster, creator and destroyer. You delight me, except for those times I could wring your neck and dance a jig on your grave.

But marriage and the family may provide the best hospital for our ancient wounds. When we vow to marry for better and worse, we implicitly pledge our willingness to reopen the terror and beauty of innocence. The promise of childhood, the birthright each child genetically claims in its flesh, the cry of life is, "I deserve to be loved unconditionally." Our innate sense of our own goodness carries with it the innocent expectation that we are lovable in our entirety. But this promise is inevitably broken. All parents, all cultures, systematically stunt the young. Love is given on the condition that we are pleasing, that we perform well, that we obey the "oughts." Every child is expelled from the paradise of perfect love. We compromise and become adults. But the hope for unconditional love does not die, it only lies dormant. When we marry it springs to life again. Before God we vow the impossible secret hope of our heart, to love and cherish, without condition, so long as we both shall live.

Inevitably, marriage vows are put to the test. Will she really love me when she sees the worst; when she sees my sadness, my insecurity, my domineering, my little-boyish whining and bullying ways? Will he really love me when he sees my anger, my aggressive demands, my guilt-tripping manipulations, my seductive little-girl ways? Sure as night follows day, when the trust deepens between a man and a woman, their infantile selves will come out of hiding. I will play the brat I was forbidden to be, and you will play the bitch. We will cease being "nice" to each other. All the unfinished business I have with women in general and Mother in particular, all the unfinished business you have with men in general and Father in particular, all of the credits and debits of the Keen and the Lovett clans, become psychic soil that we two must turn over, plow, and tend together.

The alchemy of unconditional love that heals us only takes place when a man and a woman, knowing the best and worst of each other, finally accept what is unacceptable in the other, burn their bridges, and close off their escape routes.

As a rule, men fare better in marriage than when single. Studies show that married men live longer, are healthier, and make more money. But fidelity seems to come harder to us than to women. Common wisdom tells us that we are phobic about commitment, and that even when we are well married we continue to desire many women. Maybe we want sexual variety because we are programmed by evolution to sow our seed as widely as possible. Maybe we want numerous women to bolster our sense of our own masculinity. Whatever the reasons for our resistance to monogamy, the great virtue of marriage is that it presents us with a chance to heal the split within ourselves, between passion and tenderness, between our schizophrenic images of woman as whore or virgin. Until a man can look on the same woman with both respect and desire, he remains the victim of his own ambivalence—a boy-child, a playboy.

Cocreation: Familial Love and the Fatherhood of Men

In the last generation, far too much of our thinking about men and women circled around sexual skills, romantic love, and the changing dynamics of marriage in the era of the two-career family. Both men and women have increasingly divorced the discussion of gender from our biological and spiritual destiny as the bearer, nurturers, and initiators of children. To try to distance ourselves from the only creative act that requires the unique endowments of a man and a woman is certain to cause us confusion.

Sex may teach a man and woman the delight of coming together; marriage may suffuse us with the comfort and healing that comes from knowing and being known; but it takes a child to tutor us in the virtue of hope. In sex we forget ourselves and inhabit the present moment; in marriage we remember and heal the wounds of the past; in creating a child we invest all that we are in a future that extends beyond our days.

The starting point for thinking about the mystery of gender, for cherishing the ineradicable differences between the sexes, for celebrating the coming together of the opposites, is the procreation of a child. It would be folly to try to return to the silly and repressive medieval notion that only heterosexual acts between partners desiring to conceive a child are justified. But it seems to me equally foolish to think that we can explore manhood and womanhood, male or female sexuality, without placing children at the center of our attention. To retain our humanity we need to preserve something of the ancient feeling of the awful-sweet mystery of sexuality that is reflected in the worship of the creative phallus and the fertile womb. Primitive peoples know what we are beginning to forget—sexuality is wonderful and terrible because it is our link with the creative power of being, itself. If ever we lose sight of the ontological fact that human sexuality is defined by a situation that implicitly involves the triad of man-woman-child, we neglect something of the spiritual dimension of sexuality.

A strange kind of forgetfulness seems to affect much of the recent writing and thinking about men's liberation. The men's movement has allowed men to talk about how much we have been wounded by the missing father, how we long for the fathers we never knew, how insecure we feel because our fathers never initiated us into manhood. But then, strangely, the family is seldom mentioned as a major arena within which virility is exercised. Often men who suffer from the father vacuum resolve to be intimate with their sons and spend quality time with them, but somehow the family remains on the outer edge of men's circle of values.

I had been divorced for five years when I saw a billboard, smack in the middle of the smoggy, industrial section of Richmond, with the dire message: "Nothing makes up for failure in the family." My immediate reaction was to start an argument with the billboard evangelist, to defend myself and the multitude of my fellow divorcés who had broken up families for what we considered the best of reasons. "That's asinine! What a guilt trip! A good divorce is better for the kids than a bad marriage. And, anyway, divorce is not necessarily the sign of 'failure.' And, besides that, my kids are living with me and I am 'making up' their loss to them. And, and, and . . ." Not until I had exhausted my self-defense did I simmer down and let the full weight of the proposition sink in and think about it in a calm manner.

It has now been twelve years since I saw the billboard. My daughter and son from my first marriage are grown and lovely. I am remarried and I have a ten-year-old daughter. After considerable meditation on the matter, I have come to believe that the message of the billboard is both true and prophetic. In watching my children struggle with the hurts and discontinuities that are the inevitable result of the irreconcilable differences between their parents, I have learned what many men learn only after divorce. There is nothing more precious than our children. In the quiet hours of the night, when I add up the accomplishments of my life in which I take justifiable pride—a dozen books, thousands of lectures and seminars, a farm built by hand, a prize here, an honor there—I know that three that rank above all the others are named Lael, Gifford, and Jessamyn. In the degree to which I have loved, nurtured, and enjoyed them, I honor myself. In the degree to which I have injured them by being unavailable to them because of my obsessive preoccupations with myself or my profession, I have failed as a father and as a man.

The health, vitality, and happiness of the family is the yardstick by which a man, a woman, a society should measure success and failure. I suggest that the decline of honor in family is directly related to the continuing cold war between the sexes, the escalating climate of violence and the sense of the vacuum of meaning that haunts our time. As far as I can see, there is no way for men and women to recover wholeheartedness, to become passionate and truly free, without rediscovering the central importance of the family. A man or woman without an abiding investment in family, children, and generations yet to come is a straw blowing in the wind.

To understand how crucial the existence of strong families is to the cultivation of free spirits we might meditate on the odd fact that the first target of tyrants and utopians of the political right and left is always the family. From Plato to Marx to Mao, all those thinkers who want society organized so individuals will fit into some overarching five-year plan for the ideal republic, the ideal socialist or religious state, inevitably try to replace the family and place the education of the young in the hands of state-run institutions. Under the banner of freeing women for productive work, or liberating the young from the prejudices of the old, or instilling the values necessary for an ideal commonwealth, parents and children are separated or allowed minimal contact. The motive behind this antipathy toward the family is not difficult to find. So long as men's and women's prime loyalty is to family and kin, they cannot be controlled by the state or any other institution. But if they can be convinced to switch their loyalty to some "higher" cause or institution, they will obey the dictates of their leaders.

For better and for worse, the family is the first line of defense against dehumanization and misplaced loyalty. Within the privacy of the home, we may think, speak, and worship as we please. We may educate our children in the values we cherish and teach them respect for the traditions we uphold. Because it is easiest to love our own children unconditionally, the family is the natural school of love. Loving our kin, we may gradually learn to extend kindness to strangers. And because children incarnate our hopes, they are our visceral evidence of the wisdom of investing our time and care in the lives of others.

Almost without noticing it, we are voluntarily eroding the freedoms and surrendering the loyalties that no tyrant could take from us without a fight. By our increasingly slavish devotion to the economic order, we are destroying the cradle of freedom. The iron law of profit is best served by those who are willing to depersonalize themselves by valuing efficiency above compassion, and devotion to the competitive goals of the corporation over loyalty to family.

A history of the word "economics" contains a parable that illuminates our present dilemma and offers a challenge to men and women. Originally "economics" meant "the art of managing a household" and it contained the notion of thrift and voluntary simplicity. Later, under the impact of the industrial revolution, "economics" came to mean the system of production, distribution, and consumption of commodities. When factory, store, office, and bank usurped the loyalties of men and replaced the home as the center of economic activity, women who chose to give serious attention to homemaking were given the condescending title of "home economists." And the final transformation, which is to say degradation, of the dignity of the home, is symbolized by a recent change made at the University of Iowa. What was once the College of Home Economics has now been renamed the College of Consumer Sciences.

The only revolution that will heal us is one in which men and women come together and place the creation of a rich family life back in the center of the horizon of our values. A letter I got recently from a woman makes the point: "Perhaps the real shift will come when men fully realize, in the gut and not just in the head, that they are equally responsible, with women, for the creation, nurturing, and protection of children—that children are not simple sex objects, ego trips, or nuisances, but their first responsibility—before war, money, power, and status."

You may object: "All of this is well enough in theory, but unfortunate in fact, for many people the family was a vicious trap and a cruel destiny. The place that should have been a sanctuary was often a torture house. The arms that should have held us often pushed us away. Many flee the family because it was the place of injury, captivity, disappointment, abuse. The children of alcoholics and abusive parents fear marriage and family and find their solace in becoming solitary. There are so many bad marriages and dysfunctional families it sometimes seems only reasonable to junk the institution or invent a replacement." True enough, but hopes of replacing the family with some more perfect institution, like hi-tech pipe dreams of creating space colonies into which we can escape when we have polluted the earth, have proven to be both dangerous and deluded. It is within the bonds of what is familial that we must live or perish.

Fortunately, the profusion of dysfunctional families does not necessarily predict a grim future for the family. One of the standard themes in mythology is the promise of the wounded healer. In our hurt lies the source of our healing. The bird with the broken and mended wing soars the highest. Where you stumble and fall, there you find the treasure.

One of men's greatest resources for change is our wound and our longing for the missing father. We can heal ourselves by becoming the kind of fathers we wanted but did not have. Create out of the void, out of the absence. Our best map for parenting is outlined like a photographic negative in the shadow side of our psyches. Get in touch with your disappointment, your rage, your grief, your loneliness for the father, the intimate touching family you did not have, and you will find a blueprint for parenting. Become the father you longed for. We heal ourselves by learning to give to our children what we did not receive.

If you are not married, do not have children, or are gay, find a friend's child who needs nurturing and become a part-time substitute parent. It strikes me that the lack of substantial manliness one finds in some gay communities is a result not of a homoerotic expression of sexuality, but of the lack of a relationship of nurturance to the young. To be involved in creating a wholesome future, men, gay or straight, need an active caring relationship to children. A man who takes no care of and is not involved in the process of caring for and initiating the young remains a boy no matter what his achievements. This generation of men knows by its longing for fathers who were absent that nothing fills the void that is created when men abandon their families, whether out of selfishness, dedication to work, or devotion to "important" causes. When anything becomes more important to a society than the welfare of its children, it is a sure sign of spiritual disintegration.

There is a felicitous match between what men need to learn for their own wholeness, and attitudes and skills that are necessary for fathering. The child-within-the-man can best be healed by caring for a child who is to become a man. Children are our playmates and teachers. These days many men, lamenting that they experienced no rites of initiation into manhood, are gathering in small groups and experimenting with creating new rites and rituals. This is well and good, but we need to remember that a solid sense of manhood is not something we can ultimately get from any ceremony. Male initiation may involve a ceremony, but the reality in back of it is what happens day by day in the nitty-gritty contact between a boy and the significant men in his life, especially his father. A boy naturally learns how to be a man by observing how his father treats women, how he deals with illness, failure, and success, whether he shares in the household chores, whether he cuddles and plays. We first and forever (or not at all) learn our infinite worth from the look of adoration we see in our parents' eyes. We learn the delights of sensuality from their enjoyment of our innocent bodies—cuddling, wrestling, tickling. We learn to trust in a world that contains evil when we come crying with a skinned knee and are held, hurting, in arms; and the voice that is forever assuring us, "Everything is going to be all right." We learn to give ourselves generously to create a better future that we will not live to see by the sacrifices our parents make on behalf of our becoming.

The second time around with marriage and fatherhood, I learned that the most important thing I can do as a father is to create a sense of welcome. By allowing my delight to overflow, I imprint a message on my child's psyche: "I welcome you, the world welcomes you. We appreciate your being and take joy in your becoming." Erik Erikson said in *Identity and the Life Cycle* that the first developmental task of childhood is achieving a sense of basic trust. I would rather think of the first necessity as achieving a sense of basic delight. A child whose sheer existence is a joy to its parents will begin life with a sense that it is desired, its being is a gift, the world will welcome its creativity. And one of the best ways to do this is to get down and get physical. In the beginning most of my ideas of what would be fun for Jessamyn were far too complex. I finally discovered that what she liked most was rough wrestling, and stories invented on the spot. When someone asked her what she liked about me her reply was, "I like his wrestle." It is hard to overemphasize children's need for touch, cuddling, and holding.

I am also learning to talk to children, not at them. First time round as a father I had truckloads of rules, oughts, ideals, and explanations—all of which kept me at arm's length from my children. I thought it was my responsibility to oversee and direct their experience from my superior position, to protect them from complex adult emotions and from the harsh realities of the world until they were ready to confront them. Lately I have come to believe that the best thing I can give my children is an honest account of what I feel, think, and experience, to invite them into my inner world, tell them the stories that will give them some sense of my pilgrimage as a man.

The other night I had a dream in which my father slipped, fell down the stairs, and hurt himself. As he started to get up I said to him, "You always try to be so large and tough, even when you are hurt, and you never let anybody hold you." He turned to me, curled up in my arms, and allowed me to hold him. I woke from the dream with a heaviness in my heart, a refrain from an old hymn on my lips, and a question in my mind. The line was from the hymn, "When we are strong, Lord, leave us not alone, our refuge be." The question was: Who holds the father? I have learned to allow the little boy in myself to be held. Women have often done that for me. But who nurtures and comforts the strong man when he is hurt or weary? Three days after the dream I got the answer to my question. My son, Gifford, arrived in Sonoma to help me build our house. He is the head builder. I am contractor and general workman. The circle of familiar love begins to complete itself. His coming of age ritual marks my passage into autumn. The father who once held the small boy

within his arms is now tended by the strong arms of his man-
child.

Hearth, Hospitality, and Community

The time is ripe for men and women to create a new type of
community for which there is, as yet, no single name. To get a
notion of what I mean, add together this family of words: *hearth*
(a nuclear area, a vital or creative center), *hospitality* (the cordial
and generous reception and entertainment of guests or strangers),
charity (the kindly and sympathetic disposition to aid the needy
or suffering), *celebration* (to honor by engaging in religious,
commemorative or other ceremonies or by refraining from ordinary business), *community* (a body of individuals organized into
a unit with awareness of some unifying trait).

The kinds of institutions that have evolved in modern,
urban centers are too anonymous to satisfy our need for belonging and recognition. When we live in apartments separated by
thin walls from neighbors we do not know; when we are tended
when we fall sick and our dying and burying is managed by
strangers; when our birthdays, anniversaries, and holy days pass
uncelebrated; when we depend on government to care for the
unfortunate, the elderly, and the homeless; when our kinfolk are
so widely dispersed that we can only reach out to them by
telephone, we begin to suffer from a deficiency of community.
To gain that sense of worth that comes only when our name and
story is known, we require a small group of people, perhaps no
more than a hundred, that greets us and takes an ongoing interest
in our lives. Something larger than a nuclear family but less
constricting than a tribe.

We might begin by re-creating the old sense of hearth and
hospitality. A hearth is not a house with a fireplace, or a home
shared only by members of the same family. It is more like an
extended family. As we have more and more households that are
made up of single persons, one-parent families, homosexual
couples, roommates, and other nontraditional combinations, it
becomes important to create new types of networks and nonbio-
logical kinfolk—persons who choose to create some kind of
hearth with one another, perhaps to dwell together in cohousing
units. A hearth is a place of gathering, a center where friends and
family talk about what is important; feast, laugh, and weep
together; celebrate the rites of passage that punctuate their days;
witness and pledge common troth with bride and groom; chris-

ten and initiate children; rejoice together in good fortune, new jobs, and successful undertakings; give aid, advice, and consent in handling of delinquent children, alcoholic wives, and lovers and friends with cancer; tend senile parents; and care for strangers who come into their midst.

There is nothing more urgent that men and women have to do together than to redeem ourselves from anonymous organizations, too much television, and fast food, and rediscover the enduring satisfactions that are inseparable from common meals, the communion of friends, and the gathering of community.

Ardor for the Earth: The Common Vocation

In the next few generations the major conflict is not going to be the battle between the sexes. Within a decade or so (in the overdeveloped nations) women will have won economic and political equality and will have sufficient public power to share in the decisions about war, work, and welfare.

The great struggle that is shaping up for the year 2000 and beyond will be between two tribes with opposite worldviews, values, and ways of organizing life—which earlier I called Progressives and Radicals. In each tribe men and women will stand together. We may expect that the men and women who will control General Motors will be locked in combat with the men and women who demand a radical reduction of automotive emissions. Male and female generals, members of congress, and beneficiaries of the military-industrial-welfare system will contend against men and women who want our national resources to be invested in creating a plutonium-free environment and re-creating livable cities.

Men and women can only finally come together by sharing a common erotic and earthy vocation.

The simple truth, which we have conspired to forget during the last century, is that the human species is an integral part of an incomprehensible unity of being in the process of becoming: a single organ in the body of Gaia; a cell through which universal history flows like fluid through a membrane; an Aeolian harp the spirit of life moves like the wind; a character within the dream of God; a citizen within the commonwealth of sentient beings.

The great advances in civilization in the last three thousand years have paralleled the growing awareness of and respect for the individual. By seeing ourselves as actors standing apart from nature, we have been able to create luxury for masses of people and freedoms beyond the dreams of ancient kings. But individualization and separation from nature is also becoming our disease. The medicine that once healed us now threatens to destroy. The vocation of a previous era has become the nemesis of the present age. The severed self, the conqueror of nature, the architect of a strictly human utopia, has become a species-chauvinist, a cosmic fascist, seeking to impose his/her will on all of the other species in the commonwealth. In the natural order no less than the political order, such an exercise of ruthless power combined with rational technology is certain to produce immense unhappiness and disaster.

The way forward for moderns is not to return to the simplicities of an earlier time. That route is blocked. We can't go back to hunting and gathering, or subsistence agriculture. We have no model for the type of civilization we must create in the near future if we are to survive.

In our time the journey begins when men and women hear and respond to a common vocation to come together to create a new kind of social order that is not based upon enmity and the hope of conquest.

As contentious genders engaged in sexual combat, men and women have not been kindly to one another. But far beyond the violence we have done to each other in the past is the violence we are together doing to the earth. Our common vocation now is to find a way to repent of our wasteful and consuming ways, and learn to love the limits that are necessary to respect the habitat of our neighbors. We need to discover how to nurture an ecological conscience that is sensitive and powerful enough to administer justice, and protect the hearth of all the creatures we are rapidly rendering homeless by our compulsive march toward affluence. And, as part and parcel of the same vocation, we must take on the enormous century-long project of changing the style of political and genderal relationships that keep the warfare system alive and deadly.

As overwhelming and nearly utopian as this task seems, it would certainly be an illusion to suppose that we could continue with our present alienating and destructive industrial warfare against nature, political warfare between nations, and intimate warfare between men and women.

And so, it falls to men and women today to begin a journey. As it was at the beginning of every pivotal era in human history, so it is in ours—only the starting point of the journey is known, and not its conclusion. As prodigal sons and daughters all we know is that we must leave the father's household, as we once left the mother's, and travel into a strange country. Perhaps along the way, if we make common cause, we may become true companions. And together we may enjoy some foretaste of the feast of a distant homecoming.

The great calling of our time that is worthy of men and women is to hold each other within our hearts, and to conspire to create a hearth within the earth household.

These three live or die together: The Heart. The Hearth. The Earth.

15

TRAVEL TIPS
FOR PILGRIMS

There is no how-to guide to the process of becoming a full-summed and spirited man. To suggest there are techniques to achieve authentic manhood would be to devalue the dignity we can achieve only by struggling to become conscious and compassionate. We win our souls after long years of practicing the discipline of awareness and abiding in fear and trembling until we learn, at last, to rest content with our grandeur and baseness.

Men who are beginning to nibble on the apple of consciousness often ask "Where do we start? How do we do it?" The answer is simple: Begin where you are. No esoteric cult, enlightened guru, holy ashram, secret gnostic practice, or all-knowing psychotherapist is necessary. Once a man or a woman crosses the great divide that separates unconscious living from the quest to become more conscious, any event is an invitation to awareness. In India there is an old saying: "When the student is ready the guru appears." To a man who wants to know who he is, and is willing to change in accordance with what he learns, the world and everyday experience are his teachers. If I have a fight with my wife, it is an occasion to reflect on the way I deal with womankind, conflict, anger, violence, resentment, blame, or guilt. If I find myself marooned in a blizzard at a truck stop in Wyoming, it is an opportunity to meditate on how I cope with captivity, boredom, and the inability to control circumstances.

Although there are no techniques that can guarantee us certain and safe passage, valuable assistance, and companionship in sharing the lore of the journey are available from fellow travelers. The following tips, questions, and focusing exercises are some I have found helpful and have used in various seminars.

Forming a Questing Community

In one sense the voyage of self-discovery is solitary, but that doesn't mean you have to take it all alone. A lot of men suffer silently when they are in creative chaos, and feel something is wrong with them because they don't realize other men are experiencing a similar disintegration of the old modes of masculinity. In matters of the psyche and spirit, taking the journey and telling the story go hand in glove, and that is why we need a listening community in order to make our solitary pilgrimage. The most powerful resource we have for transforming ourselves is honest conversation between men and men, women and women, men and women.

Therapy groups run by professionals provide a starting place for some men who are in crisis. The advantage of these groups is that they offer immediate, skilled help. The disadvantage is that, because they are led by paid professionals, they never achieve the spiritual democracy of leaderless groups in which all members are equally responsible for the development of the community.

To start a leaderless men's group, reach out to one person who seems ripe for friendship and risk being candid about your feelings and needs. Men you sense are in trouble with romance, marriage, family, alcohol, drugs, or work are good candidates. Go slow in gathering your community. Propose and talk about new members before inviting them. It is important to collect a group of men with whom you can be candid.

Keep the group small enough to allow time for in-depth sharing by all members, no more than twelve or fifteen, and large enough to give you some diversity, no fewer than six. In our group we found it was essential to include only men who would make a long-term commitment to meeting at least once a week.

Monthly or infrequent meetings, or a constantly changing set of participants, do not allow a group to develop the level of trust that is necessary to get beneath the facade. If someone is not ready to make regular attendance and participation a priority, don't waste the group's time by including him.

The agenda of a group will emerge naturally from the concerns of the members. Most weeks one or more men will have been wrestling with some problem that becomes the focus of the discussion. Gradually, the group will share experiences, stories, and feelings, and learn how to challenge, pursue, and nurture. Over the course of time, questions about sex, money, work, authority, power, competition, loneliness, death, guilt, addiction, fathers, mothers, children, goals, and the pains and pleasures of being male will arise. Some of the following exercises, all of which are best done in a small group or with a partner, may help you focus your reflections and deal more creatively with issues that are central for men. A more complete account, and suggestions for exploring the journey that is every person's birthright can be found in *Your Mythic Journey* by Anne Valley Fox and myself. (See footnotes, page 270)

Recovering Your Personal History of Manhood

1. How, when, and where did you learn to be a man?
   - Collect photographs from your early childhood and use them to tell the story of what you learned about boys and girls, men and women, in your family of origin. What did your father's and mother's bodies feel like? Who touched you? Comforted you? Punished you? What did you learn about sex roles in your family? Were there different rules for boys and girls in your family? What was your father's ideal of masculinity? Femininity? Your mother's?
   - Who were your early heroes and role models? What books, movies, or television programs presented you with images of men you imitated?
   - What kind of ceremonies or symbolic activities marked your passage from boyhood into manhood? Who initiated you into the male mysteries—father, brother, uncle, grandfather, the gang?
   - How, ideally, would you initiate your son into manhood? What would you say to him about the difficulties and joys of being a man? What advice would you give him?
   - What men do you most admire today? Despise?

2. The wounds and gifts of gender.
   - What is hardest about being a man? What do you resent? What difficulties, pains, and injuries have you suffered because you were male? What expectations and roles have informed and deformed your life?
   - What pleasures and privileges do you enjoy as a man?
   - In what ways do women have it easier? Harder?
   - If you could choose to be male or female in A.D. 2000, which would you choose? Why?

Warfare, Conquest, and Competition

- Outline the history of your personal battles, conflicts, and low-intensity warfare. Name your enemies, overt and covert. Who wounded you? Whom have you wounded? What is your style of self-defense? Are you active or passive, the aggressor or the victim? With whom have you fought physically? Verbally? How violent are you? Against whom have you had to defend yourself? Whom do you resent? Hate? For what causes have you fought? If you have been in an actual war, what effect has the experience of battle and killing had upon your life?
- Inner battles: me versus myself versus I. In what degree have you lived in a state of inner warfare? Who are the antagonists in your struggles with and against self? Desire versus duty? "I want" versus "I should"? Spirit versus flesh? Emotion versus reason? Compassion versus self-encapsulation? Greed versus generosity? Sometimes it helps to dramatize inner conflicts by giving the tendencies names: the homesteader versus the gypsy, the dictator versus the playboy, the intellectual versus the sensualist, the wimp versus the wild man, etc.
- How competitive do you feel with other men? To feel OK about yourself do you need to be one-up, to win, to be smarter, more powerful, more accomplished than the men around you?
- Are you afraid men would despise or take advantage of you if they knew your hidden weaknesses?
- From what fights, and situations of conflicts, have you withdrawn when you should have stood firm? How courageous and cowardly are you?
- One easy way for a group of men to examine various styles of fighting in a controlled situation is to arm wrestle. Do

you wrestle to win? Or are you more comfortable in losing? Do you use wiles, strategy, or brute force? How do you feel when you win? When you lose?

- Once you identify your basic fight-style, experiment with another. If you usually stand and fight when challenged, try running away. Or vice versa. Instead of fight or flight, try the opossum strategy—collapse and play dead.
- To locate festering resentments, fill in the blank in the following sentence with the first things that come to mind: "I'm mad as hell about . . . and I won't take it anymore."
- An honorable but rare way to end conflict is to recognize that you were wrong, repent, and make amends. Repenting, reowning our shadows, taking responsibility for the vices and varieties of evil we normally project onto our enemies, is one of the fastest, but most painful, ways to achieve psychological and spiritual integration. It is safe to assume that about half of the time you were the aggressor and your opponent the innocent victim. When have you been "the bad guy"? Greedy? Cruel? Heartless? Unjust? Insensitive? At fault? How difficult is it for you to say, "I was wrong. I am sorry"?

Power and Other Values

The obsessive quest for power (potency, domination, conquest, control) has been the linchpin of male identity. Therefore, significant change in our self-understanding as men involves redefining our relationship to power.

- Ask a group of men to rank themselves in order of power from the most to the least powerful. Be forewarned: This is always difficult and embarrassing, but it is a dynamite way to evoke discussion about power, sex, money, and other values.
- What is power? Is there a difference between strength and power?
- Do you consciously strive to accumulate power? How?
- If power is defined as the ability to overcome resistance and get what you want, what means do you use to achieve your desires? Physical? Financial? Sexual? Mental? Position? Persuasion? Imagination? Moral? Spiritual? Willpower? Do you try to influence or intimidate others, to seduce or persuade? How do you *feel* when you use various types of power?

- In what circumstances do you feel powerless? Impotent? What do you do when you can't control the situation?
- What keeps you from realizing your full potentiality? Guilt? Shame? Fear? Laziness? Fate?
- Do you empower others? How?

Work, Money, and Vocation

- Trace your work history. When did you first earn money? For what? What did your father and mother teach you by example about the relationship between manhood, work, and money?
- How much money do you make? What is your total financial worth? Notice the embarrassment, reticence, awkward silence, or evasive humor when you introduce the question of money in a group of men. Why is it so hard to talk about money?
- Sex, love, money, and power—how do you feel about each? What is most important to you?
- How much money do you need? What for?
- Do a value inventory. First, list your professional and personal values in two columns. What are your professional and economic goals? How far do you aspire to advance? What do you want to make, do, create? What are your personal, family, and communal goals? More time? More intimacy? More service? Second, beside the various items in your two columns, write the number of hours you spend each week in activities that further each of your professional and personal goals. What are you not taking the time to do? Are you shortchanging your work, your family, your friends, yourself, your community? What interests, enthusiasms, and passions have you never taken the time to pursue?
- In what ways does your profession, job, or corporation force you to do things you consider unethical?
- Does your religious or spiritual philosophy of life dovetail or conflict with your work?
- Do a life review. Are you a success? A failure? How do you measure success and failure?
- If you had all the money you needed for a comfortable lifestyle, what would you do?
- How would you like to be remembered? What would you like to have written on your tombstone? Make a will in

which you bequeath both your material goods and your psychological and spiritual gifts and achievements.
- In what ways is the world better for your having lived, labored, and loved?
- To locate some of the sources of potential burnout, complete the following sentence five or ten times with the first things that come to mind: "I'm sick and tired of . . ."
- What are the factors in your personal and work life that cause the most stress?

Sex, Love, and Intimacy

1. Exploring your sexual history and feelings.
   - Trace the history of your penis. When did you first become aware that you had a dangling destiny? As a boy were you proud, embarrassed, puzzled, awed, ashamed, pleased by your penis? What nicknames did you use for it—cock, pee-pee, wanger, thing, dick, weenie? What rules and attitudes did your parents and peers have about what you were to do and not to do with it? Do you feel your penis is too small, too large, just the right size? How often does "it" rebel against "you"—get you in trouble by irresponsible sex, or by refusing to stand and deliver when ordered? What is your experience of impotence?
   - When did you start masturbating? How did you feel about it? Did you receive any religious instruction about masturbation?
   - When did you first have intercourse?
   - How well do you integrate passion and tenderness? Under what conditions are you most sexually at ease? One-night stands? Long-term relationships? Marriage? Is sex best with or without love?
   - How much performance anxiety accompanies sex?
   - How have your sexual desires and habits changed over the years?
   - Do you have sexual feelings toward men? Feeling of tenderness?
   - Do you trust men or women more?
   - How do you deal with conflicts with women? Do you bully and intimidate? Have you ever hit a woman? Used sex to punish or demean? Have you ever forced a woman to have sex? Do you shrink and withdraw when you encounter female anger? What tactics do you use in the war between the sexes?
   - How much do you tend to divide women into whores and

Madonnas, the impure and the pure? Have you ever visited a prostitute or seduced a woman and felt that she was "trash," "dirty," "bad"?

2. Listening to women.
   - Read feminist literature with an open heart and a critical mind. Probably as much as ninety percent (SWAG statistic) of the conceptual material most of us have encountered in our formal education reflects a male point of view. This bias is gradually being corrected by a new generation of women. Go to any good bookstore and browse and you will find a wealth of information to choose from. You will have to separate those books that speak, primarily, with a passion for things womanly from those that are animated by a spirit of blame. Two that have changed my thinking are *Woman and Nature* and *Pornography and Silence* both by Susan Griffin.[11]
   - Practice listening to women without interruption. Psychological studies show that men interrupt more often than women. Hard-driving men, Type A personalities, habitually have their answer prepared before the question is finished, and have a hard time listening "with the third ear." It is a good practice to allow silence to fall between sentences to make certain that you have understood what is being said before you reply. I observe, but cannot prove, that image, emotion, and personal experience enter into women's thinking more often than men's (which is more typically abstract and impersonal). Often in mixed gatherings men vie with each other to be heard, and women can't get a word in edgewise without becoming very aggressive. Try being sensitive to the rhythm of women's conversation. The most common complaint I hear from women about men is, "They don't listen to us."
   - If you were a woman, what kind of a woman would you be? Draw a picture of yourself as a woman. Imagine what it would be like to create a child within your body, to give birth and suckle a baby. How would the experience of motherhood change the way you look at the world?

3. Practicing the art of loving.
   - Whom do you want to love better? What stops you? Whom do you want to love you better? What stops them? What do you need that you don't get? What do you have that you don't give?

- What *won't* you give up to have a more harmonious marriage or relationship, i.e., what is not negotiable?
- Ideally, how would you arrange your life? How much time would you devote to being alone, intimacy (being with a friend, a lover, family) work, service, recreation?
- Practice empathy. Sit in a public place where you can observe the passing parade and use your imagination to inhabit other people's lives. What does it feel like to be the well-dressed, cocksure man hurrying to an appointment? The policeman directing traffic? The bag lady with the shopping cart full of belongings? The teenage girl undulating down the street to the rhythm of a hard rock tune played on a ghetto blaster? If you imitate another's body stance and movement, you will discover something about the way they move through and experience their world. Place yourself *within* the events and lives of the people reported in the daily newspaper. Imagine what it is like to be the woman who is raped and beaten by two men in an alley on 19th Avenue. What does she feel when she is released from the hospital? When (or if) she reports the rape to the police? When she walks down a street at twilight and sees a strange man approaching?

Feelings and Emotions

Because the artificial gender division of our culture assigned reason to men and emotion to women, men tend to be novices in distinguishing the repertoire of their own emotions.

- Construct a chart of your emotional landscape. Imagine you are a scientist observing your life from afar. Begin by making an hour-by-hour chart of the range of emotions you experience and express on an average day. What do you feel like when you wake up? Do you anticipate the day with a feeling of excitement, or dread? Do your dreams leave you with an aftermath of fear, sexual arousal, anxiety, a feeling of flying free? What emotions dominated your workday? Frustration? Satisfaction? Resentment? Numbness? Creative joy? Boredom? Fatigue? Self-forgetful concentration on solving a problem? What do you feel when you go home? Loneliness? Relief? Contentment? What emotions come into play in your relationship with your significant others—family, lover, main squeeze? If you were writing your autobiography (as you should to recollect your lost and strayed memories) how would you characterize the emotional climate of different periods of your life? What emotions were dominant, which were missing? Were you chronically resentful, angry, numb, sad, etc.?

• Practice expressing rather than repressing your feelings. Once you have a chart of the bright and dim colors in your emotional range, habitual and tabooed feelings, you may be able to expand your repertoire by practice. To be fully alive we need the full palate of colors, from dark despair to the blues in the night, the gray in-betweens, the soaring sky blue, the red of passion, and the gold of triumph. Make a habit of identifying your feelings and expressing them in some appropriate way. The great value of a long-term intimate relationship is that it provides a companion with whom we can share the kaleidoscope of our feelings.

Useful Phrases and Opening Sentences

I want. . . .
I don't want.
Yes!
No!
I will. . . .
I won't.
Please listen.
I'm listening.
I was wrong.
I am sorry.
I think you are wrong about that.
I won't yield on this. . . .
That hurt me.
That made me angry.
It's not worth fighting over.
I'll fight for that.
I feel empty . . . sad . . . discouraged . . . blue . . . depressed . . . tired . . . disappointed . . . afraid . . . discouraged . . . bored.
I feel full . . . satisfied . . . hopeful . . . passionate . . . energetic . . . excited, happy, joyful, content.
It feels like you are blaming me. What exactly do you think I have done wrong?
I don't want to work that hard.
This job is not fulfilling.
I have better things to do.

I quit.
Thank you.

Changing the Male Body

Every emotion has a psychological as well as a physical manifestation. When we are depressed our eyes are downcast, our chest heavy, our breathing shallow. When we are anxious the chest narrows and we become breathless. When we are resentful and enraged the eyes narrow and the lips become thin and pinched. When we are angry or fearful we are flooded with adrenaline and our heart rate increases as we prepare to fight or flee. When we are joyful we are uplifted and suffused with warmth and tingling sensations. While we give different names to psyche, body, and spirit, they are, in fact, inseparable.

It follows from this that a warrior and a pilgrim psyche will have different physiological profiles. What Wilheim Reich called "the character armor of the warrior" is seen in the defense mechanisms of the body—the chronically rigid and foreshortened muscles of the chest, the tightened anal sphincter, and the narrowed visual focus—as well as in the habit of paranoid thinking and projecting of evil onto an exterior enemy. By contrast, the character armor of a pilgrim's body is softened by the habit of the free expression of grief, repentance, doubt, fear, wonder, joy, and so on. It gradually becomes breathful (inspired), sensitive, undefended, vulnerable, open, and flexible.

Eastern religious practice has always focused on psychophysiospiritual disciplines. Becoming conscious of the rhythm of breathing is both the central metaphor and the therapeutic exercise of Zen Buddhism and the more mystical forms of Hinduism. Since breath and spirit are one and the same, we discover our true identity and participate in the ultimate reality by consciously inspiring and expiring. We discover that atman (the human breath-spirit) is Brahman (the universal breath-spirit). In addition, the martial arts—judo, kung fu, akido—are meditations in motion that aim at creating a responsive rather than an aggressive body. The disciplined martial artist is lithe but not limp, aware enough to keep out of harm's way but able to respond to danger. He, or she, does not initiate the use of force.

Recently, body-oriented therapies and disciplines have come into their own in the West. Jogging, nutrition, yoga, and different forms of meditation (mostly aimed at reducing stress) are commonplace. Sensory awareness, massage, rolfing (Structural Integration), Feldenkries's work, and the Alexander technique are widely accepted ways of working with the physical component of repressed emotion and constricted ways of thinking and living.

If you are trying to make the transition from warrior to pilgrim you may find it helpful to practice a martial art, yoga, or one of the body therapies. If you are spring-tight, intense, and always on the go, you may learn more by having a massage than by entering yet another marathon and trying to beat the competition or your previous best time. Competition may be good for General Motors, and may be fun on the racquetball court, but it makes for a soul-wearying style of life.

Cultivating Solitude

- If you are in one of those long-term marriages where you have become joined at the hip, try taking separate vacations. Travel alone. Rediscover your own rhythms—when you like to rise and go to bed, what you like to eat, what you think about when you are solo.
- Design a sanctuary of solitude—a room, a cabin, a place in the wilderness—into which you may retreat to nurture your relationship to yourself. In what kind of place do you slow down and come to quietude?
- Keep a journal, an ongoing record of your questions, conversations with yourself, observations, stories.
- Pay attention to your dreams. If you don't remember your dreams begin by telling yourself, before going to sleep, that you will dream and remember. Keep a pad and pencil or a tape recorder beside the bed and, if you wake with any portion of a dream, write or record it. When you wake, remain in the position in which you were sleeping. Do not be in any hurry to get out of bed. As Howard Thurman said to me, "Simmer." Let any images that remain from your dreams play and replay in your mind and imagination before you occupy yourself with the tasks of the day. Several times during the day, stop for a moment or two and remember the most startling, troubling, or exciting images from your dream of the previous night. If you are trying to solve any problem in your personal or professional life, rub the images from the dream against the problem and see if, like flint and steel, they produce a spark that might ignite a solution.
- For me, the greatest resource in cultivating my relationship

with myself is walking. The philosopher Friedrich Nietzsche once said that the only ideas that were worthwhile were those that came when he was walking under an open sky. My breakthrough ideas inevitably slip into mind when I have given up thinking and problem solving and taken to the woods or the beach for a long hike, or when I amble mindlessly around a strange city.

Rituals, Ceremonies, and Symbolic Events

Rituals and ceremonies stand midway between reflection and action. Symbolic acts, like sacraments, are outward and visible signs of inner and invisible psychological and spiritual realities. They punctuate our lives and provide a testimony to what we find most meaningful. Recently, groups of men and women have begun to gather to create rituals that express their newfound self-understanding and identity. Many have borrowed the native American customs of drumming, dancing, and sweat lodges. The group with which I belong has little taste for formal rituals but has an annual white-water rafting and camping trip. We find that the adventure on the river, the cooking, eating, and sitting around the fire together create shared memories and a powerful feeling of community.

Spirited and Virile Action

Reflection without social action, the inner journey without the practice of virtue, is sterile. And vice versa. Introversion and extroversion are the yin and yang of a balanced life.

There is no end to the ways we can express a spirited and careful sense of manhood. Recently I have come across men who have chosen to exercise their care by: becoming big brothers to fatherless boys; creating a breeding program that rescued Peregrine falcons from extinction; going into hospitals and holding abandoned babies born to drug-addicted mothers; helping to finance a shelter for battered women; working as a volunteer in a hospice; teaching English to recent immigrants; growing gardens in vacant city lots; creating a computerized system of communication for mute children; rejuvenating a local Democratic party; lobbying to make television more interactive and responsive to community needs.

Find an appropriate vehicle for your passion. In general, it seems best to focus your attention and energy on one social ill so you may become effective.

In the end, there are only two rules: Remember yourself. Practice compassion. And, now that I think about it, they amount to the same thing.

APPENDIX

Perfect 10s:
What Makes an Ideal Man?
A *Psychology Today* Survey[1]

Mirror, mirror on the wall
Who's the best and brightest
of us all?

Heroes are the translation of our ideals into flesh and blood, the incarnations, the historical mirrors, in which we see our ideals reflected.

Every age has its pantheon of heroes and heroines, models, ideal types, icons, beautiful people, stars, demigods. We are by nature a worshipful species. We cast our dreams into Olympian fields, stained-glass firmaments, and celluloid heavens, and project our need for perfection onto saints and beautiful people. Each generation stands in awe before its version of the lifestyles of the rich and the famous.

The realm of heroes and heroines is filled with paradox and contradiction. It contains representatives both of the kinds of people we in fact admire, and those we think we *should* admire. Lovable rogues, colorful sociopaths, and sexual outlaws mix freely with wise leaders, compassionate healers, great inventors, and saints. At any banquet of modern heroines and heroes, Mae West and Mother Theresa, Donald Trump and Norman Lear, Sean Penn and Paul Newman, Ronald Reagan and Mikhail Gorbachev, Oliver North and Ralph Nader would all rub elbows. Also included would be whatever new stars and notorious personages have been elevated to the weekly Hall of Fame by *People* magazine, *U.S. News and World Report, Time, Newsweek*, etc. In a society dominated by mass media, heroism is systematically confused with notoriety. Anyone who appears regularly in commercials or on talk shows also enters into the company of heroes. Even the obsequious Ed McMahon, and Martha Ray with her shining dentures, seem to qualify.

Have modern men and women been brainwashed by media? Have we lost our values? Have we become so superficial that we confuse notoriety with virtue? Have we lowered our ideals to coincide with what we can manage at the moment?

I had a hunch that most men and women have well-defined ideals of both manhood and womenhood that are far more discriminating than we might imagine if we judge by popular heroes. I set out to test this hypothesis, with the help of my colleague Dr. Ofer Zur, by constructing a questionnaire that probed people's judgments about ideal men, good men, average men, and inferior men. The questionnaire first appeared in *Psychology Today* in March 1989. We received and analyzed over six thousand replies, many accompanied by letters, and published the results in a second article in November 1989. I include both of these articles with due credit and many thanks to my coauthor, constant companion in dialogue, and friend, Dr. Zur.

You may want to pause at this point, fill out the questionnaire, and later, compare your answers with those of *Psychology Today* readers.

WHAT MAKES AN IDEAL MAN?

Prepared by Sam Keen and Ofer Zur

In the heyday of John Wayne—or Alan Alda, his 1970's opposite—we all seemed to have strong opinions about what made for an ideal man.

Do we still? In a world full of best-sellers about "men who hate women," one might well wonder. What are our ideals of manhood today? Who is a "10," not just in looks? Are there still rites of passage for men? Can you point to anyone you know (or know of) who is an ideal man? And what makes an ideal man different from a good man? (Or from an average or inferior man?)

PHILOSOPHIES OF LIFE

Everyone lives by certain basic ideas. The question is, which philosophies are held by an ideal man, and which by less exceptional or even inferior men? Read and rate the following statements on an A to D scale, *circling the appropriate letter,* where:

A represents the philosophy of an ideal man (a hero, a mensch, a "10" in the whole-person sense, one of the exceptional few whom you admire most).

B is a good man (above average, someone you respect).

C is an average, run-of-the-mill man.

D is an inferior man, someone you'd avoid.

His Philosophy	Rating	
Do unto others as you'd have others do unto you.	A B C D	(1:6)
Don't rock the boat.	A B C D	(7)
Look out for Number 1.	A B C D	(8)
Life is hard, and then you die.	A B C D	(9)
If it feels good, do it.	A B C D	(10)
Time is money. Money is power.	A B C D	(11)
Take whatever you can, any way you can get it.	A B C D	(12)
Take it easy. Go with the flow.	A B C D	(13)
Life is a gift to be shared.	A B C D	(14)
From each according to his ability, to each according to his need.	A B C D	(15)
Do your duty and obey the law.	A B C D	(16)
Leave the world better than you found it.	A B C D	(17)
Question authority.	A B C D	(18)
My country right or wrong.	A B C D	(19)
Whoever has the most toys wins.	A B C D	(20)
A man's most important duty is to his family.	A B C D	(21)
God helps those who help themselves.	A B C D	(22)
Reverence for life.	A B C D	(23)
Jesus is my personal savior.	A B C D	(24)

RITES OF PASSAGE

Every society has experiences it views as necessary for a boy to achieve manhood—and special kinds of experiences that mark the lives of extraordinary men. *Circle the appropriate letter* for any of the following experiences you consider essential for a boy to become:

A: an ideal man.

B: a good man.

C: an average man.

If you don't consider the experience a rite of passage, skip to the next item.

His Experience   Rating

Experience	Rating	
Circumcision	A B C	(25)
Fighting to defend himself	A B C	(26)
Getting a gun	A B C	(27)
Becoming sexually active	A B C	(28)
Marriage	A B C	(29)
Establishing personal values, rather than relying on those set by his parents or society	A B C	(30)
Moving away from home	A B C	(31)
Undertaking an adventure	A B C	(32)
Fathering a child	A B C	(33)
Standing up for his ideas	A B C	(34)
Completing his education	A B C	(35)
Being able to support himself	A B C	(36)
Being able to support a family	A B C	(37)
Going to war	A B C	(38)
Finding his life's work	A B C	(39)
Achieving career success	A B C	(40)
The death of his parents	A B C	(41)
Defying authority on a matter of conscience	A B C	(42)
Achieving spiritual grace	A B C	(43)
Forming strong friendships with other men	A B C	(44)
Achieving mastery over women	A B C	(45)
Enjoying equality with women	A B C	(46)
Taking an active part in community affairs	A B C	(47)
Becoming a mentor for the young	A B C	(48)
Becoming aware of personal shortcomings	A B C	(49)
Becoming compassionate	A B C	(50)
Developing patience, wisdom, the long view	A B C	(51)
Facing death with dignity	A B C	(52)
Other _____	A B C	(53)

WHAT'S AN IDEAL MAN LIKE?

Which of the following best describe the beliefs, attitudes, or behaviors of an ideal man? *(Check as many as apply.)*

A doer, takes charge	☐ 54
Receptive, responsive to the initiative of others	☐ 55
Extroverted	☐ 56
Introverted	☐ 57
Usually focuses on practical matters	☐ 58
Stops often to wonder, appreciate, dream	☐ 59
Pragmatic, commonsense approach to life	☐ 60
Involved in some kind of spiritual quest	☐ 61
Predictable, reliable, orderly	☐ 62
Can be wild and full of surprises	☐ 63
Self-contained, self-sufficient	☐ 64
Willingly accepts help from others	☐ 65
Type A personality: Hard-driving	☐ 66
Type B personality: Easy-going	☐ 67
Always self-confident	☐ 68
Has self-doubts and questions	☐ 69
Follows inner authority	☐ 70
Seeks a guide, mentor, teacher	☐ 71

Acts only after careful planning ☐ 72
Spontaneous ☐ 73

Never shows pain ☐ 74
Expresses feelings of sadness ☐ 75

Critical ☐ 11:6
Nonjudgmental ☐ 7

Suave, urbane ☐ 8
Casual, earthy ☐ 9

Easy to be with ☐ 10
Stimulating, sometimes difficult ☐ 11

Always where the action is ☐ 12
Seeks and enjoys solitude ☐ 13

Even-tempered, moderate ☐ 14
Has mood swings ☐ 15

Strong physical presence ☐ 16
Strong intellectual, moral, or spiritual presence ☐ 17

Pays attention to diet, exercise, health ☐ 18
Basically ignores his body ☐ 19

Loves the outdoors and physical challenge ☐ 20
Is urban, culturally sophisticated ☐ 21

Charismatic, enthusiastic, animated ☐ 22
Cool, rational, self-controlled ☐ 23

Commanding presence ☐ 24
May go unnoticed in a crowd ☐ 25

Handsome ☐ 26
Looks don't matter ☐ 27

An ideal man finds his primary sense of meaning in *(check one only)*:
His work ☐ 28-1
His family ☐ -2
Self-exploration and personal growth ☐ -3
Play, sports, leisure ☐ -4
Helping others ☐ -5
Artistic pursuits ☐ -6
Political action/power ☐ -7
Financial success ☐ -8
Religion ☐ -9
Other _____ (29)

LOVE, SEX, AND POWER

How macho is the ideal man? How nontraditional? In the following section, *please check only the statements you think express the beliefs, attitudes, or behaviors of an ideal man.*

His Attitudes Toward Women

Compared to men, he thinks women are:

	More	Equally	Less
Intuitive	☐ 30-1	☐ -2	☐ -3
Nurturing	☐ 31-1	☐ -2	☐ -3
Rational	☐ 32-1	☐ -2	☐ -3
Aggressive	☐ 33-1	☐ -2	☐ -3
Sexually aggressive	☐ 34-1	☐ -2	☐ -3

The ideal man believes *(check as many as apply)*:

Businesses will become more humane when more women share management
    power.   ☐ 35
Business will change women more than women will change business.   ☐ 36
A man who is financially supported by a woman loses a measure of his
    masculinity.   ☐ 37
Women who work outside the home are more interesting than women who do
    not.   ☐ 38
Women with young children should stay home if they can afford to.   ☐ 39
Women should be drafted and share the dangers of combat.   ☐ 40
In general, men are more suited to leading corporations and nations than
    women are.   ☐ 41
If more women were in positions of political power there would be less war. ☐ 42

His Sexual Attitudes

The ideal man believes *(check as many as apply)*:

Sex is an essential source of pleasure.   ☐ 43
Intimacy is more important than sex.   ☐ 44
Homosexuality is abnormal.   ☐ 45
Homosexuality is a legitimate choice.   ☐ 46

The ideal man *(check as many as apply)*:

Has nonsexual friendships with women.   ☐ 47
Has close friendships with other men.   ☐ 48
Prefers one-night stands and casual sex.   ☐ 49
Is sexually loyal to his wife or lover.   ☐ 50
May be celibate.   ☐ 51
Is heterosexual.   ☐ 52
Is homosexual.   ☐ 53
Is bisexual.   ☐ 54

The ideal man is most sexually attracted to *(check one)*:

Physically beautiful partners   ☐ 55-1
Nurturing partners   ☐ -2
Powerful, accomplished partners   ☐ -3
Partners more low-key than himself   ☐ -4

His Views on Family

The ideal man *(check as many as apply)*:

Sees being a good father as central to being a man.   ☐ 56
Sees being a good husband as central to being a man.   ☐ 57
Chooses not to marry or have children so he can devote himself to his work. ☐ 58
Provides his family with a high standard of living.   ☐ 59
Is willing to be a full-time househusband.   ☐ 60
Would refuse a job that required him to be away from his family a great deal. ☐ 61

His Reaction to Anger and Violence

The ideal man *(check as many as apply)*:

Is highly competitive in business and sports.   ☐ 62
Is noncompetitive, cooperative.   ☐ 63
Expresses anger, but is not violent.   ☐ 64
Never strikes a woman, even if she hits him.   ☐ 65
Sometimes fights physically with other men.   ☐ 66
Would fight an intruder who threatened his family.   ☐ 67
Enjoys watching violent sports—ice hockey, boxing.   ☐ 68
Is a skilled hunter.   ☐ 69
Is a pacifist.   ☐ 70
Would go to war for a cause he believes in.   ☐ 71

MEN, FAMOUS AND INFAMOUS

Name two famous men, living or dead, fictional or real, who most embody the ideal, good, average, or inferior man. On the line below each name, list some of the qualities that characterize him.

Ideal man #1: _____ (72)
His qualities: _____
_____ (73)
Ideal man #2: _____ (74)
His qualities: _____
_____ (75)
Good man #1: _____ (III:6)
His qualities: _____
_____ (7)
Good man #2: _____ (8)
His qualities: _____
_____ (9)
Average man #1: _____ (10)
His qualities: _____
_____ (11)
Average man #2: _____ (12)
His qualities: _____
_____ (13)
Inferior man #1: _____ (14)
His qualities: _____
_____ (15)
Inferior man #2: _____ (16)
His qualities: _____
_____ (17)

ONE VERY PERSONAL HERO

If you can, name one man you know personally who is as close to an ideal as possible, and describe the qualities that make him so:

_____
_____
_____ (18)

WHERE DO YOU FIND HIM?

In what kind of job, occupation, or profession are you *most* likely to find an ideal man?

_____
_____ (19)

In what kind of job, occupation, or profession are you *least* likely to find an ideal man?

_____
_____ (20)

An ideal man is most likely to live in a:

Large city (1 million		Small town	☐ -4
or more)	☐ 21-1		
Small city	☐ -2	Rural area	☐ -5
Suburb	☐ -3	Anywhere	☐ -6

YOUR OWN ATTITUDES

How do *you* see the changes in our culture? Indicate your agreement or disagreement with the following questions by *circling the appropriate number.*

Modern men are less masculine than men a generation ago.

Strongly agree   **Strongly disagree**
1   2   3   4   (22)

There is nobody in the movies these days as manly as Clark Gable or Gary Cooper.

1   2   3   4   (23)

These days men seem to be confused about masculinity.

1   2   3   4   (24)

Now that women are entering the workforce and earning more money, life is better for men.

1   2   3   4   (25)

Men would be happier if they devoted themselves more to their families and communities and less to their work.

1   2   3   4   (26)

Women would be happier if they devoted themselves more to their families and communities and less to their work.

1   2   3   4   (27)

Now that most women work outside the home, both men and women are worse off.

1   2   3   4   (28)

Women have a more secure sense of their identity than men.

1   2   3   4   (29)

Even in the 1980's, it's still easier to be a man than it is to be a woman.

1   2   3   4   (30)

In general, women these days seem happier than men.

1   2   3   4   (31)

ABOUT YOU

Are you: Male ☐ 32-1   Female ☐ -2

Your age: _____ (33)

Highest level of education you've completed: _____ (34)

Are you currently a full-time student?   Yes ☐ 35-1   No ☐ -2

Your marital status: _____ (36)

Your ethnic background:

    Caucasian ☐ 37-1   Afro-American ☐ -3

    Hispanic   ☐ -2   Asian   ☐ -4

    Other _____ (-5)

What is your total annual income, and (including the other people you live with, if any) what is the total annual income of your household?

	Your Income (38)	Household Income (39)
Under $20,000	☐ -1	☐ -1
$20,000–29,999	☐ -2	☐ -2
$30,000–39,999	☐ -3	☐ -3
$40,000–59,999	☐ -4	☐ -4
$60,000–74,999	☐ -5	☐ -5
$75,000 or more	☐ -6	☐ -6

Do you have children: Yes ☐ 40-1   No ☐ -2

Your occupation: _____ (41)

Your job title: _____

_____ (42)

You live in a:
Large city (1 million
 or more)   ☐ 43-1   Small town   ☐ -4
Small city   ☐ -2   Rural area   ☐ -5
Suburb   ☐ -3

Your region:
Northeast   ☐ 44-1   Southwest   ☐ -4
South   ☐ -2   West Coast   ☐ -5
Midwest   ☐ -3

Your political orientation:
Conservative   ☐ 45-1   Liberal   ☐ -3
Moderate   ☐ -2
Other _____ (-4)

Your religious affiliation:
Protestant   ☐ 46-1   Jewish   ☐ -3
Catholic   ☐ -2   Agnostic/Atheist ☐ -4
Other _____ (-5)

Your sexual preference:
Heterosexual   ☐ 47-1   Bisexual   ☐ -3
Homosexual   ☐ -2   Celibate   ☐ -4

FOR MEN ONLY: If you had to rate yourself according to the scale we've been using, would you call yourself:
An ideal man   ☐ 48-1
A good man   ☐ -2
An average man   ☐ -3
An inferior man   ☐ -4

FOR WOMEN ONLY: Please rate the man you're closest to according to the scale we've been using.

Is he your:
Husband   ☐ 49-1   Father   ☐ -4
Lover   ☐ -2   Brother   ☐ -5
Friend   ☐ -3
Other_____ (-6)

Would you call him:
An ideal man   ☐ 50-1
A good man   ☐ -2
An average man   ☐ -3
An inferior man   ☐ -4

WHAT AN IDEAL MAN IS . . .

Most Like

Receptive, responsive to the initatives of others	89%
Strong intellectual, moral, or physical presence	87%
Pays attention to diet, exercise, health	87%
Expresses feelings of sadness	86%
Stops often to wonder, appreciate, dream	82%
Follows inner authority	77%
Even-tempered, moderate	77%
Easy to be with	75%

Nonjudgmental	74%
Willingly accepts help	70%
A doer, takes charge	68%

Least Like

Basically ignores his body	2%
Never shows pain	6%
Has mood swings	10%
Critical	14%
Introverted	16%
Always where the action is	20%
Type A personality	20%
Suave, urbane	22%

Percentages listed reflect the proportion of survey respondents who consider each of these factors descriptive of "the beliefs, attitudes, or behaviors of an ideal man."

THE MEN OF OUR DREAMS . . .

One of the few places where men and women differ is in the famous men they choose to list (we asked for two) as most embodying the ideal, good, average, and inferior man—and in the qualities they attribute to those men. The percentages are small because this was a write-in—we've listed the top 10 ideal men and everyone in the other categories mentioned by 5% of either men or women. One conclusion: We have an easier time agreeing about who we hate than who we admire.

Ideal Men

Women Say		Men Say	
Jesus	14%	Jesus	17%
Gandhi	8%	Gandhi	11%
Alan Alda	7%	John F. Kennedy	10%
Tom Selleck	6%	Abraham Lincoln	9%
Abraham Lincoln	6%	Martin Luther King, Jr.	9%
Paul Newman	5%	Thomas Jefferson	4%
Martin Luther King, Jr.	5%	Ronald Reagan	4%
Bill Cosby	4%	Winston Churchill	3%
John F. Kennedy	3%	George Bush	3%
George Bush	3%	Billy Graham	3%

What Makes Them That Way . . .

Caring/loving	65%	Caring/loving	55%
Intelligent	34%	Intelligent	28%
Moral/honest	29%	Moral/honest	25%
Sensitive	29%	Leadership	19%
Family man	20%	Courage	19%

Good Men

George Bush	7%	Jimmy Carter	11%
Ronald Reagan	7%	John F. Kennedy	10%
Alan Alda	6%	George Bush	7%
Bill Cosby	6%	Martin Luther King, Jr.	7%
Martin Luther King, Jr.	6%	Ronald Reagan	6%
Jimmy Carter	5%	Abraham Lincoln	5%
Michael Dukakis	5%	Gandhi	5%
Abraham Lincoln	4%	Dwight D. Eisenhower	5%
John F. Kennedy	3%	Bill Cosby	3%
Gandhi	2%	Alan Alda	1%

Women Say		*Men Say*	
What Makes Them That Way . . .			
Caring/loving	41%	Caring/loving	46%
Moral/honest	35%	Intelligent	26%
Intelligent	30%	Moral/honest	19%
Family man	25%	Leadership	15%
Humor	24%	Courage	11%

. . . AND OF OUR NIGHTMARES

Average Men

Women Say		*Men Say*	
George Bush	19%	Ronald Reagan	19%
Ronald Reagan	17%	George Bush	15%
Jimmy Carter	5%	Oliver North	7%
Dan Quayle	5%	Jimmy Carter	5%
Gerald Ford	5%	Dan Quayle	4%
Oliver North	2%	Gerald Ford	3%

What Makes Them That Way . . .

Family man	17%	Caring/loving	16%
Bland/dull	15%	Bland/dull	11%
Moral/honest	13%	Family man	10%
Caring/loving	12%	Moral/honest	10%
Intelligent	12%	Hard worker	8%

Inferior Men

Adolf Hitler	15%	Adolf Hitler	28%
Ronald Reagan	9%	Ronald Reagan	12%
Richard Nixon	7%	Richard Nixon	10%
Jim Bakker	7%	Jim Bakker	7%
Ayatollah Khomeini	6%	Ayatollah Khomeini	7%
Donald Trump	6%	Charles Manson	7%
Charles Manson	5%	Donald Trump	3%
Archie Bunker	5%	Archie Bunker	3%
Morton Downey, Jr.	5%	Morton Downey, Jr.	3%
Sean Penn	5%	Sean Penn	2%
Mike Tyson	5%	Mike Tyson	1%

What Makes Them That Way . . .

Egocentric	34%	Immoral	32%
Immoral	30%	Egocentric	23%
Violent	19%	Greedy	17%
Greedy	15%	Bigoted	16%
Insensitive to others	15%	Exploitive	14%
Stupid	15%	Insensitive to others	13%

Who Is the New Ideal Man?
A Report

Here is what six thousand men and women who replied to the questionnaire think about what differentiates ideal, good, average, and inferior men.

Some wondered whether the search for an ideal man, like the quest for the Holy Grail, might be mythic at best and presumptuous at worst. Ideal men exist only in platonic heavens or romantic novels. And the notion itself may be dangerous. Among the chorus of objections were the following: A woman from Seattle writes, "My husband is an excellent man. His problem is he thinks he ought to be ideal. He says to me, 'Good enough isn't good enough.' He is tortured by the idea of perfection." Another reader of pragmatic temperament said, "There aren't any ideal men, and the good ones I encounter occasionally in the gym are facing everyday reality. They don't affect national policy, negotiate peace treaties, show people the way to heaven, make a fortune in the stock market, kiss strange women. They are too busy paying for the new car and balancing budgets." " 'Ideal' for whom?" asked a music lover. "It is all relative. For a Viking to be shy, unassuming, gentle, and sensitive would be dysfunctional. My ideal man was once arrested as a Peeping Tom, had a terrible temper, and spat in mirrors thinking they were windows—Beethoven."

Some women confessed that even if they could find an ideal man, they probably wouldn't like him. One woman writes, "Most women claim to want good, solid, dependable men. When they have one, after a time, they come to regard him as boring. The very traits we claim to prize in theory will be the fodder for our resentment in the future. Why?" Another writes, "I want a few endearing imperfections. I admire intelligent men, but it doesn't bother me if a man thinks Thornton Wilder and Friedrich Nietzsche were receivers for the New York Giants." In a more troubled vein, many women wrote that, while they admired ideal and good men, they were sexually attracted to ones who had many qualities they judged as inferior, if not evil. A woman executive from the Midwest wrote, "Thinking about the ideal man invites a lot of paradox. In our fantasy the ideal man may be a Renaissance man. Trouble is they seldom seem predisposed to committed relationships. The men I have loved don't stack up. But because we loved them, they seemed ideal, didn't they?"

We shouldn't wonder that the quest for the ideal man met with some resistance. De Tocqueville noted more than a century ago that the American character is constitutionally suspicious of elitism and aristocratic virtues. Our faith in the common man predisposes us to reject the notion of what Aristotle called the "great-souled man." In our brave new world all men are considered equal even if some (mostly WASPs) are more equal than others. While we admire heroes, we are not entirely comfortable with men who aspire to the heights. The ancient virtue of "honor" as a defining characteristic of a man was mentioned by only one respondent.

In defense of the quest we are pleased to report that while a few who answered the survey were skeptical about "ideal" men, the vast majority have captured the unicorn, found the Grail, or at least managed to kiss a frog and turn an ordinary man into a prince. Of the men who responded, 15% consider themselves ideal, 74% think of themselves as good, a mere 9% rate themselves as average, and practically no one (00.8%) judges himself inferior. Lest you think this is a bit of male vanity, you may be startled to learn that women rate the men closest to them even higher than they rate themselves. A generous 37% of women consider their husband-lover-main squeeze, friend, father, or brother to be ideal. More than half, 52%, consider him good. We received an exaltation of letters in praise of men. Listen to the larks: "My father made me feel so loved and so important that I feel ideal enough about myself to enjoy living and growing." "My ideal man is out in the backyard playing ball with his gifted children." A clerk from North Carolina writes, "I couldn't think of any man, famous or infamous, living or dead, who could hold a candle to my husband. He supports me no matter what I choose to do." Susan writes of her dad, "This man would go to the ends of the earth for us." And Margie, who is a mechanical engineer, says, "My husband has always stood by me, and his bywords are, 'you can do it.' After eleven children he changed jobs so we could relocate, and sent me off to obtain my university degree. He may not be a '10,' but neither am I, and he's all ours."

Philosophy of Life

What is the bottom line? What defines a man? Does it matter what he believes, or only how he acts and how much he accumulates? Our working hypothesis was that heroes, average guys, and villains have fundamentally different worldviews. G.K. Chesterton was right when he said that a practical landlord should always ask a prospective tenant about his philosophy of life, because a man who thinks time is money and time is running out is likely to run out on the rent. So, in the questionnaire, we boiled down different philosophies of life to a series of bumper stickers, clichés, or rules of thumb to see if a man's beliefs mattered.

When we tabulated the responses we found they fell neatly into three distinct philosophies of life—categories or factors—which we named the idealistic/conscientious, the authoritarian/conformist, and the cynical/materialistic. A surprising 98% of respondents agree that an ideal man is an idealist who believes that his life is a gift he should reverence; that he should leave the world better; and that he should follow the golden rule. A majority of those polled judge that while a good man may question authority, he is loyal to his family, continues to obey the law, and does his duty. The average man doesn't rock the boat, believes money is power, and may consider Jesus his personal savior although he acts as if God helps those who help themselves. Inferior men are cynical and materialistic. They look out for number one, take whatever they can, believe that life is hard and then they die, and that whoever has the most toys wins.

Rites of Passage

In formulating our questions about rites of passage, we wanted to find out what kind of pivotal events, experiences, and social rituals were necessary to turn a boy into a man and to transform an average man into an extraordinary man. We wondered whether an ideal modern man still has to undertake something like what Joseph Campbell called "a heroic journey" to discover his uniqueness.

The survey told us that average men are still defined by the traditional rites of the warrior—initiation into manhood by the ordeal of circumcision, getting a gun, going to war, and achieving mastery over women. A step up the scale, good men are practitioners of what might be called the householder's virtues. They have successfully completed the biological tasks of becoming sexually active, moving away from home, entering into marriage, fathering a child, supporting a family, forming friendships with other men, and becoming active in community affairs. Very good men dare to defy authority, undertake an adventure, have found a lifework, and have achieved spiritual grace. At the top of the scale is a kind of ideal that is heroic and spiritual but not specifically religious. The two virtues that rank highest as characterizing the ideal man are wisdom and compassion—exactly the virtues held in highest regard in both Buddhism and Christianity. The ideal man must have established his own values, be aware of his shortcomings, become a mentor for the young, and face death with dignity. Indeed, the only new virtue of the hero is that he must enjoy equality with women.

Attitudes and Behaviors

At this point the portrait of the hero begins to take on a distinctly modern hue, not exactly narcissistic but definitely introverted and apolitical. Here numbers speak more eloquently than words. When asked where an ideal man finds his primary sense of meaning (what Paul Tillich called "ultimate concern") readers replied:

Self-exploration and personal growth	48.7%
His family	26.4%
Helping others	11.6%
Religion	06.8%
His work	04.0%

Artistic... 01.2%
Financial 00.6%
Play, sports, leisure 00.2%
Political action/power 00.2%

These responses suggest it is no longer the "me" generation. But it may be the "me-and-mine" generation. If self is first,
family still ranks well above play, money, work, or religion. Does
this mean we are beginning to turn inside out, convert the ideal
of technical progress and economic growth into a psychological
ideal of personal growth?

The other qualities listed stress receptivity, feeling, willingness to accept help, and sensitivity. It is not until we reach
the eleventh place—a doer—that we find qualities that have
traditionally been thought of as cornerstones of masculine identity. ("Men do. Women are.") Harry, who gets the prize for the
shortest letter, overstates the point only a little: "What makes
an ideal man? A good woman!" One woman put it this way:
"Most men I know seem to identify masculine traits with violence. Those traits that make us human are considered feminine." Another woman, noting but lamenting the same trend,
wrote, "We have convinced men that to be men is somehow not
optimal. They should try very hard to be, well, sort of, women.
But not wimps, you understand, just not quite so much the way
they are. It's a damn shame." We seem to have reversed Henry
Higgins's question and now want to know: Why can't a man be
more like a woman?

Furthermore, the straight-ahead, damn-the-torpedos, Type
A personalities that have characterized the best and the brightest,
or at least the most financially successful men, now rank near
the bottom of the list of qualities of this "new age" ideal man.
Although we can't quite bring ourselves to admit he is an intro-
vert (16%), he is more interested in his health than where the
action is, and in cultivating his feelings (evidently mostly positive since he doesn't have mood swings), than in being critical or
urbane.

Attitudes Toward Women

Surprisingly, both men and women believe the ideal man has
relatively traditional attitudes toward women. He thinks women
are sugar and spice, slightly more nurturing and intuitive than
men, and less aggressive in general and in the bedroom than

men. One of the very few items in the entire questionnaire on which we found a significant difference between the responses of men and women concerns expectations about women in business. The majority of men (53%) but only a small minority of women (15%) think business will change women more than women will change business. (I.e., women still believe in the capitalist myth that individual consciousness creates social structures, while the men—who have the most experience of corporate culture—have become Marxists and believe that social structures create individual consciousness.) Women believe that women can change the system. Men believe that power corrupts regardless of gender. Inconsistently, only 37% of men and women believe that if more women were in positions of power there would be less war. Why women believe women would humanize the workplace but not the political battlefield we do not know. Maybe it's the examples of Golda Meir, Indira Gandhi, and Margaret Thatcher.

Love and Sex (in That Order)

The good news is that 91% say the ideal man cultivates intimacy and friendships. The bad news is that he is not terribly sexual. Good-bye Don Juan, Lady Chatterley's lover, James Bond, and Warren Beatty. He doesn't go in for one-night stands, and only 58% think that sex is an essential source of pleasure for him. Only 13 women and not a single man in our entire sample listed "sexy" as the first defining quality. Among the hundreds of letters we received, only one was sexually explicit. Theresa from Texas, who is 28, married, and thinks Tom Selleck is both terrific and humble, says her ideal man is uninhibited. He loves to play different roles in the bedroom, all the way from aggressive to lazy. "He doesn't mind when his lover chases him around the bedroom wearing nothing but thong underwear . . ." and he might well "walk into a dark bedroom wearing nothing but a glow-in-the-dark condom." Herewith a more typical response from Deborah, who is a homemaker, lists her job titles "Mommy" and "Honey," and says her husband is ideal. "There are many times I find him sexually attractive, but when he is at the sink, preparing dinner or doing dishes at the end of a particularly tiring day, somehow that hip action at the sink or that genuine concern for me is the ultimate turn-on." Sue, a retired teacher, whose first choice for ideal man is John Kennedy, pinpointed some of the ambivalence we feel about sexuality and ideal masculinity. She wrote that the charismatic men with the take-charge personalities who achieve great success also have another side—a built-in capacity for infidelity, the need for challenge. They seem to have an enormous sexual drive which goes along with their drive to achieve in other areas of their lives.

Quite unexpectedly when it comes to judgments about the kind of women ideal men would find attractive, men seem to be more "feminist" than women. According to men, the ideal man will be more sexually attracted to partners who are powerful and accomplished than to those who are physically beautiful. Women believe the opposite. Since men's responses seem a reversal of the commonly accepted wisdom that says men are more interested in looks than women, it is puzzling. Notice, for what it is worth, that when it comes to naming ideal men, women picked 62% of their candidates (men 20%) from the category of entertainers, i.e., men who are known only by sight and fantasy.

Anyway, you get the drift of things. This new sexual ideal for men reflects the values of a generation that has passed through the sexual revolution, ceased playing musical beds because of herpes, AIDS, and other STDs, lost its obsession with orgasms, and is beginning to learn that women prefer men with slow hands and warm hearts to hot rods and hunks.

The news about attitudes on homosexuality will not delight the gay community: 34% of respondents think an ideal man considers homosexuality an abnormality. A scant 8% believe that an ideal man is homosexual (9% bisexual) although, as one woman wrote, "Gay men come closer to the ideal because they are generally more sensitive to women's viewpoints, more inclined to accept women as friends and equals." We suspect that the letter from a male professor of religion in Florida expresses some of the tangled sentiments about homosexuality that the majority of our respondents continue to feel, liberal rhetoric notwithstanding. He writes: "I was surprised to find that I did not believe that homosexuality would characterize an ideal man, though I believe upon reflection that it can characterize a good man."

Family

The ideal man has strong family ties. No Marlboro men need apply. Being a good husband and father (75%) is central to his view of masculinity. And 62% want Dad—no Willy Loman—to refuse any job that will require him to be away from his family a great deal. But 70% are not yet ready for him to become a househusband. The ideal man is still supposed to remain the breadwinner although he doesn't have to strive to provide his family with a high standard of living. Strangely, Jesus was number one on the hit parade but only 6% believe an ideal man might choose not to marry in order to devote himself to his work.

Anger and Violence

Wise and compassionate he may be, but the ideal man is neither wimp nor Dirty Harry. Most (85%) agree that he can feel, and expresses his anger without resorting to violence unless he must fight an intruder. "My ideal man," writes a woman educator from Philadelphia, "rarely raises his voice in anger, refuses to fight even verbally, has a keen sense of humor, and is able to adapt to the crisis of the moment. He hardly ever criticizes but offers helpful, tactful suggestions." A majority (59%) say he would go to war for a cause he believes in but 22% think he may be a pacifist. More than 90% agree that he no longer engages in those ritualized forms of violence that were a crucial part of the education of the warrior. The ideal man does not enjoy violent sports, doesn't fight with other men, does not hunt (probably is not a member of the NRA) and is noncompetitive.

Conclusions

Historically speaking, the most startling finding of our survey is the degree to which the current ideal of manhood is apolitical. The new ideal man may be compassionate and wise, but the sphere of his caring and action is very narrow. Like the Epicureans, he is more likely to be tending his own garden and looking after his own family than he is to be involved in political action. As we considered these findings we couldn't help thinking of Aristotle's definition of man as a "social animal." During the time in classical Greece when democracy was born, manhood was defined by political participation. During the writing of this report, we paused frequently to watch the dramatic news of revolution in China, where thousands of young men and women without weapons were facing down armed soldiers and tanks. Their example made us wonder what would become of a nation whose "ideal men" remain within the ghetto of privacy. Can an ethic of personal growth create a sufficiently strong sense of community to preserve freedom? We doubt it. We note that, inconsistently, few (.02%) consider that an ideal man finds his primary sense of meaning in politics or religion (6.8%) and yet Jesus and Gandhi are at the top of the list of admirable men. Furthermore, political figures occupy the first nine places in men's affections and six out of ten in the women's list. Evidently we are content to admire visionaries and revolutionaries from afar but do not want to emulate them. Up close we prefer men who are more domesticated and easy to be with.

Whenever ideals, paradigms, worldviews, and gender roles shift, we must expect both gain and loss.

At long last, the ideal man has escaped the compulsive extroversion that has shaped the minds of men since somebody invented clocks and scorekeeping. He has lost some of his involvement in the public world—his striving for success at any cost, his obsession with power—but has gained access to the inner world of feeling, receptivity, and spirituality. He is more sensitive, has more self-doubts, and is no longer such a tower of strength—unbending, substantial, and solid. As Steve, a writer from Pennsylvania, suggests: "The ideal man is not hard and unyielding as a piece of granite, but is rather fluid like a body of water, able to change shape, freeze, or boil, yet still retain the watery essence. He can become what the situation demands. If there is a need for an authoritarian leader, he can play that role. If there is a need for a diplomatic peace-finder, he can be that too. Inherent here is the ability to discern the need of the moment." The new ideal man is more androgynous than autonomous. No rugged individualist. He is close kin to the Taoist ideal expressed in the Chinese classic, the *Tao te ching:* "The ancient masters/ . . . were careful as someone crossing an iced-over stream/ Alert as a warrior in enemy territory./Courteous as a guest./Fluid as melting ice./Shapable as a block of wood./ Receptive as a valley./Clear as a glass of water."

We seem to want the obsolete but habitual connection between masculinity and violence to be severed. But we have not yet found a way to connect the kinder and gentler virtues we admire with that untamed quality—wildness and passion—that seem necessary for virility. Yes, Zorba, "a man needs a touch of madness." We sometimes get the feeling that the new ideal man is a bit too tame. Even in feminist circles one sometimes hears the plaintive cry, "A hard man is good to find." All too few men or women told us, as Deborah did, that the ideal man "must have passion, compassion, and honor; a passion for his music, art, writing, thinking, discovering, spiritual understanding; must honor himself."

In these days of rapid change in gender roles, men no less than women are faced with impossibly high expectations. If the new superwoman is supposed to combine all the aggression, dedication, and ruthlessness necessary to succeed in business, with the ability to nurture and create hearth, the new superman is supposed to be oh-so-sensitive and self-actualizing, not too concerned with money or career, but still ready to fight to protect home and country, and competitive enough to provide a good living for his family. No one says how these contradictory qualities fit within the same psyche. Many readers commented on the double bind men face. Jodi, a married college student from White Plains, told us, "Men have it rough emotionally. Women want them to be strong, rugged, tough, aggressive, and very successful at their careers, but if they are, they are thought of as overly macho or sexist." John, an inmate in a North Carolina prison, wrote: "Many young southern women seem to hold mixed ideas of an ideal man. A warm, considerate man to give her all the space she needs for career and personal ambition, yet, strong-willed and somewhat dominant (when appropriate) like her father. This somewhat incompatible set of standards and expectations has kept me ill at ease with where I fit 'in the scheme of things.' "

A final word of caution. We think the vision of the ideal man presented here—kinder, gentler, receptive, apolitical—is widespread in American culture. Karen L., for instance, who writes romance fiction, told us that the trend in romance fiction has "moved away from the tall, dark, wealthy, powerful, enigmatic, moody, macho hero to ones who are successful (not necessarily rich), friendly, compassionate, humorous. The macho, John Wayne types seem to be on the wane (no pun intended), but neither are the editors looking for too-wimpy Alan Alda types." But it is altogether possible that our findings tell us more about the ideals of men and women who have a strong interest in feeling and the inner world (and therefore read *Psychology Today*) than the population at large. We suspect that in less affluent, blue-collar, and military populations, we would find that the differences between classes will be greater than the minimal differences between genders within any single class that we found in this study.

The portrait of the ideal man that has emerged from this questionnaire should make us pause to consider and critique the ideals that are being promoted and celebrated within the psychological community. In the eighteenth century, the American ideal was a man like George Washington or Thomas Jefferson who risked his life for political principles and ideals, a man "who devoted himself to the good of the community" while he "lived a life of piety" and "mild religion." By the nineteenth century this had changed and the ideal man became one, like Theodore Roosevelt, who was intent on self-cultivation, hard work, high moral conscience, robust health, and physical courage.[2] A generation ago Phillip Reiff warned against "the triumph of the therapeutic," the subtle tyranny created by the new religion of psychology in which our focus turned excessively inward. There is a danger that dedication to self-exploration and personal growth may replace a larger vision of a just commonwealth that includes humans, rich and poor, and other species with feathers, fins, and fur. Our age cries out for men filled with prophetic rage, men daring and political enough to husband the fragile and succulent earth and protect the weak and disenfranchised. In the mythology of Buddhism the ideal man, the bodhisattva, takes a vow to save, or heal, all sentient beings. It requires a bit of madness and a lot of compassion to aspire to such a goal. But as long as we are talking about ideals, shouldn't our reach exceed our grasp?

NOTES

SECTION I:

1. "Guns and Dolls," *Newsweek* (May 28, 1990).
2. Susan Forward and Joan Torres, *Men Who Hate Women and the Women Who Love Them* (New York: Bantam, 1987); Dan Kiley, *What to Do When He Won't Change* (New York: Fawcett, 1988); Dan Kiley, *The Peter Pan Syndrome* (New York: Avon, 1984).
3. Joseph Campbell and M.J. Abadie, *The Mythic Image* (Princeton, NJ: Princeton University Press, 1981).
4. Herb Goldberg, *The New Male: From Self–Destruction to Self–Care* (New York: New American Library, 1980); *The Inner Male: Overcoming Roadblocks to Intimacy* (New York: New American Library, 1987); Warren Farrell, *Why Men Are the Way They Are: The Male–Female Dynamic* (New York: McGraw-Hill, 1986).

SECTION II:

1. Parts of this summary taken from David Gilmore, *Manhood in the Making: Cultural Concepts of Masculinity* (New Haven, CT: Yale University Press, 1990), p. 38.
2. Joseph Campbell, *The Hero With a Thousand Faces* (Princeton, NJ: Princeton University Press, 1949).

3. For more on this process see Sam Keen and Anne Valley Fox, *Your Mythic Journey* (Los Angeles: Tarcher Books, 1989).
4. Mark Baker, *Nam: The Vietnam War in the Words of the Men and Women Who Fought There* (New York: Morrow, 1982), p. 22.
5. Phillip Caputo, *A Rumor of War* (New York: Ballantine, 1978), p. 120.
6. *American Handbook of Psychiatry*, Vol. 1 (New York: Basic Books, 1974), p. 750.
7. Larry Dossey, M.D., *Recovering the Soul* (New York: Bantam Books, 1989).
8. This chart is taken from Sam Keen, *Faces of the Enemy* (New York: Harper & Row, 1986), p. 133.
9. *Newsweek* (July 16, 1990); *New York Times* (August 6, 1990).
10. Gilmore, op. cit., p. 230.
11. Ayn Rand, *For the New Intellectual* (NY: Signet Books, 1961) p. 130.
12. *American Health* (September 1988).
13. Timothy Haight, "Living in the Office," *Whole Earth Review.* (Summer 1989), p. 75.
14. Earl Shorris, *The Oppressed Middle: Politics of Middle Management* (Garden City, NY: Doubleday, 1989). Now in print under a different title: *Scenes from Corporate Life* (NY: Penguin, 1990).
15. David J. Rogers, *Waging Business Warfare: Lessons from the Military Masters in Achieving Corporate Superiority* (New York: Scribner, 1987).

SECTION III:

1. Robert Oppenheimer, *Familiar Quotations*, John Bartlett, ed. (Boston: Little Brown & Company, 1980) p. 861.
2. E. Anthony Rotondo, Jr., "Body and Soul: Changing Ideals of American Middle–Class Manhood, 1770–1920," *Journal of Social History* (Spring 1983).
3. Todd Gitlin, "Postmodernism Defined, at Last!", *Utne Reader* (July/August 1989).
4. Albert Camus, *Neither Victims Nor Executioners*, Dwight MacDonald trans. (New York: Continuum Publishing Co., 1980), p. 51.
5. John C. Murray, *We Hold These Truths: Catholic Reflections on the American Proposition* (Kansas City, MO: Sheed & Ward, 1985).
6. Quoted in J. Glenn Gray, *The Warriors* (New York: Harper & Row, 1956).
7. Excerpts from George Gilder, "Microcosm: The Quantum Revolution in Economics and Technology," *Fortune* (August 28, 1989).

SECTION IV:

1. Rainer Maria Rilke, *Rilke On Love and Other Difficulties* (New York: W. W. Norton, 1975), p. 25.
2. Søren Kierkegaard, *The Journals of Kierkegaard 1834–1854*, Alexander Dru, ed. (Huntington, NY: Fontana Publishing, 1958).
3. Gerard Manley Hopkins "No Worst, There Is None . . .", *The Norton Anthology of Poetry* (NY: W. W. Norton, 1970) p. 903.

4. Laurens Van der Post, *Patterns of Renewal*, Pendle Hill Pamphlet Number 121 (Wallingford, PA).
5. Martin Luther, cited in N. O. Brown, *Love's Body* (New York: Random House, 1966), p. 237.
6. Sam Keen, *Apology for Wonder* (New York: Harper & Row, 1969).
7. Dag Hammarskjöld, *Markings* (NY: Alfred Knopf, 1964) p. 56.
8. Aldous Huxley, *Ape and Essence*, (NY: Harper & Row).
9. Norman Maclean, *A River Runs Through It* (Chicago: University of Chicago Press, 1979).
10. *Psychology Today* (April 1974).
11. Ernest Becker, *The Denial of Death* (New York: Free Press, 1985); *Escape From Evil* (New York: Free Press, 1976).
12. Albert Camus, *Resistance, Rebellion and Death*, Dwight MacDonald, trans. (New York: Alfred Knopf, 1961), p. 71.
13. Jim Autry, *For Love and Profit* (New York: William Morrow, 1991).
14. Etty Hillesum, *An Interrupted Life: The Diaries of Etty Hillesum 1941–1943* (New York: Washington Square Press, 1985), p. 157.
15. Jim Fowles, "The American Male in 1990," *Futures Research Quarterly* (Fall 1985).
16. Wendell Berry, *A Continuous Harmony: Essays Cultural and Agricultural* (New York: Harcourt Brace Jovanovich, 1975), p. 42.
17. Chief Seattle speech, probably given January 1855, published first in *Seattle Sunday Star*, 1887; different texts in John M. Rich, *Chief Seattle's Unanswered Challenge* (Fairfield, WA: Galleon Press, 1977).

SECTION V:

1. Marion Woodman, *Addiction to Perfection* (Toronto: Inner City Books, 1982).
2. Betty Reardon, *Sexism and the War System* (New York: Teachers College Press, Columbia University Press, 1985), p. 15.
3. Charlene Spretnak, *The Politics of Women's Spirituality* (New York: Anchor Books, 1982), p. 554.
4. Sally Miller Gearhart, "The Future—If There Is One—Is Female" in *Reweaving the Web of Life*, Pam McAllister, ed. (Philadelphia: New Society Publishers, 1982), p. 271.
5. Spretnak, op. cit. and McAllister, op. cit.
6. Monica Sjoo and Barbara Mor, *The Great Cosmic Mother* (New York: Harper & Row, 1987).
7. Unpublished paper. Lori McElroy and Tana Dineen, "Women and Peace: A Feminist Dilemma."
8. Joen Fagen, "Mythology, Psychotherapy, and the Liberal Arts Tradition," *Pilgrimage* (March 1989).
9. Jean S. Bolen, *Goddesses in Everywoman: A New Psychology of Women* (San Francisco: Harper & Row, 1989).
10. John Moyne and Coleman Barks, trans., *Open Secret: Versions of Rumi* (Putney, VT: Threshold Books, 1984).
11. Susan Griffin, *Woman and Nature: The Roaring Inside Her* (New York: Harper & Row, 1979); *Pornography and Silence: Culture's Revolt Against Nature* (New York: Harper & Row, 1981).

APPENDIX:

1. Published by special arrangement with *Psychology Today* and my co-author, Dr. Ofer Zur.
2. See E. Anthony Rotondo, "Body and Soul: Changing Ideals of American Middle–Class Manhood 1770–1920," *Journal of Social History* (Spring 1983).